Journal of Research
of the
American Federation
of Astrologers

2016

Copyright 2016 by American Federation of Astrologers

No part of this book may be reproduced or transcribed in any form or by any means, electronic or mechanical, including photocopying or recording or by any information storage and retrieval system without written permission from the author and publisher, except in the case of brief quotations embodied in critical reviews and articles. Requests and inquiries may be mailed to: American Federation of Astrologers, Inc., 6535 S. Rural Road, Tempe, AZ 85283.

ISBN-10: 0-86690-660-6
ISBN-13: 978-0-86690-660-9

Cover Design: Jack Cipolla

Published by:
American Federation of Astrologers, Inc.
6535 S. Rural Road
Tempe, AZ 85283

www.astrologers.com

Contents

From the Editor	v
A Hybrid Design Proposal for Research in Astrology By Glenn Perry	1
Using the Developmental Age Method to Interpret Significant Experiences in the Lives of Winston Churchill and Franklin Delano Roosevelt By Julie Grant	19
The Origins of the System of Twelve Houses By Jose Luis Belmonte	65
Vrddhayavanajataka By Ronnie Gale Dreyer	83
History of the Astrological Technique of Solar Arc Directions By Peter Gadek	103
Outer Planet Conjunctions and the ~1500 Year Climate Cycle By Bruce Scofield	151
Adolescent Behavior and Lunar Phase By Alex Trenoweth	181
The Ukraine Crisis Seen as an Event in the History of Post-Soviet Countries By Lutz Rathke	201
Significant Aspects of the Reality and History of the Sidereal Zodiac By Rui Miguel Fernandes	223
About the Authors	255

From the Editor

The American Federation of Astrologers is proud to publish the papers from the first recipients of the Catharine and Ernest Grant Trust Astrological Research Grants. They represent the investigations of astrologers from around the world, with submissions from Spain, Germany, Portugal, England, as well as the United States. The monetary awards from the Grant Trust were made to those in the astrological community who are members of the American Federation of Astrologers (AFA), the International Society of Astrological Research (ISAR), the Association for Astrological Networking (AFAN), and the National Council for Geocosmic Research (NCGR) in order to further astrological research. In addition, this Research Journal includes several noteworthy papers from the general membership of the AFA. The broad categories of research that these papers address employ quantitative and qualitative methods and historical approaches that further the body of astrological knowledge.

One of the goals of the Grant Trust is to develop educational materials and programs about how to do astrological research. Our first paper is entitled *A Hybrid Design Proposal for Research in Astrology* by Glenn Perry, Ph.D who is the research director of ISAR. He acknowledges the many problems that quantitative research presents for astrological research due to the multiple ways in which astrological variables can manifest while still being true to the principle. His paper presents a methodology for a hybrid qualitative/quantitative design that is consistent with the way astrology actually works and can generate important insights into the specific astrological factors behind human behavior.

The next paper, *Using the Developmental Age Method to Interpret Significant Experiences in the Lives of Winston Churchill & Franklin Delano Roosevelt* is by Julie Grant, ISAR's recipient for a Grant Award. She combines hermeneutics and historical inquiry to test the premise that signs and houses signify developmental stages of fixed duration within the human life cycle. Planets in these houses specify an exact month and year in which that configuration is felt and expressed, and aspects connect various periods across time.

In addition to the testing of hypotheses, research into the origins and history of the astrological tradition along with the translations of ancient texts is an invaluable contribution to the body of astrological knowledge. This allows contemporary astrologers to better understand the foundations of the practice.

Jose Luis Belmonte from Spain is one of AFA's recipients of the Grant Award. His paper, *The Origins of the System of Twelve Houses* looks into both the Babylonian theory of the rising times of each sign as well as the Greek philosophical meanings behind the original names of each house in order to explore what can deduced about the significations of the houses.

Ronnie Gale Dreyer is AFAN's recipient of the Grant Award. Her research project is a first time translation and commentary of the introductory verses of the *Vrddhayavanajataka* by Minaraja, a classic Sanskrit text on Indian horoscopy. Ronnie also discusses how Hellenistic and Indian concepts combined to formulate the iconography, symbolism and meaning of the zodiac in Indian astrology.

Peter Gadek, one of NCGR's recipients of the Grant Award, has investigated the *History of the Astrological Technique of Solar Arc Directions*. His exhaustive study shows how this technique developed over the course of two millennia from Primary Directions first discussed by Claudius Ptolemy. He traces and explains the many variations of this method as used by multiple historical astrologers.

Bruce Scofield, Ph.D., one recipient of NCGR's Grant Award, presents a scientific study in which he investigates *Outer Planet Conjunctions and the ~1500 Year Climate Cycle*. Reviewing the latest scientific studies from NOAA/NGDC Paleoclimatology Program and NASA solar data, he analyzes the possible correlations between the conjunctions of Saturn, Uranus, and Neptune and solar irradiance that drive periodicity in climate change.

Adolescent Behavior and Lunar Phase is the title of a paper submitted by Alex Trenoweth from the United Kingdom. She is one of AFA's recipients of the Grant Award. She analyzes a middle-school's daily data reports of poor student behavior incidents recorded over two academic years and examines how incidents correlate to sleep cycles timed by lunar phases and lunar latitude.

The *AFA Journal of Research* also accepts papers from its members at large. Another branch of historical research is the analysis of political and intellectual movements as timed and described by the cycles of the outer planets.

Lutz Rathke from Germany in *The Ukraine Crisis Seen as an Event in the History of Post-Soviet Countries* explores the 1989 Saturn-Neptune and 1993 Uranus-Neptune conjunctions in the light of the ideological conflicts that govern world politics, with particular reference to the Ukraine.

Significant Aspects of the Reality and History of the Sidereal Zodiac by Rui Miguel Fernandes from Portugal examines the sidereal zodiac from both a historical and mathematical perspective. He looks at the challenges in identifying primary reference stars given the phenomena of precession as well as star drift and he offers a mathematical model by which to establish an anchor point.

The American Federation of Astrologers extends its appreciation to these contributors for their hard work and dedication in furthering the body of astrological knowledge.

Demetra George
Research Director for the AFA

A Hybrid Design Proposal for Research in Astrology

By Glenn Perry, Ph.D

ABSTRACT: Quantitative research in astrology is fraught with problems due to the unique nature of astrological causality. The usual design chooses a specific event-outcome and then postulates an astrological signature for that outcome. An experiment is devised to determine if the astrological variable(s) can be shown to cause the effect. The problem with this approach is that an astrological archetype can manifest in multiple ways while still remaining true to itself. By adding additional astrological variables, potential outcomes increase exponentially. Accordingly, a quantitative design that attempts to statistically correlate astrological factors with singular outcomes is inherently flawed. Conversely, it is possible to create a hybrid qualitative/quantitative design that is consistent with the way astrology actually works. A phenomenological study of a specific astrological factor will yield a wide range of behavioral and event outcomes. Data analysis can organize these outcomes into key themes, and a series of statements can then be created that describe attitudes, beliefs, behaviors, and experiences that match these themes. These statements can be incorporated into a Likert scale administered to an experimental group of individuals that have the astrological factor in question, and a control group that does not have the factor. The hypothesis would be that the experimental group would score higher on the survey instrument than the control group.

In the most general sense, there are two ways of approaching astrological research. The first is to choose an outcome and then attempt to correlate that outcome to a presumed astrological factor. The second approach is to choose an astrological factor and then investigate how that factor might manifest as behavioral and event outcomes. In this article, I will propose a hybrid design that utilizes both methods.

In the first approach, called quantitative research, the event itself is the primary focus, for it determines the hypothesized astrological correlation. The goal is to measure the statistical likelihood of the event correlating to a hypothesized astrological signature. For example, a researcher may attempt to discern the probability that people diagnosed with paranoia will have Sun opposed Pluto in their natal charts. The researcher first chooses paranoia as his research topic, and then hypothesizes the astrological cause of Sun opposed Pluto. An experiment is designed to determine if the proposed astrological cause produces the predicted effect. If an experimental group of individuals with Sun opposed Pluto can be shown to have a higher incidence of paranoia than a control group without this aspect, then the hypothesis is confirmed—to wit, Sun opposed Pluto causes (or correlates to) paranoia.

In the second approach, called qualitative research, the astrological configuration is the primary focus, for it determines the means for researching the possible outcomes *of* that signature. This approach does not postulate one specific outcome for a given configuration, but recognizes many possible outcomes. Moreover, the goal is not to determine the probable cause of a condition, but to deepen our understanding of a particular astrological factor.

For example, a researcher may attempt to learn about the experience of individuals who have Sun opposed Pluto. Through various types of questionnaires and interviews, s/he might ask subjects to describe their experience of their father, their capacity for self-expression, their susceptibility to power struggles, tendencies toward distrust or suspicion, experiences of betrayal or abuse, resultant shame and guardedness, self-destructiveness, an urge to provoke or transform others, attraction to the healing professions, vulnerability to the dark side of life, engagement in heroic battles against corrupt adversaries, the wish to eliminate evil and vice, conflict between the need for self-esteem and self-reform, encounters with danger and death, sexual preoccupation, the capacity to regenerate or empower wounded systems (people, organizations, conditions), and other potential outcomes.

Again, qualitative research is grounded in the assumption that there is no one particular outcome for an astrological variable like Sun opposed Pluto. Moreover, the number of potential outcomes increases exponentially by adding more variables into the mix—such as, the Sun's sign, house, and total aspects. Potential outcomes are determined not merely by the entire configuration and its embeddedness in the chart as a whole, but by a host of other factors as well, including the individual's gender, education, family background, cultural milieu, maturity, level of awareness, degree of self-actualization, and free will. Because these factors are not predictable from the chart alone, their effect is largely indeterminate.

Conversely, quantitative research is based on the assumption that for any given effect, such as paranoia, there is an astrological cause. Experiments are designed to test the hypothesized relationship between the astrological signature (cause) and the predicted effect. In theory, any number of astrological variables, singularly or in combination, might be postulated as the "signature" of a particular condition. The experimental method lies in the attempt to establish and measure the hypothesized connection.

This is certainly a worthy objective, although the presumed relationship between an astrological factor and a behavioral or experiential outcome has been notoriously difficult to prove. Meanwhile, a qualitative study has entirely different goals. The researcher would not strive to establish an astrological cause or corollary to paranoia that could be expressed quantitatively; rather, she would seek a deeper understanding of the actual experience of subjects who *have* a particular astrological signature.

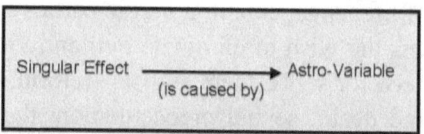

Figure 1: Quantitative Research

In effect, qualitative research of the type proposed here is the inverse of quantitative methods. Quantitative research chooses an outcome—a singular effect—and then tries to correlate that effect to a presumed astrological variable/cause (see Figure 1).

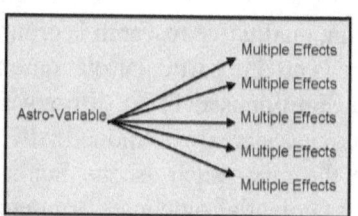

Figure 2: Qualitative Research

Conversely, qualitative research chooses an astrological variable and then investigates how that factor might manifest as multiple behavioral and event outcomes (see Figure 2).

Problems with Quantitative Research

Proving astrology via application of the experimental method has been the ever elusive goal of astrological research. Quantitative, statistical research derives from the "hard" sciences of physics and chemistry and divides the world into causes and effects. The experimental method has privileged status because it is associated with greater certainty of knowledge.

Since astrology gives the appearance of being a hard science, with its planetary "forces" (causes) and specific outcomes (effects), astrologers have assumed that it can be researched with methods that ape the hard sciences.

Yet, experimental research is designed to determine causal relationships between physical things. As a qualitative language of consciousness, astrology is less about things than about symbols, meanings, and values. These reside at an interior, subjective realm and slip through the nets of quantitative methods the way sea slips through the nets of fisherman. An astrological aspect like Sun opposed Pluto may correlate to a physical object such as an abusive father, but it can also symbolize a process of "self-healing," a meaning of "corrupted relations," a value of "depth," and a quality of "intensity." Such outcomes are not easily measured or quantified.

More importantly, chart symbols are polyvalent and multidimensional, meaning they are capable of combining and manifesting in an endless variety of ways. Whereas quantitative research reduces the meaning of an astrological "signature" to one outcome only, such as "paranoia," chart configurations are inherently ambiguous and cannot be collapsed into fixed and singular definitions without destroying their essential meaning. A planetary aspect, for instance, has a *breadth* of meaning that includes subjective and objective correlates, a *coincidence* of meaning between inner and outer manifestations (synchronicity), a *depth* of meaning contingent upon level of integration, a *historical* meaning that changes in response to growth over time, and an *uncertainty* of meaning due to the indeterminate nature of human behavior.

Every variable in astrology—sign, planet, house, and aspect—has a wide range of meanings. The sign Leo, for example, can symbolize a motive (self-esteem), a feeling (confidence), a behavior (creativity), a person (hero), an event (a play), a place (theatre), or a thing (trophy). When signs are combined with planets, houses, and aspects, the sheer number of variables coalesces into so many possible outcomes that settling upon one meaning is like trying to reduce the ocean to a wave. No one would presume to understand the ocean with its currents, tides, and endless variety of life forms by scooping up a few gallons of seawater. Likewise, we cannot understand the depth and complexity of an astrological configuration by collapsing it into a single outcome.

Consider Sun opposed Pluto, which, like any aspect, has subjective and objective manifestations. Subjectively, it symbolizes a psychological conflict between antithetical needs, an unconscious belief with related affects, an aptitude for a specific kind of activity, and a wide range of behavioral traits. Objectively it can manifest as an event pattern from childhood, an external situation or predicament, and a relationship with a specific type of person that recapitulates childhood precursors.

Moreover, subjective and objective correlates mirror one another synchronistically. This means that personality attributes that are unacceptable and thus unrecognized can be projected onto people and events. Unconscious, unactualized psychological potentials tend to manifest outside as "fate." A woman with Sun opposed Pluto, for example, is just as likely to attract a paranoid husband as be paranoid herself.

The vertical dimension of astrological aspects further compounds the interpretive picture (see Figure 3). Every astrological configuration has a depth of meaning that reflects its level of integration. Meanings change in accord with degree of functionality; thus, there are higher and lower levels of expression for any planetary aspect. At lower levels of the hierarchy, an aspect will manifest in a more conflicted way, such that resultant behavior is more primitive, compulsive, rigid, and dysfunctional. At higher levels of integration, the same aspect is characterized by greater freedom of choice,

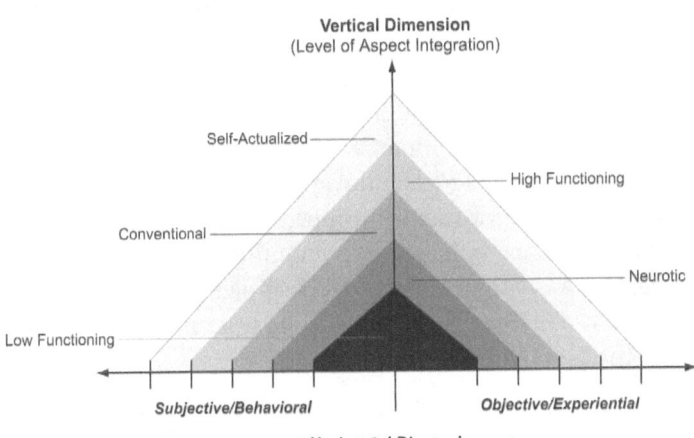

Figure 3: Horizontal & Vertical Dimensions of Planetary Aspects. The above graph shows two basic dimensions of astrology—horizontal and vertical. The horizontal dimension depicts the range of behavior and experience that correlates to any given configuration. Conversely, the vertical dimension depicts level of integration and overall quality of functioning. The left side signifies the subjective aspect of consciousness, which includes drives, beliefs, affects, and behavioral traits. The right side shows the objective side of life—synchronistic events, people, and experiences. There are five levels of functionality—low functioning, neurotic, conventional, high functioning, and self-actualized. Each level is inclusive of behavior and experience that accrues to lower levels while adding new possibilities of expression. As level of integration rises, there is 1) increasing degrees of freedom 2) a broader range of potential experience, and 3) enhanced functionality.

expanded options, more flexibility of expression, improved functionality, less inner and outer conflict, enhanced need satisfaction, and a wider range of potential experience. The point here is that ignorance of the vertical dimension of an astrological variable obscures its depth of meaning.

Not only do people express aspects at higher and lower levels of functionality, but they change over time. At one stage, a person may express the aspect in a severely dysfunctional way. As he continues to mature, heal, and evolve, the same aspect can manifest at a more functional level. The Black Muslim and heavyweight champion boxer, Muhammed Ali, who has Sun opposed Pluto, was reviled as a young man for his hostility and antagonism toward the United States government. He was subsequently stripped of his title and arrested for refusing to be inducted into the military. Later, however, he became a U.S. ambassador overseas and is now recognized as a beloved national hero. In 1996, he was chosen to light the torch for the Olympic Games in Atlanta.

From the foregoing we can see that collapsing a multi-dimensional variable like Sun opposed Pluto into a single, concrete outcome constitutes a radical narrowing of its range of meaning. In fact, it could be argued that reliability of interpretation (accuracy) is inversely proportional to concreteness (specificity). Again, astrology is a language of abstract qualities and developmental processes, not concrete things. A chart/person is an indeterminate system that is only relatively predictable. Moreover, at higher levels of integration, freedom of expression actually increases. Thus there is an inherent and inescapable uncertainty to astrological meanings.

Not only can astrological configurations express themselves through different outcomes, but the same outcome can be a product of different types of configurations. Paranoia, for example, is but one of many outcomes associated with Sun opposition Pluto; yet, it can also be a product of innumerable other astrological factors. These would be too many and varied to speculate on here. Suffice to say that paranoia could conceivably involve dozens of different combinations of variables.

Some astrologers might argue that a viable method of astrological research would entail: 1) adding all combinations of variables together to create a hypothesized "astro-signature" for paranoia, and 2) conducting an experiment to test whether individuals diagnosed as paranoid are more likely to have such a signature than a non-paranoid control group. The problem here, however, is defining the dependent variable—paranoia—in such a way that it can be clearly operationalized for research purposes. There are many types and degrees of paranoia, so operationalizing it would be difficult. Moreover, as stated earlier, the number of potential outcomes increases exponentially the greater the number of astrological variables. An "astro-signature" for paranoia, which could conceivably involve dozens of astrological variables, would also correlate to innumerable *other* potential outcomes. In my opinion, this is not likely to lead to confirmation of the hypothesis. It follows that attempts to correlate precise outcomes to specific astrological signatures is stacking the proverbial deck against astrology.

Given the difficulties of utilizing a strictly quantitative method to test astrological precepts, the question arises: *how can a design be created that takes into account the unique nature of astrological causality and provides the best chance of demonstrating astrology's validity?* The answer, I believe, lies in finding a way to combine qualitative and quantitative methods into a unified design. It is to that goal that we now turn.

A Phenomenological Approach

A qualitative method that is uniquely qualified for astrological research is the phenomenological approach. The purpose of the method is to investigate the essential nature of an experience, such as an astrological configuration or transit. In this regard, the method is descriptive rather than predictive. It focuses on a subjective, non-empirical realm by asking participants to describe, as fully as possible, their actual experience of a phenomenon.

First, a basic question is formulated, such as "What is your experience of natal Sun opposed Pluto?" Once participants are selected that have the required configuration, the researcher engages them in a series of individual, open-ended interviews by asking pertinent questions. Interviews may be supplemented by questionnaires, biographical material, or other means of acquiring relevant data. Meanwhile, researchers are required to suspend preconceptions, beliefs, or expectations about the meaning of the aspect. Subjects, in turn, are asked to engage in a process of self-reflection in which they draw upon their memories, feelings, and linguistic abilities to describe their experience with maximum clarity. The goal is to acquire observation statements of directly apprehended experience on both subjective and objective dimensions. Respondents describe attitudes and behaviors that relate to the aspect, as well as relevant experiences involving external events and relationships. Interviews are recorded and later transcribed.

The next step is data analysis. The goal here is to deduce from the evidence the essential form, structure, and meaning of the phenomenon. Having amassed a sufficient quantity of information, generalizations are derived from the descriptions offered and the data is organized into themes and categories. Hopefully, a structure emerges that entails basic units of meaning that hold across research participants. In other words, the goal is to discern and articulate commonalities of experience. No attempt is made to be objective; rather, such information is intrinsically intersubjective; that is, capable of being shared by different people, thus allowing for confirmation or disconfirmation of meaning by a community of others who have had the same experience.

The final step is to interpret the data from multiple perspectives. What does the interpreter conclude from data analysis? Although the data might coalesce into five or six basic themes, a larger, more inclusive understanding can be abstracted that subsumes the units under a more general heading. Quotes from participants should be included in order to provide persuasive evidence to substantiate interpretations. Eventually, it may be possible to formulate a final hypothesis as to the meaning and probable experiences of individuals that have natal Sun opposed Pluto. For example, a researcher might conclude:

Individuals with this aspect seem to undergo recurrent identity crises and transformations in order to heal a shame-based, wounded sense of self. In one form or another, they must face evil and conquer a fear of death that is implicit in their relations with others. This often requires a confrontation with the dark side of life and a willingness to be vulnerable. Standing up to the dark leads to restoration of self-esteem, empowerment, and wounded-healer status.

All of this, of course, does not necessarily constitute a proof of astrology. To make inroads toward that end, a researcher would have to convincingly demonstrate that individuals that have Sun opposed Pluto are more likely to have certain experiences than those without the aspect.

Testing the Hypothesis Quantitatively

The final stage of our qualitative-quantitative hybrid design is to create a Likert-type scale that measures the degree to which an experimental group with Sun opposed Pluto scores higher than a control group that does not have that configuration.

The instrument would consist of approximately twenty to thirty statements that describe subjective and objective correlates of Sun-opposed-Pluto. Each statement would be no more than a few sentences, and would draw upon the core themes and categories of meaning revealed in the phenomenological stage of research. Subjective statements would describe impulses, feelings, conflicts, attitudes, beliefs, expectations, interests, aptitudes, and actual behaviors. Objective statements would cover experiences, events, situations, predicaments, and relationships with Sun-Pluto others.

For example, a subjective statement might be:

I frequently find it difficult to trust. Experience has taught me that people often have ulterior motives and covert intentions that thwart my objectives. I must be vigilant and guarded in my relationships.

An objective statement might be:

My relationship with my father was somewhat painful. He was consistently cruel, shaming, or harshly disapproving of my behavior. Sometimes it felt as if he wanted to make me over into someone else.

Each statement can be graded in a Likert scale multiple-choice format that measures the respondent's intensity of agreement or disagreement.

- ☐ Strongly agree (2 points)
- ☐ Somewhat agree (1 point)
- ☐ Uncertain (0 points)
- ☐ Somewhat disagree (-1 point)
- ☐ Strongly disagree (-2 points)

Clearly, the success of the instrument in measuring Sun-Pluto responses would derive from the accuracy and psychological sophistication of the statements themselves. Care would need to be taken to devise statements in a gentle, value-neutral way so as to avoid evoking responses based on self-esteem needs. It would not be effective, for example, to state:

I behave in ways that are shameful, disgusting, and hurtful to others. Vindictiveness and cruelty are tactics that I frequently employ to let others know that I am someone to be feared.

While some respondents might actually feel and act this way, the statement as phrased is too extreme and thus likely to evoke a disagreement response.

Statements concerning specific issues and themes could be

phrased in a variety of ways, both positive and negative. Some statements should be included that are precisely opposite of what might be expected from a Sun-Pluto person. These statements would be graded in the reverse; thus, disagreement responses would be scored as earning points. An example could be:

I tend to be rather optimistic and positive in my interactions with others. In my experience, most people have an immediately positive first impression of me, and are apt to like who I am.

If the Sun-Pluto person disagrees with this statement, this would count as points *earned*, since such a statement constitutes a reverse way of describing the hypothesized Sun-Pluto oppositional attitude. In this case, the scoring would proceed as follows:

- ☐ Strongly agree (-2 points)
- ☐ Somewhat agree (-1 point)
- ☐ Uncertain (0 points)
- ☐ Somewhat disagree (1 point)
- ☐ Strongly disagree (2 points)

Not only would statements need to cover a sufficient *breadth* of meaning to encompass subjective and objective permutations of the aspect, but other statements should address the *depth* dimension of meaning. Some would lean toward less integrated, more primitive expressions of the aspect, whereas others would represent the more functional, integrated version. By providing a range of statements that describe both the breadth and depth of the aspect, the probability is increased that respondent scores will confirm the hypothesis. A statement at the low end of the continuum might be expressed as the following:

A recurrent theme in my life has been a tendency to behave in a self-destructive way toward others. By being resistant, provocative, or even hostile, I get other people to react negatively toward me. I suspect that sometimes I am my own worst enemy.

A statement at the high end could be:

I am unusually sensitive to the human tendency toward self-destructiveness. Often, people are so afraid of being hurt or violated that they behave with hostile defensiveness, thereby getting others to respond in ways that confirm their fears. I have a strong interest in helping people with this sort of problem.

Other statements would address the historical dimension of the aspect; that is, how it evolves over time. At earlier developmental stages, hard aspects tend to operate in a more conflictual, less integrated fashion. Behavior tends to be relatively dysfunctional, which, in turn, leads to frustrating experiences. Outer figures that embody Sun-Pluto are likely to behave in a manner that frustrates the subject's need for approval, validation, and self-esteem. For example, an envious sibling or parent might persecute the child for any attempt at self-expression. A statement might say:

As a child, I frequently felt unjustly accused of wrongdoing. Some family members chose to see me in the worst possible light and would blame, disparage, or shame me. This made me wonder if there was something wrong with me.

An adult version might be:

One of my challenges has been to overcome a fear that any attempt at self-expression is likely to evoke a negative response. At times I suffer from performance anxiety; I fear that efforts to be myself will cause others to shun, attack, or reject me. However, I've made progress in healing this fear, and now feel more empowered to express my true self.

Once a sufficient number of statements are created, the researcher would administer the test to an experimental group of subjects that have the aspect, and a control group of subjects who do not. One way of selecting the experimental group would be to advertise for individuals born on days when the Sun was in opposition to Pluto within an orb of three degrees. This would entail approximately 7 days per year over perhaps a thirty span, ages 30 to 60, or 210 total days. Ideally, test respondents would be individuals with no high-level knowledge of astrology and no knowledge of the configuration being tested. This would help to assure that respondents are not predisposed to identify with the statements out of loyalty to astrology. In fact, the experiment would not need to be advertised as a test of astrology, but as a type of sociological research.

With regard to the control group without the aspect, special care would need to be taken to select out participants who have features in their charts that might predispose them to respond in ways that mimic the Sun-Pluto experimental group. These subjects would unnecessarily contaminate the data. It would be important to eliminate, for example, respondents that have a conjunction, square, or quincunx between Sun-Pluto. Also, perhaps participants should be eliminated who have an inner planet in hard aspect to Pluto; or Sun or Moon or Ascendant in Scorpio; or more than two personal planets in Scorpio; or a stellium in Scorpio; or the Sun or Moon in the 8th house. While these configurations are subtly different from Sun opposed Pluto, there is enough overlap of meaning to create a problem in clearly differentiating the two groups. This would necessitate, of course, that participants in the study have accurate birth data.

Discussion and Conclusion

Two types of astrological research methods were discussed. Quantitative designs attempt to determine if a specific effect can be correlated to a precise astrological cause. Conversely, qualitative designs explore how a particular configuration can manifest in a variety of outcomes.

Quantitative research in astrology was criticized on the basis of its narrowness of interpretation. Particular configurations can produce many and varied outcomes; and outcomes can be the product of many and varied configurations. This makes it extremely difficult to correlate singular effects to hypothesized astrological causes.

Conversely, qualitative methods capture the full range and depth of meaning of an aspect. Yet, they lack the robust precision of experimental designs, and are weak in their ability to confirm astrology.

To solve the deficiencies of each method, a hybrid design was proposed that integrates qualitative and quantitative components. Emphasis was placed on how astrological configurations like Sun opposed Pluto are indeterminate and multidimensional, meaning they express themselves on multiple dimensions concurrently—subjective, objective, synchronistic, horizontal, vertical, and historical. By utilizing a phenomenological method, these dimensions can be precisely articulated for any astrological aspect. The wealth of data that results can then be organized into various themes and categories of meaning. Finally, a survey instrument—a Likert scale—comprised of statements that result from the phenomenological study can be administered to test subjects. The hypothesis is that an experimental group with the aspect will score higher on the Likert scale than a control group. In effect, the phenomenological stage of the study is combined with the survey instrument so that it becomes possible to actually quantify test scores.

By providing a sufficiently broad range of cognitive, emotional, behavioral, and experiential descriptors, which reflect the full range of possible expressions of a given configuration, this hybrid design avoids the pitfall of assuming that an astrological signature corresponds to a singular trait or experience. Proposed descriptive statements capture an array of psychological traits and synchronistic events; thus, both inner and outer manifestations of the aspect can be scored. Horizontal, vertical, and historical dimensions can also be graded. Even if subjects do not identify with every Sun-Pluto statement, the chances of confirming the hypothesis are increased by providing a broad range of Sun-Pluto descriptors. Although astrology is a qualitative language of consciousness, the proposed design affords a means of quantifying scores on a specified configuration.

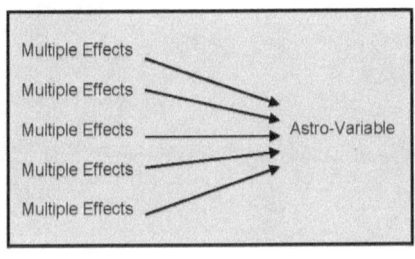

Figure 4: A Hybrid Design

While still being quantitative, this design is precisely the opposite of conventional quantitative designs, and more in accord with how astrology actually works. Rather than postulate complex, multi-variable "astro-signatures" to correlate to singular outcomes, a single astro-variable is tested against a complex, multi-dimensional "effect." This is reflected in the graphic shown above:

Figure 4 depicts a method that is experimental in the same way that Figure 2 was, except now the "effect" being measured is the full spectrum of qualitative outcomes that the variable entails. Rather than broadening the astro-signature by adding more and more factors, we have expanded the definition of the effect instead. That is, we are not measuring a single, concrete effect, but a multidimensional expression that reflects the aspect as a whole.

Our qualitative-quantitative design cuts both ways. The qualitative component affords the opportunity to gain useful information that clarifies and deepens our knowledge of an astrological configuration. Its quantitative component provides a means for using statistics to confirm the experimental hypothesis, thus providing greater certainty of knowledge.

Using the Developmental Age Method to Interpret Significant Experiences

By Julie R. Grant, M.A.

ABSTRACT: This study uses a combination of hermeneutics and historical inquiry to analyze the individual natal charts of Winston Churchill and Franklin Roosevelt according to the Developmental Age Method (DAM) developed by Glenn Perry, Ph.D. The basic premise of the DAM is that signs and their corresponding houses signify developmental stages of fixed duration within the human life cycle. Planets falling within these houses specify an exact month and year during which the meaning of that configuration is acutely felt and expressed. The quality of the planetary period can extend backwards and forwards from that point for several months or more. Planetary aspects connect different periods diachronistically—a coincidence of meaning across time—such that an earlier period is analogous to a later one. In this paper, particular focus is on historical data related to the beginning of Churchill and Roosevelt's legendary relationship during 1940-1941 at the inception of America's entry into World War II. The study centers on Churchill's Uranus age of 66.8 in August 1941 when he was British Prime Minister, and Roosevelt's Moon age of 58.6

in June 1940 when he was America's president. Planets, signs, houses, and aspects are analyzed using readily available historical data. The study confirms that each man's experiences at their respective developmental ages were strikingly in accord with the relevant planetary configuration. It also consistently demonstrated diachronistic relationships between planetary ages connected by aspect. That is, experiences at the earlier age appeared to be analogous to and preparatory for experiences at the later age.

Research Topic and Question

The natal charts of Franklin D. Roosevelt and Winston Churchill are analyzed utilizing the Developmental Age Method[1] (DAM) developed by Glenn Perry, Ph.D. Particular focus is on historical data related to when Roosevelt and Churchill began their consequential relationship at the inception of America's entry into World War II.

My research entails an analysis of the individual natal charts of Roosevelt and Churchill with a focus on discerning correlations between planetary placements and the period of 1940 to 1941. This examination specifically involves Roosevelt's Moon in Cancer in the tenth house, signifying age 58 in June 1940, and Churchill's Uranus in Leo in the eleventh correlating to age 66 in August 1941. My primary goal was to discern if the meaning of these placements clearly correlated to Roosevelt and Churchill's individual goals, intentions, and experiences during the period cited.

The DAM provides a means for determining the meaning of exact ages that planets signify in the native's life. I also examined natal aspects to these planets that might potentially relate to earlier events based on the DAM ages, looking for diachronistic relationships between the two periods of time. Perry asserts:

"If a planet forms a significant aspect to another planet that resides at an earlier or later developmental stage, those two stages are apt to be connected in a diachronic way—that is, a formative event in the earlier stage may form the basis for an analogous event in the latter stage since the same aspect unites the two periods of time."[2]

My hypothesis is that earlier events that correspond with planets that aspect Roosevelt's Moon and Churchill's Uranus were in some way preparatory for, and analogous with, the seminal events that occurred during 1940-1941.

Purpose of Research

The purpose of this research is to examine evidence that the Developmental Age Method can determine "the precise periods that planets signify in a native's life."[3] Highly credible empirical evidence can be derived from well-researched events of people with very public lives. Positive evidence that is supportive of the applicability of the DAM will ideally contribute to the field of psychological astrology.

Research Method

My research method entails a combination of hermeneutics with historical inquiry. Hermeneutics is a technique used to interpret textual information. In the context of this paper, relevant information includes autobiographical and biographical data about meaningful events in the lives of Churchill and Roosevelt respectively, as found in books and on websites.

I also use the theoretical lens of astropsychology as taught at the Academy of AstroPsychology. This lens includes the notion that astrological signs symbolize specific needs, that planets are designed to fulfill the needs of the signs they rule, and that houses provide the environment in which the action takes place.[4]

The orbs used for the interpretation of aspects between planets are as follows:

Aspect	Applying Orb	Separating Orb
Conjunction	10	8
Opposition	9	7
Trine	8	7
Square	7	6
Sextile	4	3
Quincunx	4	3

Overview of Key Astrological Concepts

Developmental Zodiac

To understand the Developmental Age Method, one must first understand Perry's AstroPsychology model. According to Perry, the proper function of planets is to fulfill the psychological need of the signs they rule, whereas houses symbolize the environments within which planetary actions occur. Theories from developmental psychology are used to support correlations between sign meanings and specific stages of the human life cycle. Each sign signifies a progressively more advanced stage as one moves around the zodiac.[5] In Perry's own words:

> "Evidence suggests that the zodiac not only symbolizes the structure and dynamics of the psyche, but also the evolutionary unfoldment of consciousness. That is, the structure of the zodiac exactly parallels the stages of the human life cycle. Each sign can be understood as a developmental stage of specific quality and duration. And because houses are based on the same angular dynamics as the signs to which they correspond, they also represent the same 12-stage process.
>
> "While the zodiac shows the generic unfolding of consciousness, houses reveal the native's actual ex-

perience during particular periods. This occurs by virtue of planets signaling not only where but when that planetary process will be most acute."[6]

To illustrate, Aries symbolizes needs for freedom, independence, and survival. The developmental stage at which these needs are prominent is the first two years of life. Infants are concerned primarily with fulfilling needs for immediate gratification associated with survival. Providing an environment for the fulfillment of Aries needs, the first house symbolizes births, new beginnings, adventure, spontaneity, and how we assert ourselves; the first house thus aligns with ages 0-2.

Similarly, Taurus symbolizes needs for safety, security, and sensual gratification. Taurus needs for attachment are fulfilled through second house circumstances, which includes things that one acquires that provide a source of security. Taurean needs are paramount during the stage of 2-5 when toddlers become concerned with feeling safe, form intense attachments, and begin to acquire toys and transitional objects that provide a sense of comfort and security. As a corollary to the sign Taurus, the second house signifies ages 2-5 as well. Planetary factors associated with the second suggest how the individual might have navigated this particular developmental stage.

As a final example, Gemini symbolizes needs for information, learning, and mental stimulation. The third house signifies the environment (early schooling and mentally stimulating experiences) through which these needs can be fulfilled. Gemini/third house needs are foremost during age 5-9, at which time children learn to read and write.

Planets are associated with particular types of action because they naturally strive to fulfill the needs of the signs they rule. These actions will be noticeably apparent in the house the planet occupies. Moreover, a planet's action will be qualified by its sign position.[7] Thus, for example, if Mercury in Scorpio inhabits the second house, the native might associate learning with security, leading to a habit of collecting books with a desire to ensure there will always be material available for knowledge acquisition. Because Mercury is in Scorpio, the need for this data may have a quality of life and death urgency. The person may dig deep with intense curiosity and develop a sense of power from the knowledge gained, as in "knowledge is power."

Dispositors

Although each sign is ruled by one particular planet, any planet can be in any sign. A dispositor is a planet that rules the sign that another planet occupies. In the example, Mercury is in Scorpio; thus Pluto, as the ruler of Scorpio, disposes Mercury. Pluto acts on behalf of Mercury, carrying forward Mercury's intentions. When studying, for example, the native may associate learning (Mercury) with some sort of crisis (Scorpio) that threatens his sense of security (second house). This association, in turn, activates Pluto, which will strive to resolve the crisis through its own actions in the sign and house it occupies. Pluto (transforming, healing) symbolizes the next step after Mercury (studying).

Astropsychology also considers aspects to dispositors. If Mercury is opposed Pluto, then Mercury is "ill-disposed" because it is in conflict with its own dispositor. Although Pluto is the next planet in the sequence of unfolding action, its opposition to Mercury creates tension and potential conflict.[8] Perhaps the native's way of acquiring information, and/or the nature of the information gained, evokes a reaction in the environment that exacerbates the sense of danger associated with learning and communication. Later we will see how this exact sequence applies to Winston Churchill.

Developmental Age Method

The Developmental Age Method (DAM) takes the developmental zodiac one step further and calculates the age at which planets reside in the natal chart. For instance, Mercury in the second house will fall within the range of two to five years of age. The precise location of Mercury within the second house will determine the exact age. The DAM postulates that "planets at specific positions within houses may correspond to critical events that occurred during the period that planet signifies within the house."[9] In other words, distinct and meaningful events that correspond to the meaning of the planet/sign/house will be seen in the life at the age calculated. Additionally, the DAM posits that there is a diachronic relationship between planets in aspect with each other. As Perry writes, "diachronistic patterns show meaningful relationships between events from different stages that are expressions of the same planetary aspect."[10] According to the DAM, earlier events are often analogous to, and preparatoy for, challenges and experiences that occur during the stage that the later planet symbolizes.

The following is a table of the developmental age ranges by sign/house:[11]

Sign-House Developmental Ages

Sign/House	Age Range
Aries/first house	0-2
Taurus/second house	2-5
Gemini/third house	5-9
Cancer/fourth house	9-14
Leo/fifth house	14-20
Virgo/sixth house	20-27
Libra/seventh house	27-35
Scorpio/eighth house	35-44
Sagittarius/ninth house	44-54
Capricorn/tenth house	54-65
Aquarius/eleventh house	65-77
Pisces/twelfth house	77-90

Winston Churchill

Concerning Churchill's life, I have focused my study on Uranus' sign, house, and aspects for the relevant time periods. Uranus' aspects include square aspects to Mercury in the second house and Pluto in the eighth, as well as an opposition to Saturn in the fifth house (see Figure 2). I will outline the time and quality of significant events correlating to each planetary placement, along with diachronicities between these events and those of the Uranus period.

Mercury Age of 4.4 in April 1879

Churchill's Mercury is in Scorpio in the second house. The second house correlates to ages 2-5 and signifies the developmental stage at which the child develops the ability to trust that parents and other significant attachment figures will be stable, safe and sufficiently constant in their affections that an internal sense of security can develop. In developmental psychology, this is referred to as the attainment of self and object constancy.

Churchill's Mercury age of 4.4 corresponds to April 1879. According to the DAM, Churchill would have had a "pivotal or noteworthy event" during a one to two year period centering about April 1879 that would correlate to the meaning of Mercury Scorpio opposing Pluto Taurus.

As the planet of learning and competence, Mercury rules the cognitive functions. In Scorpio, it may be intense, focused on depth, and perhaps somewhat guarded. In the second house, Mercury in Scorpio suggests a passionate student with a penetrating intellect, and for whom intellectual competence is necessary for a sense of security to develop.

Pluto is intense, vigilant and powerful. Pluto's imperative is to descend into the shadows so that it can expose what lurks below. Since it occupies the sign of Taurus in the eighth house, this suggests a deep concern about financial stability that may

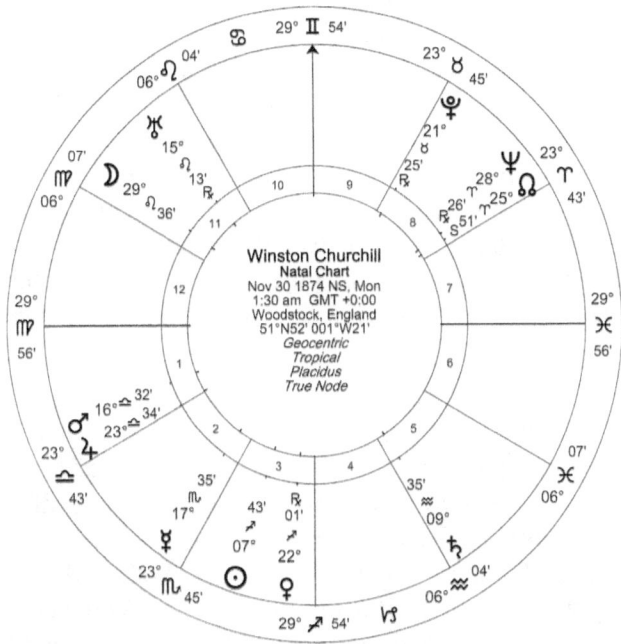

be affected by factors beyond Churchill's control.

According to Perry, the opposition is a Libra aspect. Thus, Churchill's Mercury-Pluto opposition requires a harmonizing of the respective planetary functions. If operating in a functional way, each planet balances the other. However, since Mercury is ill-disposed by Pluto, this correlates to an unbalanced excess of Scorpio-Pluto energies impinging upon Mercury, which increases the likelihood of Mercury dysfunction. The challenge for Churchill will be to keep his wits about him even as events rattle the ground beneath him.

Like many of his social class, young Churchill had a governess who was hired to tutor him in reading and math when he was 4-6 years of age. The tutoring occurred when his family lived in Ireland at a home they called "The Little Lodge."[12] One can only imagine a four-year-old Winston trying to penetrate the tortured vagaries of math at such a young age. In his autobiography, he described his oppression by the tyrannical requirements of his instructress in a manner consistent with Mercury's opposition to Pluto. According to Churchill, the menacing numbers terrorized him as they moved around in unpredictable ways. His governess seemed a virtual embodiment of evil, forcing him to probe a mystery beyond his ability to grasp. Fearing she would expose his inadequacies, young Winston would hide in the dark woods to avoid the torments of schooling. Churchill colorfully recounts his memory of this experience:

> "Letters after all had only got to be known, and when they stood together in a certain way one recognized their formation and that it meant a certain sound or word which one uttered when pressed sufficiently. But the figures [numbers] were tied into all sorts of tangles and did things to one another which it was extremely difficult to forecast with complete accuracy. You had to say what they did each time they were tied up together, and the Governess apparently attached enormous importance to the answer being exact. If it was not right, it was wrong. It was not any use being 'nearly right'. In some cases these figures got into debt with one another: you had to borrow one or carry one, and afterward you had to pay back the one you had borrowed. These complications cast a steadily gathering shadow over my daily life".[13]

All of this is consistent with the two-year period surrounding his Mercury age-point of 4.4, or April 1878 to April 1880. In April 1880, right on schedule, Churchill's family moved to London.[14] Since Churchill's trauma of being schooled by his detestable governess at the Little Lodge took place before the London move, it is reasonable to assume it occurred between

April 1878, when Churchill was only three, and April 1880 when he turned five. As I will show, the underlying psychological dynamics expressed during this second house period will thread their way through significant events that occurred during the eighth house Pluto period of his early forties. In fact, his use of the term "shadow" in the quote above foreshadows the difficulties he will encounter at his Pluto age.

Saturn Age of 14.4 in April 1889

Churchill's Saturn resides in Aquarius in the fifth house opposing Uranus in Leo in the eleventh. In the astropsychology model, the fifth house correlates to adolescence, the primary tasks of which are developing a sense of identity, winning approval, and enjoying time with friends. The fifth house age range is 14 to 20.

Churchill's Saturn age of 14.4 corresponds to April 1889. According to the DAM, between approximately April 1888 and April 1890 he would have experienced noteworthy event(s) signifying Saturn Aquarius in the fifth house opposing Uranus in Leo in the eleventh. Saturn is the planet of achievement, discipline and structure. In Aquarius, Saturn may express itself in a nonconformist or even revolutionary manner with an eye on the big picture. Its placement in the fifth suggests an unconventional young man who strives to be successful in his performance. Since Saturn is opposed Uranus, however, it has to strike a point of balance with its Uranian counterpart.

Uranus signifies liberation and innovation. Uranus in Leo in the eleventh house opposing Saturn suggests a person aligned with a heroic cause in resistance to tyrannical control. We might surmise that Churchill's instinct was to awaken a sense of pride in his eleventh house compatriots, especially in opposition to what he perceived as cold, totalitarian oppression. In fact, by the time Churchill reached his Uranian age of 66, this is precisely what he did: instill pride (Leo) in allied forces

(Uranus) that were opposing German oppression (Saturn). Churchill led the movement to resist Germany in WWII by championing the cause of freedom.

However, Churchill's Saturn in Aquarius was ill-disposed by Uranus, causing additional challenge to the opposition in a manner that was especially apparent during his Saturn period of 13-15. Saturn Aquarius opposed Uranus can result in too much Aquarius-Uranus, at least as perceived by Saturn. In effect, Saturn is evoking a Uranian response that actually frustrates Saturn's aims. For example, Churchill's urge to excel by adopting a global, holistic perspective may backfire if such a perspective upsets the established order. Accordingly, Churchill may find that his confident drive to shake things up may impact his ability to succeed.

Recall that Churchill's Saturn signifies age 14.4 in April 1889, a period extending approximately one year before and after that date. Winston took the entrance exam at the Harrow School in March 1888. His favorite subjects were history, poetry and writing (essays). However, the exam included sections on two topics he disliked: Latin and Math. Having no interest in those subjects, he refused to make any effort to learn them. He could not answer a single question on the Latin exam; thus, when he entered Harrow in April 1888, he was placed in the Third Form (lowest division) of the school.[15] In effect, Saturn at this fifth house stage of Churchill's life manifested as an oppressive authority that devalued his performance and against which he wanted to rebel (Uranus).

Nevertheless, Churchill had successes at the Harrow School. For example, he flawlessly recited 1,200 lines of Macaulay's narrative ballad, the *Lays of Ancient Rome*. But his achievements were on his own terms; that is, when he *chose* to apply himself.[16] Conversely, he rebelled against things he did not want to do. Young Winston was accused by his superiors of being inconsistent, careless, forgetful and irregular in his efforts and accomplishments, as befits Saturn in Aquarius opposed to its own dispositor.[17] In fact, his inconstancy caused him to remain in the lowest form despite his potential for much higher level performance.[18]

Because of his academic placement, he was not allowed to study Latin and Greek. The administrators at Harrow thought that Third Form students lacked the intelligence to comprehend foreign languages. Consequently, he was enrolled in an English program and studied with a man, Robert Somervell, whom he credited as the finest English language educator that he could have encountered. Regarding Somervell's instruction, Churchill recounts:

> "Each [sentence component] had its colour and its bracket. It was a kind of drill. We did it almost daily. As I remained in the Third Form three times as long as anyone else, I had three times as much of it. I learned it thoroughly. Thus I got into my bones the essential structure of the ordinary British sentence—which is a noble thing."[19]

In effect, Churchill's strong oratorical foundation (Saturn) was a direct result of his rebellion (Uranus) against studying subjects that disinterested him. Ironically, while he struggled to comply with the structure of Harrow's academic programs, he delighted in the structure of the English language. As his fifth house peers were learning Latin and Greek, he was mastering (Saturn) the English language, a mastery that would become a famously crucial part of his accomplishments throughout his career. Uranus provided the clinical detachment and overview of Saturnian structure (syntax and grammar). At 14, his Saturn-Uranus opposition provided the requisite training for the fame Churchill was ultimately to achieve with Uranus' dispositor—Sun Sagittarius in the third. It was precisely Churchill's capacity to speak heroically and persuade convincingly that elevated him to the status of the world's greatest orator at a critical period in human history.

Note again that Churchill began his Harrow schooling in April 1888, so his first two years fall perfectly into the DAM timeframe of April 1888 to April 1890. This timeframe included his rebellion and subsequent mastery of English.

Diachronistic Relationship Between the Mercury Age and the Pluto Age of 43.3 in March 1918

Churchill's Pluto age of 43.3 corresponds to March 1918. Generically, the eighth house signifies ages 35 to 44 when individuals frequently struggle with issues of integrity, power, shared financial arrangements (loans, debt, investments), and personal transformation, often associated with a mid-life crisis. Churchill's Pluto in Taurus in the eighth opposing Mercury in Scorpio in the second corresponds to 1917 to 1919. According to the DAM, this period is likely to entail intense and conflicted negotiations involving financial transactions of a high-risk nature.

Just prior to this period, Churchill had been Secretary for the Admiralty in the British Armed Services. In 1915, during WW I at Gallipoli (in what is now Turkey), the English were engaged in a disastrous military campaign that cost 50,000 British lives. Churchill was largely held responsible and subsequently demoted to a minor cabinet post, resulting in one of the two most severe depressions of his life.[20]

In 1917, just as the start of Churchill's Pluto period, the Bolshevik (communist) forces of Vladimir Lenin and Leon Trotsky gained control of the Russian government through a successful rebellion. Given the Communist threat to the stability and values of Western Europe, Britain and its allies needed to determine the best strategy concerning Russia at the conclusion of World War I. As Minister of Munitions in December 1918, Churchill was pushing for increased engagement in the region. In January 1919, still in his Pluto-age period, his career was reborn (Pluto) when Prime Minister David Lloyd George appointed him Secretary for War and Air, the most responsible position he had obtained since the Gallipoli campaign.[21]

The Allies initially intervened on behalf of the anti-Communist faction, but it was short-lived. American President Woodrow Wilson blocked Churchill's efforts to defeat the Bolsheviks when he decided to withdraw allied troops. Neither the U.S. nor the other Allies would agree to Churchill's admonitions to increase engagement. Churchill was relentless in his efforts to overturn the decision, despite having no official standing in the decision process. Lloyd George found it necessary to act swiftly and decidedly to crush Churchill's attempts at making war.[22]

As Secretary of War and Air in 1919, Churchill's job was to oversee the withdrawal of British forces from North Russia. Instead, he used the authority and flexibility of his position to increase military resources under the guise of needing additional forces to safeguard retreating troops. Lloyd George was fearful that Churchill's obsession was devouring Britain's economic means. He also bemoaned Churchill's compulsive preoccupation with the Bolsheviks, charging that it incapacitated him for other work.[23]

Churchill's fixation on the dangers represented by the Bolsheviks was obvious, and he used his abundant rhetorical skills to demonize Russia to the British public. He portrayed the Bolsheviks as:

> "... a poisoned Russia, an infected Russia, a plague-bearing Russia, a Russia of armed hordes smiting not only with bayonet and cannon, but accompanied and preceded by the swarms of typhus bearing vermin which slay the bodies of men, and political doctrines which destroy the health and even the soul of nations... the mob are raised against the middle

class to murder them, to plunder their houses, to debouch their wives and carry off their children. . . ."[24]

Note the heavy use of Plutonic imagery in the above quote—plague-bearing, armed hordes, destroy, mob, murder, plunder, rape—all of which bear testament to Churchill's immersion in Plutonic depths precisely at his Pluto age point. In fact, he was so singularly identified with the goal of armed intervention against the evil Bolsheviks that the British press referred to it as "Mr. Churchill's Private War."[25] In the end, however, Churchill had to acquiesce. It is arguable that his estimation of the extent of the Bolshevik threat was clearer than that of his colleagues. Nevertheless, his attempt to increase military investment in the region was unrealistic given the state of Britain's treasury and the Allies' lack of appetite for another military ordeal on the heels of the First World War.[26] In other words, it was a time of intense and vocal opposition for Churchill, as befits Pluto opposed Mercury.

While Churchill used his oratorical (Mercury) skills to expose the menacing, Plutonic Bolsheviks, he was also ignoring his accountability to ensure Britain's financial security while obsessing about the need to overpower the enemy to secure British interests. Again, this perfectly reflects the second-eighth house polarity—the houses of savings and debt—while also highlighting the life-and-death intensity of Mercury Scorpio opposed to its own dispositor.

Consistent with what the DAM would predict, Churchill's experience in his role as Secretary for War and Air during his Pluto period of 43-44 was analogous to his Mercury-age 3-5. In the earlier period, he feared the ire of his governess and parents for his stupidity. Now it was the Prime Minister of the United Kingdom, Lloyd George, who cast an ominous shadow over him. This time, however, there was no running to hide in the woods from his adversary. Churchill faced off against Lloyd George without flinching, trading intellectual blows with one of the most powerful men in the world. At the same time, his obsession with Russia undermined his credibility and demonstrated his need to integrate further the Mercury-Pluto opposition.

Uranus Age: 66 Years in August 1941

In Perry's astropsychology model, the eleventh house corresponds to ages 64-77 when focus shifts from career ambitions to humanitarian concern for the collective. The individual joins with others of like mind to foster change and reforms for the benefit of the broader community. Churchill's Uranus is located at 66.8 years, corresponding to August 1941. It is square Mercury in Scorpio in the second house and opposition Saturn in Aquarius in the fifth.

The DAM posits that Churchill could experience significant events between approximately August 1940 and August 1942 that reflect the Uranus-Saturn opposition, Uranus in square aspect to Mercury and Pluto, and with diachronistic connections to the earlier periods that Mercury, Pluto, and Saturn signify.

Diachronicity Between Uranus Age 66 and Saturn Age 14

Generically, Uranus opposition Saturn suggests a tendency to rebel against authority and to challenge the status quo with a more enlightened, progressive view. Initially we saw this during Churchill's Saturn age of 14, when he refused to conform (Uranus) to the Harrow School's oppressive regime (Saturn). Recall that they required him to study subjects in which he had no interest. As an aspect of marriage the opposition suggests that in addition to rebelling against an ominous threat, a yet more integrated version would involve Churchill finding a partner to help liberate the group with which he is identified (Uranus in the eleventh) from oppression and control by a totalitarian other (Saturn in the fifth). For that is precisely what was needed in relation to Fascist Germany in August 1941.

Over the years Churchill had developed a reputation for disrupting government and military structures by speaking out against prevailing views whenever he perceived serious threats to which others were not responding. Given the threat from Nazi Germany, Churchill was concerned throughout the 1930s with the inadequate level of funding for Britain's military. He continually made his apprehensions known to the British parliament. By 1940, his perspective proved visionary.[27]

Neville Chamberlain was appointed Prime Minister in 1937. Despite disagreeing with Winston's point of view, he felt compelled to include the prophetic Churchill in his cabinet and appointed him as the first lord of the Admiralty.[28] In 1940, Chamberlain's policy of appeasement led to a vote of no confidence in his leadership. He subsequently recommended to King George VI that Churchill succeed him as Prime Minister. Churchill began his appointment on May 10, 1940, precisely at the start of his Uranus age period of 65-67 (1940-1942).[29]

Churchill knew that Britain could not stand up to the mighty Third Reich alone. Beginning in 1939, he was in secret correspondence with Franklin Roosevelt, providing him information about the state of the war in anticipation that Britain would ultimately need help from the U.S.[30] In August 1941, they had their first in-person meeting while in their respective leadership roles. Churchill sailed on the *Prince of Wales* and met Roosevelt at Placentia Bay of Newfoundland. The meeting had profound meaning for Churchill. In words that evoke images of a marriage ceremony, Churchill describes the occasion:

> "On Sunday morning, August 10, Mr. Roosevelt came aboard H.M.S. Prince of Wales and, with his Staff officers and several hundred representatives of

all ranks of the United States Navy and Marines, attended Divine Service on the quarterdeck.

"This service was felt by us all to be a deeply moving expression of the unity of faith of our two peoples, and none who took part in it will forget the spectacle presented that sunlit morning on the crowded quarterdeck—the symbolism of the Union Jack and the Stars and Stripes draped side by side on the pulpit; the American and British chaplains sharing in the reading of the prayers; the highest naval, military, and air officers of Britain and the United States grouped in one body behind the President and me; the close-packed ranks of British and American sailors, completely intermingled, sharing the same books and joining fervently together in the prayers and hymns familiar to both."[31]

While Churchill had been speaking out against authority for much of his life, he was now fighting the oppressive racial superiority of the Nazi war machine. His primary goal: to liberate Europe from German occupation. However, as heralded by his Uranus-Saturn opposition, he needed a powerful partner to stand by Britain and fight for the world's freedom. Democratic America was a potential ally (eleventh house) and partner (opposition) who until recently had withheld the critical military support that Britain needed. Churchill's description of the Newfoundland meeting depicts both friendship (Leo/fifth house) and alliance (Aquarius/eleventh). He felt optimistic that the U.S. and Britain were uniting against a common enemy, and that his friendship with Roosevelt would lead to a critical partnership in liberating the world from Nazi tyranny. Notably, this meeting occurred precisely at Churchill's Uranus age in August 1941, and is entirely consistent with an integrated version of Uranus in Leo in the eleventh house opposition Saturn in Aquarius in the fifth.

Diachronicity Between Uranus Age 66, Mercury Age 4, and Pluto Age 43

As noted, Uranus not only opposes Saturn but is also square the Mercury-Pluto opposition. Recall that Mercury's opposition to Pluto manifested as Churchill's obsession with obtaining financial support for defeating England's enemies. The Uranus square to his Mercury-Pluto opposition suggests that Churchill's ability to reconcile Mercury and Pluto would have a direct impact on the altruistic, humanitarian objectives of Uranus in the eleventh during the period of 1940-1942. Moreover, his eleventh house Uranus "cause" might benefit from what he previously learned during his Pluto period of 1917-1919 when he was obsessed with the Bolsheviks.

In fact, a distressing lack of military armament significantly challenged Churchill's first years as prime minister from 1940 to 1942. Britain's "10 Year Rule" assumed there would never be another world war, which curtailed resources allocated to the military and left the war chest at insufficient levels in the face of another historical conflict. The British public was battle weary, and the government did not heed Churchill's calls for war preparation until late in the game.[32]

During this period Churchill had been imploring Roosevelt to send military supplies that Britain desperately needed. However, Roosevelt was navigating complex politics at home with an isolationist Congress, which made it politically difficult for him to oblige. Eventually, the exchanges between the two leaders led to an innovative (Uranus) solution to Churchill's second-eighth house resource problems.[33] This would appear to reflect a successful integration of the T-square from Uranus in the eleventh house to Mercury in the second and Pluto in the eighth.

The exact solution was the Roosevelt administration's Lend-Lease Act that was passed in March 1941. The act allowed the United States to "lend or lease war supplies to any nation deemed vital to the defense of the United States."[34] This enabled President Roosevelt to provide needed supplies to Britain while remaining officially neutral in the war.[35]

It was a critical time that exactly corresponded to Churchill's Uranus period of 1940-1942 as calculated by the DAM. In an effort to change (Uranus) the course of the war, Churchill befriended and partnered with Roosevelt as a key Saturn ally (fifth-eleventh axis). He provided secret information (Mercury in Scorpio) so that Roosevelt could innovatively (Uranus) provide what was needed to secure Britain's safety and solvency (second house). Together they resolved England's financial crisis via America giving Britain a loan (Pluto in eighth).

What started out as an issue with learning numbers, as expressed by Churchill in financial terms of borrowing and lending at his Mercury age of 4.4, now culminated in borrowing from the U.S. to ensure that Britain had adequate military supplies to defeat Germany. At his Pluto age of 43.3 in 1918, Churchill's obsession with England's safety overpowered his sense of fiscal responsibility. But by his Uranus age of 66 in 1941, an integrated Uranus-Mercury-Pluto T-square enabled a solution that accomplished both defense and financial solvency on the path to ensuring an allied victory. Again, the significant event of March 1941—Roosevelt's Lend-Lease agreement with Churchill—occurred precisely within the DAM timeframe of August 1940 to August 1942.

Franklin Delano Roosevelt (FDR)

Examination of Roosevelt's life and astrological corollaries will focus on Moon Cancer in the tenth and planets in direct aspect to the Moon, including a quincunx from Venus in Aquarius in the fifth house and a sextile from Saturn in Taurus in the eighth. Emphasis will be on Roosevelt's experiences at the developmental ages of each planet and how they relate diachronistically to one another.

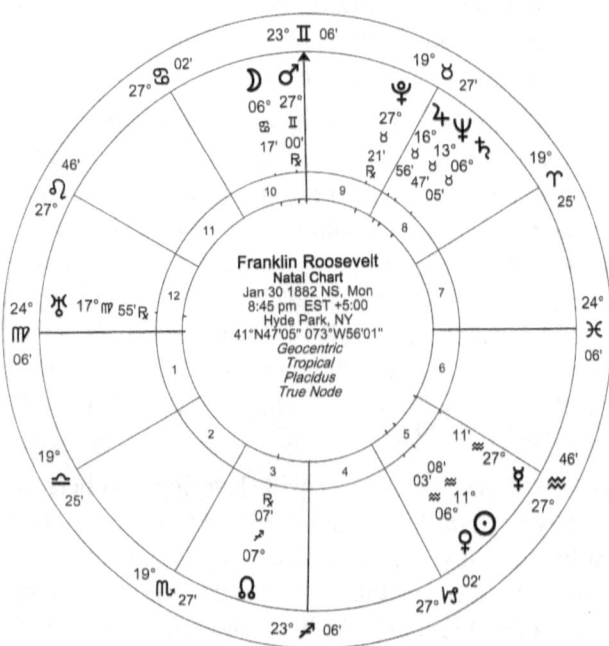

Venus Age of 15.9, December 1897

Roosevelt's Venus is in Aquarius in the fifth house. As noted previously, Perry's astropsychology model holds that the fifth house correlates to ages 14 to 20. This is the period of adolescence, and includes activities and concerns that are predominant at that stage of development. The primary task of adolescence is creation of a positive identity and sense of self-esteem. This is largely pursued through peer-to-peer social relations. Adolescent activities tend to focus on games, sports, parties, entertainment, and performance.

FDR's Venus age of 15.9 corresponds to December 1897. His Venus period would therefore range from roughly December 1896 to December 1898. During this time we would expect significant events that encapsulate the meaning of Venus conjunction Sun in Aquarius in the fifth house square Saturn in

Taurus in the eighth and quincunx the Moon Cancer in the tenth.

Venus symbolizes functions of relating, socializing, and partnering. In the sign of Aquarius, the person may socialize in a cool, detached manner, perhaps being somewhat unconventional in his relational style. He might be attracted to people who are different, rebellious, or progressive (such as Winston Churchill!). Venus Aquarius in the fifth house also implies someone who experiments with relational styles so that he can develop a sense of ease with his friendships.

Venus is conjunct the Sun in Aquarius in the fifth house. Conjunctions symbolize action and new beginnings. The two planets combine to assert something that is consistent with their respective functions and sign position; thus, Sun and Venus act as one unit in Aquarius. The Sun signifies performance, self-expression, and exercise of will. Venus-Sun in Aquarius suggests someone who may perform in an unusual, even an odd way in an attempt to relate to his peers. Venus square Saturn suggests that from ages 15 to 17 Roosevelt might have felt socially awkward and ill at ease, as if he had a steep hill to climb. Yet, fifth house peer relations will be essential to development of his identity and self-esteem. In sum, Venus conjunction Sun in Aquarius in the fifth house suggests a boy who feels out of place with his friends and who might experiment with different behaviors to find a style that facilitates his popularity.

Again, Venus is square Saturn in Taurus in the eighth house. The eighth house correlates to wounds and that which needs to be transformed, whereas Saturn signifies a striving for success. Saturn in Taurus in the eighth might suggest that Roosevelt felt wounded in his capacity for success, especially in relation to his body and capacity to form stable, meaningful attachments (Taurus). Since Saturn is square its own dispositor (Venus), we can anticipate that Roosevelt's Venus period of ages 15-17 was fraught with frustration and social difficulty with peers.

Venus is not only square Saturn but also quincunx the Moon in Cancer in the tenth house. Moon in Cancer would indicate that Roosevelt had a tender, soft side; yet its quincunx to Venus implies that social needs rendered his true feelings problematic. Lunar feelings and dependency needs were likely repressed for the sake of maintaining a pseudo mutuality in personal relationships. Similar strains might have extended to interactions with his father as well since the Moon is in the tenth house. Perhaps during his Venus period Roosevelt felt emotionally disconnected from his father and family (Moon Cancer). Venus' exact square to Saturn further underscores that at Groton Roosevelt might initially have felt lonely, frustrated, and inadequate in his ability to form comfortable relationships with his peer group (fifth house). Together, these two Venus aspects indicate that from ages 15 to 17 young Roosevelt struggled to belong and achieve social success.

In fact, Roosevelt was reared an only child in the embrace of two unusually devoted parents who showered him with continual validation and approval. They resided on a large estate in Hyde Park, New York, where there were few children his age, so he was accustomed to interacting solely with adults, such as the tutors with whom he worked during the early years of his schooling. He was cradled in this nurturing existence until the age of 14, at which time he was dislodged from his comfortable life and sent to the Groton School in Massachusetts as a boarding student, precisely at the start of his Venus period in September 1896.[36]

Roosevelt was one of 110 boys at the school.[37] Used to being an only child, one might imagine that he felt like an alien in a strange land, as befits Venus in Aquarius. Groton's headmaster, Endicott Peabody, was known for emphasizing discipline in his students, keeping a rigid schedule and expecting the boys to abide by it. Naturally well behaved, Roosevelt was comfortable with this Saturnian structure. However, he was not used to interacting with peers. To make matters worse, he entered the school at the third-year stage, exacerbating his discomfort with boys that had already established lunar, family-like friendships with each other. Not only did he need to learn how to live with other boys, he needed to figure out how to relate to them.[38]

FDR made efforts to ingratiate himself with his classmates, but not understanding the basics of how adolescent boys behave, it took him a while to comprehend group norms. For example, when he first arrived he thought that winning the Punctuality Award and setting a perfect behavior record would increase his popularity, but it didn't have the intended effect. Once he figured this out, he changed his strategy to fit in more with what the other boys were doing, committing an offense against the rules to integrate better into the social fabric.[39]

Not wanting to alarm his parents, Roosevelt withheld how he was faring in his new environment. His father was ill, and FDR wanted to spare him the burden of his struggles. So he wrote cheerful letters indicating that he was in high spirits and getting along well, regardless of the actual situation. He knew they expected him to succeed (Moon in Cancer in the tenth house), and he didn't want to disappoint.[40]

An experience he had with a group of bullies at the school reflects his ability to adjust his performance to the requirements of a particular situation. Some older boys whacked him with hockey sticks, causing him to leap back and forth to avoid being struck on the ankles. Instead of becoming agitated or trying to escape, he jumped around with a big smile on his face performing as if he was dancing with delight. His extraordinary ability to put on a show saved him from physical harm.[41]

Roosevelt's social difficulties during his Venus period are entirely consistent with Venus being in an exact square to Saturn and quincunx to the Moon. Uncomfortable relating (Venus) with his peers (fifth house), he struggled with a sense of belonging (quincunx Moon). In response, he changed the way he acted and found that breaking the rules (square Saturn) resonated better with his contemporaries. He was able to engage, adapt, and perform (Venus in Aquarius in the fifth house) in whatever manner the situation required, regardless of how he truly felt inside (quincunx Moon). He also protected his parents from knowing about his social difficulties (Venus quincunx the Moon).

All of this is especially significant given that Roosevelt's primary concern from ages 15 to 17 was upgrading his social skills. These efforts occurred within the DAM time frame of December 1896 to December 1898, marking his Venus period.

Sun Age of 16.9 in December 1898

Roosevelt's Sun is also in Aquarius, in the fifth house, signifying age 16.9 in December 1898. This means the relevant date range for Roosevelt's Sun is approximately December 1897 to December 1899, or 16 to 18. During this time, we would expect significant events that symbolize Sun conjunction Venus in Aquarius in the fifth house square Saturn-Neptune-Jupiter in Taurus in the eighth.

The Sun in Aquarius in the fifth house suggests someone who is viewed as unusual by his peers and who must develop his own unique, unorthodox identity. However, the squares to Saturn, Neptune, and Jupiter indicate this would not be an easy time for Roosevelt. Saturn in the eighth house suggests that the rigid formality of tradition and authority could feel frightening and oppressive, perhaps stunting his confidence and evoking fears of failure. Neptune square the Sun may incline him to fantasize a life of extraordinary accomplishment; yet, also diffuse his sense of self, weaken his will, and undermine his self-esteem. Finally, Jupiter in Taurus square the

Sun in Aquarius suggests that young Franklin might struggle to reconcile his emerging identity as a nonconformist with a stultifying, rigid morality imposed from above. While these aspects were daunting, Roosevelt more than rose to the challenge.

Roosevelt admits that he felt like an outsider at Groton[42] where he was not particularly popular. Young Franklin had a slight build and had developed a bit of a British accent while traveling every summer for six weeks in Europe with his parents. The other boys thought he talked strangely. These characteristics formed an image that seemed peculiar to his new contemporaries.[43]

Nevertheless, Roosevelt took advantage of the opportunities Groton offered to shape his self-expression and foster his evolving identity. He made choices regarding which school activities he wanted to join. In some he would be successful; in others, not so much.

Headmaster Peabody cultivated a physically competitive environment, believing that football was "the most spiritual of all games."[44] Since by custom the boys could not differentiate themselves by dress or financial means, athletics was an important way for them to distinguish themselves. With his slight build, however, Roosevelt was not naturally gifted as an athlete. He suffered minor injuries and struggled to succeed on the field, failing to make the first string football squad and participate in most interscholastic competition.[45]

FDR did have success with debating, however. He was a member of the junior and senior debating clubs and, according to biographers, his performance in January 1898 regarding the annexing of Hawaii provided evidence of his mental dexterity.[46]

Peabody bestowed to his Groton students a firm foundation in Christianity, and preached to them on a daily basis.[47]

Roosevelt actualized those teachings by participating in the School's Missionary Society. In addition to assisting an elderly 84-year-old widow of a Civil War drummer living near the school, he played the organ at the Society's services and worked at a summer camp for disadvantaged boys.[48] In this regard at least, he was successfully adapting to the squares from Saturn (responsibility), Neptune (charity), and Jupiter (religion) to his Sun.

Consistent with the square from Saturn, life was especially Spartan at the school, without any of the luxuries the boys had known from their family life. Roosevelt handled himself well, however, not suffocating in self-pity but instead finding the determination to work diligently and carve out an identity of which he could be legitimately proud.[49]

Groton clearly provided a vehicle for Roosevelt to develop his self-esteem and validate his emerging identity (Sun). Although he felt like an outsider (Aquarius), he worked hard to make a place for himself (Sun square Saturn-Neptune-Jupiter). He persevered despite the setbacks he had with athletics (Sun square Saturn), taking comfort instead in his emergent debating skills (Sun square Jupiter). In addition, he intentionally offered himself to charitable undertakings and sought to abide by the spiritual values he was learning at Groton (Sun square Neptune).

By the time he left Groton, Roosevelt was a charming, self-confident, and ambitious young man who had "pulled himself up by his bootstraps."[50] His solar period from December 1897 to December 1899 correlates to the second half of his sophomore year through the first semester of his senior year. Roosevelt's formative experiences in athletics, debating, and charitable activities all took place within this timeframe and perfectly reflect the meaning of the Sun in Aquarius in the fifth house square Saturn-Neptune-Jupiter in Taurus in the eighth.

Saturn Age of 40.3 in March 1922

Roosevelt's Saturn is in the eighth house at 40.3 years old, correlating to March 1922. As mentioned, the eighth house corresponds to ages 35 to 44 in the DAM. This is the stage during which the native is likely to experience issues of personal power, wounding, mid-life crisis, healing, and transformation. The DAM posits that during the Saturn period of March 1921 to March 1923, or 39-41, Roosevelt would experience significant events consistent with Saturn in Taurus in the eighth house square Venus-Sun in Aquarius in the fifth and sextile the Moon in Cancer in the tenth.

As stated, Saturn in Taurus in the eighth suggests that Roosevelt felt wounded in his capacity for success, especially in relation to his body and ability to form stable, meaningful attachments that could provide a sense of grounding and security (Taurus). In August 1921, FDR was struck with poliomyelitis, a disease that robbed him of the use of his legs.[51] Polio is defined as "an acute viral disease . . . and resulting in a motor paralysis, followed by muscular atrophy and often permanent deformities."[52] Roosevelt's affliction seriously restrained his ability to control his body (Saturn in Taurus square Sun).

In March 1922, the exact month of his Saturn in Taurus in the eighth house, both his legs were fitted with 14-pound steel braces, which is peculiarly fitting given that Saturn rules skeletal structures like bones and braces. He thus began the long process of learning to move without the use of a wheelchair. He was determined to walk again, and his determination was buoyed by an abiding faith that he would succeed. He spent a lot of time slowly and laboriously swinging his hips side to side to give the illusion that he was walking. Sweat pouring from his face, he would take hours to reach the end of the driveway. FDR endured lengthy sessions of excruciating physical therapy, insisting that they be held daily instead of the usual rhythm of three times per week.[53]

Frequently depressed during the months following his illness (depression is Saturnian), Roosevelt nevertheless put on a cheerful display for those around him. Instead of dwelling on his affliction when friends visited, he chose instead to bolster their spirits. He maintained a psychological distance by detaching from his suffering, which again reflects Venus-Sun in Aquarius quincunx his Moon. He contained his despair and shielded his family from the emotional impacts of his paralysis, which perhaps also reflects Saturn's exact sextile to his Moon.[54] Biographer Jon Meacham quotes FDR's son, James: "Terrible as it was for him, he had the mental depth and the compassion to realize how overwhelmingly frightening it was for his children, and he tried to lighten our fears."[55] Once again, Roosevelt was compelled to put on a brave face in order to hide his discomfort and fears, just as he had as an adolescent during his residence at Groton. This diachronistic connection reflects Saturn's square to Venus-Sun, showing the relationship between ages 15 to 18 and 39 to 41.

Regarding his relationships, Roosevelt always kept the big picture in mind. At this time, Eleanor became involved in politics to keep FDR's options open after he rehabilitated. Before this time, she had involved herself with the League of Women Voters in a non-partisan manner, but now she began to participate in mainstream politics in a more partisan fashion. She thought it essential that FDR's interest in the Democratic Party was kept alive and that they likewise remained interested in him.[56]

Roosevelt's conjunction of Saturn-Neptune in Taurus in the eighth house underscores that the very structure (Saturn) of his being was dissolving (Neptune) from beneath him. In effect his life was in danger of complete collapse and disintegration. He was afflicted with a dreadful disease (Neptune) that severely restricted (Saturn) the use of his legs, leaving him physically insecure and ungrounded (Taurus). Despite all this, he labored diligently to contain his despair (Saturn sextile Moon) and project a calm and cool confidence (Venus-Sun in Aquarius) to those around him. Ultimately, Neptune's conjunction with Jupiter in Taurus in the eighth house seems to symbolize a transcendent if not unrealistic faith in his capacity to heal his disabled body, and harkens back to the missionary work he performed as a teen at Groton.

An interesting corollary to Saturn's sextile to Moon in Cancer in the tenth house is Franklin's wife, Eleanor, who cemented bonds with the Democratic Party to preserve her husband's career during the period that he was recuperating from paralysis. The Moon, of course, pertains to women, whereas both Saturn and the tenth house signify career; thus, Eleanor proved instrumental in Roosevelt's success as a politician. Her significance as a political ally is further symbolized by the fact that Neptune signifies the seventh house. Saturn, therefore, is not only conjunct the actual ruler of the seventh house but square Venus, which is the natural ruler of the seventh. For Roosevelt, career and partnership were indissolubly linked, which is reflected not only in the importance of Eleanor to his career but also later in his political partnership with Churchill.

All of these events surrounding Saturn and its aspects began in August 1921 at the start of Roosevelt's Saturn period of 1921 to 1923. Remarkably, he began using his braces in March 1922, the exact age that Saturn signifies in the DAM.

Diachronicity Between Saturn Age 40.3 and Venus-Sun Ages of 15.9/16.9

As previously discussed, Saturn square Venus implies the need to work diligently to achieve solid, enduring relationships with others. Likewise, Saturn square Sun requires discipline in an effort to perfect skills that build self-esteem. At his Saturn age of 40, Roosevelt was able to capitalize on skills he developed at Groton while benefitting from a more integrated and mature version of his Sun-Saturn functions.

Recall that at Groton during his Venus-Sun period, Roosevelt endured without self-pity the austere environment and rigid structure of the School. And as befits the squares from Saturn, he worked hard to improve his Venus-Sun social skills. Now, during his Saturn period, he once again silently and willingly suffered the long hours of physical discomfort that came with the regimen needed to improve his debilitated condition. In effect, he had to *will* himself to recovery.

Recall how he performed at Groton for the bullies despite his internal discomfort (Saturn square Venus-Sun). And now with polio, he again performed successfully, projecting a calm and confident persona in the face of tremendous physical pain and difficulty. Just as at Groton he metaphorically pulled himself up by his bootstraps, so at his Saturn age he used his determination, stamina, and patience to literally pull himself up out of his wheelchair.

Yet another parallel entails the theme of protecting loved ones from worry. At Groton, he protected his parents from knowing the frustrations he suffered establishing relationships with peers in a new environment (Venus-Sun quincunx Moon). By his Saturn age, he used his considerable self-discipline to protect his family again (Saturn sextile Moon), this time from knowing the depth of despair and physical pain he was experiencing from the effects of Polio.

At Groton, FDR worked hard to build social skills that were sorely lacking. At his Saturn age of 40 in 1922, his affliction prevented him from staying engaged with the Democratic Party. Thus once again he was socially challenged, albeit for a different reason. Nevertheless, both of these conditions reflect Saturn's square to Venus. By his Saturn age, however, he was able to enlist the help of his wife, Eleanor, to cultivate and maintain the social relationships he would need for resurrecting a political career that had all but collapsed. Which brings us to Neptune.

Neptune Age of 42.6 in June 1924

Roosevelt's Neptune in the eighth house correlates to June 1924 when he was 42.6. It is conjunct Saturn on one side and Jupiter on the other, while also forming a close square to Sun in Aquarius in the fifth house. According to the DAM, Roosevelt's Neptune period of approximately June 1923 to June 1925 (ages 41-43) should include events that highlight Neptune's overall significance in his chart.

Neptune signifies our capacity for compassion and transcendence, often correlating to experiences that entail loss, suffering, and grief that bring us to our knees and require surrender to the divine. As a spiritual faculty, Neptune signifies not only the impulse to let go and let God, but also those places—institutions, hospitals, and retreats—that allow for rest and recuperation from the stresses and rigors of everyday life. With Neptune's square to Sun in Aquarius, we can expect that FDR's Neptunian experiences from 1923-1925 will present a significant challenge to his identity, while ultimately providing a vehicle for deepening compassion and developing self-esteem through some sort of charitable, humanitarian undertaking.

We have already seen how Neptune conjunct Saturn in Taurus in the eighth house appears to correlate to the breakdown of Roosevelt's body, afflicting him with polio and paralysis. In October 1924, precisely at his Neptune age point, Roosevelt visited a spa called Warm Springs that had thermal waters and an old inn. Delighting in his newly discovered mobility in the buoyant springs, he ended up staying for three weeks. Warm Springs became an important place for Roosevelt as a result of this visit. He decided to purchase and expand the retreat.[57]

Certainly this is consistent with Neptune's square to the Sun, for not only was Warm Springs a watery retreat (Neptune rules liquidity and flow), but Roosevelt's *decision* to purchase Warm Springs correlates to Venus (a purchase), Saturn (a business), and the Sun (an opportunity for play, recreation, and self-expression). Warm Springs represented an environment in which Roosevelt could be completely in command while not subject to the formality associated with his other residences where he needed to cooperate with his mother and wife. He plunged into the Saturnian details of planning, building and hiring appropriate medical personnel to supervise the rehabilitative care of the patients who visited. Again, his ability to be in charge at Warm Springs helped his self-esteem (Sun) because it provided an opportunity to create something on his own.[58]

His compassion flowed freely at Warm Springs, and his spirit was contagious to the people who traveled there to enjoy the healing effect of the waters. He took immense pleasure in chatting with everyone who visited. Roosevelt explored the local area and personally engaged with the people. It was also his first opportunity to witness abject poverty, and he never forgot it. Roosevelt came to know many of the residents by name. His experiences in Georgia broadened his appreciation for those in need and deepened his compassion for their difficult circumstances.[59]

FDR ensured that all needy people with polio could utilize Warm Springs. He established a foundation and assigned the property to it. He used two-thirds of his net wealth on the spa, causing his wife to fear that their children's needs would go unmet. His mother alleviated this fear, however, supporting Roosevelt's vision with her customary generosity.[60]

Over the course of his life, FDR would spend considerable time at Warm Springs, as much as 50 percent in some years. After attaining the presidency in 1932, he even built a house on the property that came to be called "The Little White House".[61]

In sum, not only did Warm Springs perfectly encapsulate the meaning of FDR's Neptune configuration, its discovery coincided with his Neptune age point of 42.6. Warm Springs provided Roosevelt with the opportunity to build (Saturn) a comfortable, idyllic environment for patients afflicted with polio (Neptune in Taurus in the eighth house). Warm Springs stoked the fires of his compassion by exposing him to people of different classes and economic circumstances. While run like a business (Saturn), the playful, social nature of Warm Springs reflects Saturn's square to the Sun in the fifth house. Its humanitarian group focus is clearly Aquarian while also enabling FDR to create an enduring legacy of charitable service (Sun Aquarius square Neptune-Saturn). Again, this clear and compelling symbol of FDR's Neptune configuration commenced in October 1924, at the heart of the DAM period of June 1923 to June 1925.

Diachronicity Between Neptune Age of 42.6 and Sun Age of 16.9

Generically, Neptune square Sun in Aquarius suggests a compassionate humanitarian. As an adolescent, Roosevelt found himself working with the Groton Missionary Society. Headmaster Peabody planted a seed of benevolence during those formative years. By Roosevelt's Neptune age, Warm Springs fertilized that seed, and FDR's compassion flowered. He became intimately familiar with the suffering of people that lived lives he would have never been able to imagine without such contact. The experience enlightened him and honed his skills and identity as an altruistic leader.

Moon Age of 58.6 in June 1940

Roosevelt's Moon is in Cancer in the tenth house, sextile Saturn in Taurus in the eighth house and quincunx Venus in Aquarius in the fifth. Within the DAM timeframe, FDR's Moon correlates to June 1940 (age 58.6), constituting an approximately two-year period from June 1939 to June 1941. As is well known, the tenth house signifies career wherein one ideally makes an enduring contribution to the larger community. According to the DAM model, the tenth house ranges from ages 54 to 65.

The Moon in Cancer in the tenth house reveals a strong protective instinct brought to bear in public service—as in protecting the homeland. It suggests that caring for American citizens would be FDR's first and foremost responsibility. The Moon's exact alignment with both Venus and Saturn is certainly consistent with Roosevelt's presidency, which was afflicted by a series of contractions that paralyzed the economy from 1929-1942. During his lunar period of 1939 to 1941, Roosevelt was still dealing with low unemployment and an anemic recovery. Even more importantly, he was preparing the country for what appeared to be an inevitable war with Germany.

Moon sextile Saturn reflects how FDR used discipline and authority to organize government forces in the service of protecting the homeland. Venus-Sun in Aquarius indicates a global perspective, but the Moon in Cancer suggests a sensitive, ingrown self-protectiveness. As a personal sign, Cancer is notoriously provincial and family-centric. Accordingly, it's not surprising that Roosevelt's Moon in Cancer in the tenth house corresponded to the isolationist mood of the nation during his lunar period of 1939-1941 prior to America entering WWII. To succeed as a leader, Roosevelt would have to solve the dilemma symbolized by his Cancer-Aquarius quincunx. For his altruistic concern for the plight of Europe was problematic when it came to his responsibility to protect the American people.

Roosevelt had been in active communication with Churchill since 1939, and was carefully observing events in Europe as Hitler invaded one country after another. Since the end of World War I, the U.S. populace had been predominantly isolationist, taking a dispassionate view of the conflicts in Europe.

Again, the Moon in Cancer in the tenth house suggests an ingrown "America first" isolationist policy that clearly conflicts with the broader, more universal and collaborative perspective of Venus-Sun in Aquarius.

During his lunar period, Roosevelt grew increasingly concerned and realized that eventually the U.S. would need to join the allied forces in resisting Germany.[62] However, he was also responsible for protecting the homeland. He was managing the Cancer-Aquarius tension by modulating public statements about his foreign policy intentions and reassuring the American people that their safety was his top priority—yet, all the while working politically behind the scenes to assist Britain and the Allies.[63] As is typical with the quincunx, the one planet didn't know what the other was doing.

Churchill implored Roosevelt to provide military resources for Britain. FDR wanted to be responsive to England's needs, but had to contend with a Congress that was not ready for another war. Consistent with his Venus-Moon quincunx, he was artfully navigating conflicting needs and slowly bringing the country along politically, providing to Churchill what he could without requiring authorization from Congress. He was also sensitively reassuring Churchill that he understood the danger represented by Hitler and that the U.S. remained an ardent friend to Britain.[64]

On June 10, 1940, exactly corresponding to Roosevelt's lunar age of 58.6, Italy declared war on France and Britain. FDR was scheduled to speak at his son's graduation at the University of Virginia that day. After hearing of Mussolini's actions, and despite concern from the State Department, he strengthened his speech noting that "On this tenth day of June, 1940, the hand that held the dagger has struck it into the back of its neighbor."[65] This famous "stab in the back speech" was a defining moment in U.S. history and in Roosevelt's life as well. For he could no longer abide the increasing threat in Europe.[66]

That day he asked the U.S. populace to abandon its isolationist position by providing to the allies material resources for their security and accelerating America's preparation for battle.[67]

One week later, on June 19, 1940, Roosevelt restructured his cabinet, appointing two prominent Republicans to lead the Navy and War Departments. Inviting a partnership across party lines, he was sensitive to the need to have broad political support and thus chose people with powerful influence in foreign policy and with views consistent with where he wanted to lead the nation.[68] While a U.S. declaration of war would not occur until December 1941, Roosevelt's new stance changed the dynamic as he prepared the nation for war.

With the Moon, Saturn, and Venus all in exact aspect to one another, it is noteworthy that FDR was structuring a political partnership with Churchill (Saturn square Venus) to help bring an end to America's isolationist (Moon Cancer) position. He recognized that to protect the country, he needed to forge tight political alliances with world leaders that would potentially assure the safety and security of humanity at large (Aquarius), not merely the homeland (Cancer).

To summarize, Roosevelt's Moon-age of 58.6 in June 1940 was, strikingly, the month in which the defining event—Italy's declaration of war on France and Britain—triggered a pivot in Roosevelt's public stance. The speech he made led to the restructuring of his cabinet and he began to resolve the Aquarius-Cancer quincunx problem that dominated this period of his life.

Diachronicity Between Moon Age of 58.6, Saturn of 40.3 and Venus-Sun of 15.9 and 16.9

Moon sextile Saturn suggests the application of discipline and structure for the purpose of caring and protection. During his Saturn period of 40.3, Roosevelt was determined to conquer his polio through long hours of disciplined self-care. Now, at his lunar period of 58.6, Roosevelt utilized his organizational skills in the service of preparing the nation for the grim ordeal of war. Likewise, the social skills he developed at Groton empowered him to negotiate agreements with Congress and the Allies that strengthened America's capacity to protect itself. All of this shows correlations between three different time periods signified by Sun-Venus, Saturn, and Moon.

The self-discipline he employed to endure long hours of physical therapy at age 40 were again required to navigate his way through the political obstacles he encountered at 58. During the latter period, he methodically worked the system (Saturn) to establish the infrastructure needed for America's defense (Moon). He patiently built the necessary structures and acquired the requisite resources (Saturn in Taurus in the eighth house) so that when called upon the homeland (Moon in Cancer) would be ready.

His ability to detach from feelings of vulnerability and adapt his performance (Moon quincunx Sun) to the situation was critical to his success. He provided a calm, reassuring tone for the country at a time when it was still recovering from the Depression and World War I. The Venusian equanimity he so artfully displayed to friends and family while at Groton and during his physically challenging years with polio was especially critical to the emotional well-being of the nation during his lunar period of 1939-1941. As Roosevelt famously said, "The only thing we have to fear is fear itself."

Ever conscious of the big picture, Roosevelt cultivated relationships as needed. At Groton, he developed and honed his style of relating. During his Saturn age, he recruited his wife Eleanor to engage with the Democratic Party on his behalf while he recuperated from his illness. And now, in his lunar period, he cemented the legendary ties with Churchill that would be so pivotal to the outcome of the war.

Utilizing his Saturn sextile Moon to full advantage, FDR

had been patient and disciplined in pulling himself up by his bootstraps after the debilitating effects of polio crippled him in 1922. Later he helped the country lift itself up after the economy was crippled by the great Depression. And in 1939-1941, precisely at his lunar period, America needed to stand tall again after it was laid low by the 1941 Japanese attack on Pearl Harbor. Roosevelt had to galvanize the American will in a fight to the death. In effect, FDR's previous life experience provided exactly the right preparation to inspire his fellow Americans to rise together as one.

Saturn-Neptune-Jupiter square the Sun encapsulated Peabody's vision for the Groton School. As headmaster, he strove to create an environment in which he could "develop in them [students] the powers and interests that will make them in later life the masters and not the slaves of their work".[69] He did this by enforcing discipline (Saturn), inculcating ideals (Neptune), and fostering a strong faith in Christianity (Jupiter). In FDR's words, writing to his old rector in 1940:

> "More than forty years ago you said, in a sermon in the Old Chapel, something about not losing boyhood ideals in later life. Those were Groton ideals—taught by you—I try not to forget, and your words are still with me and with hundreds of others of 'us boys.'"[70]

Peabody had infused in Roosevelt the ability to integrate his fifth and eighth house planets. This was the true foundation for the work Roosevelt was ultimately called upon to do as president. In combination with his Moon, the resulting amalgam of his experience and skills was crucial to his leadership of the United States during one of the most challenging periods of its history.

Summary

The Developmental Age Method was used to identify periods in which it was hypothesized that important events would occur that correlated with natal configurations of Winston Churchill and Franklin Roosevelt. In the years 1940-1941, both men reached the developmental age symbolized by a significant natal planetary placement. Churchill reached his Uranus age of 66.8 in August 1941, and Roosevelt reached his lunar age of 58.6 in June 1940.

This research shows that both Roosevelt and Churchill experienced critical events that symbolized these planetary placements and their aspects during the 1940-1941 period. Furthermore, the study revealed diachronic connections between these events and experiences at earlier developmental ages signified by planetary aspects To Churchill's Uranus and Roosevelt's Moon.

Churchill's Uranus in the eleventh house opposed Saturn in the fifth correlates with the inception of his partnership with Roosevelt, which commenced in August 1941. Uranus square his Mercury-Pluto opposition from the second to the eighth houses correlates with the Lend-Lease agreement the U.S. approved in March 1941 to provide military supplies to England. Both these events occurred in the timeframe the DAM predicts.

Likewise, Roosevelt's Moon in the tenth house quincunx Venus in the fifth correlates to a famous speech he made on June 10, 1940, that represented a pivot from isolationism toward a partnership with the allies, securing the safety of the homeland. His Moon in Cancer sextile Saturn in Taurus in the eighth house correlates with a structural change he made in his cabinet in June 1940 to facilitate and expedite war preparations. Both of these events correspond exactly to his Moon age of 58.6 in June 1940.

The study also shows that all these experiences have a diachronistic relationship with events that happened at earlier ages corresponding to planets in aspect with Churchill's Uranus and Roosevelt's Moon. Examining critical time periods identified by the DAM explained the psychological development of these two prominent men as symbolized by relevant planetary placements. In explaining that development, it showed clearly that earlier experiences were analogous to, and preparatory for, the events and circumstances of 1940-1941 that were so momentous in their respective lives.

Endnotes
[1] Perry, G., *The Developmental Age Method* (unpublished manuscript, 2015).
[2] Ibid, 5.
[3] Ibid, 1
[4] Perry, G., *An Introduction to Astropsychology: A Synthesis of Modern Astrology and Depth Psychology* (AAP Press: East Hampton, CT: AAP Press, 2012).
[5] Ibid.
[6] Ibid, 1.
[7] Ibid.
[8] Ibid.
[9] Perry, G., *The Developmental Age Method*, 3.
[10] Ibid, 5.
[11] Ibid, 2.
[12] Churchill, W., *My Early Life: 1874-1904* [Kindle Version 4.15.1], retrieved from http://www.amazon.com/Early-Life-1874-1904-Winston-Churchill.
[13] Ibid, 3.
[14] Primary residences of WSC: Owned, leased or provided officially, retrieved from http://www.winstonchurchill.org/support?catid=0&id=897.
[15] Churchill, W.
[16] Norman, A. (2012). *Winston Churchill: Portrait of an Unquiet Mind* [Kindle Version 4.15.1], retrieved from http://www.amazon.com/Winston-Churchill-Portrait-Unquiet-Mind.
[17] Winston Churchill (n.d.), retrieved from http://spartacus-educational.com/PRchurchill.htm.

[18]Norman, A.
[19]Churchill, W., 17.
[20]Ritala, M., "The love of power and the power of love: Churchill's Childhood," *Political Psychology*, 5(3), 1984, 375-390. http://dx.doi.org/10.2307/3790883.
[21]Norman, A.
[22]Rose, N., *Churchill: An Unruly Life* [Google Books], 2009, retrieved from https://play.google.com/books
[23]Ibid.
[24]Ibid, 146.
[25]Ibid, 144.
[26]Ibid.
[27]Murray, W., "Winston Churchill's Prewar Effort to Increase Military Spending," 2001, retrieved from http://www.historynet.com/winston-churchills-prewar-effort-to-increase-military-spending.htm.
[28]Meacham, J., *Franklin and Winston: An intimate portrait of an epic friendship* [Kindle Version 4.15.1], 2003, retrieved from http://www.amazon.com/Franklin-Winston-Intimate-Portrait-Friendship
[29]Keegan, J., *Winston Churchill: A Life* [Kindle Version 4.15.1], 2002, retrieved from http://www.amazon.com/Winston-Churchill-Life-Penguin-Lives.
[30]Meacham, J.
[31]Churchill and Roosevelt pray together. (n.d.). Retrieved from http://ww2today.com/10th-august-1941-churchill-and-roosevelt-pray-together.
[32]Murray, W.
[33]Meacham, J.
[34]Lend Lease Act 1941. (n.d.), retrieved from http://www.ourdocuments.gov/doc.php?flash=false&doc=71.
[35]Meacham, J.
[36]Smith, J. E., *FDR* [Kindle Version 4.15.1], retrieved from http://www.amazon.com/FDR-Jean-Edward-Smith.
[37]Ibid.

[38] Ibid.
[39] Hamby, A., *Man of Destiny:FDR and the Making of the American Century*, [Kindle Version 4.15.1], 2015, retrieved from http://www.amazon.com/Man-Destiny-Making-American-Century/.
[40] Ibid.
[41] Ibid.
[42] Ibid.
[43] Wasserman, B., *Presidents Were Teenagers Too* [Google Books], 2007, retrieved from https://books.google.com/books/about/Presidents_Were_Teenagers_Too.html?id=2zEtEPmrIZkC&hl=en.
[44] Hamby, A., 14.
[45] Ibid.
[46] Ibid.
[47] Ibid.
[48] Roosevelt Scholar Shares Presidents' Groton Stories, 2015, retrieved from http://www.groton.org/page/NewsDetail?pk=760950&fromId=187770.
[49] Hamby, A.
[50] Ibid.
[51] Smith, J. E.
[52] Ibid.
[53] Ibid.
[54] Ibid.
[55] Meacham, J., loc. 642.
[56] Smith, J. E.
[57] Ibid.
[58] Ibid.
[59] Hamby, A.
[60] Ibid.
[61] Smith, J.E.
[62] Meacham, J.
[63] Hamby, A.
[64] Ibid.

[65] Smith, J. E., 435.
[66] Smith, J. E., *FDR*.
[67] Roosevelt, F., "Stab in the Back Speech," June 10, 1940, retrieved from http://millercenter.org/president/fdroosevelt/speeches/speech-3317.
[68] Smith, J. E.
[69] Hamby, A., 14.
[70] Ibid, 28.

The Origins of the System of Twelve Houses

By José Luis Belmonte, M.A.

ABSTRACT: Even though the Greek name for house is *oikos*, an astrological house was called in Greek *topos* which means place. The early system of twelve astrological houses was the *dodekatropos* (δωδεχάτροπος), meaning twelve places. Before Ptolemy, there is no evidence of any astrologer using any system of houses but the Whole-Sign system, in which the signs of the zodiac are used as a house system. The rising becomes the first house from the very beginning of the sign until the end of it, regardless where in the sign the rising degree may fall. By using Whole-Sign houses, placing the twelve places was straightforward once the rising sign was known. The first part of the article explores the rising signs theory developed by Babylonians. Presupposing the use of zodiac as twelve equal thirty degree parts, the Babylonians discovered that the length of daylight was the time it takes for six signs to rise. Then they developed simple arithmetical series to calculate the rising time of each sign. The article also discusses whether the *dodekatropos* was an evolution from the system of eight astrological houses or *octotopos*, "eight places", or whether the early system of houses started as the four angles, the cardinal directions, which would became a system of twelve houses by adding two houses to each angle. The second part of the article explores Greek names of astrological houses as a source for tracing dates and its possible origin. Terms such as *moira, daimon, theos,* and *thea* are discussed along with *tyche* and *arche,* the last two did not appear in writing before the fourth century B.C.

The Rising Sign

Late Babylonian astrological texts from 500 B.C. to 50 B.C., spanning the Achaemenenid, Seleucid, and Arsacid periods, include a wide variety of celestial omens, nativity omens, and horoscopes. The earliest cuneiform evidence for the existence of the zodiac is in fifth century B.C. astronomical diary texts, and in horoscopes dated as of 409 B.C.[1] After the first Babylonian horoscopes were translated, A. Sachs assumed that the zodiac was invented in Mesopotamia in the fifth Century B.C. and set up the hypothesis that horoscopic astrology was first propounded in Babylonia.[2] Yet Babylonian horoscopes register only the date of birth, the position of the sun, moon and five planets in the zodiac. Since there is no rising sign, midheaven, or even places (houses) in those Babylonian nativities it would be more appropriate to classify them as zodiacal astrology, in line with a three-stage scheme propounded by Van der Waerden for the development of astrology: Omen Astrology, Primitive Zodiacal Astrology, and Horoscopy.[3]

In the final phase of Babylonian astronomy, the use of the zodiac of 12 equal 30-degree signs allowed Babylonian astronomers to discover that the length of daylight was the time it takes for six equal consecutive signs to rise, and the length of daylight could be calculated by summation over the rising times of 180 degrees of the ecliptic. Therefore the concept of longest and shortest daylight became directly related to rising signs. The length of the longest (M) and the shortest (m) daylight was the length of daylight at summer and winter solstices. Its origin is Babylonian because the ratio present in extant fragments show a relation $M : m = 3 : 2$ which corresponds to the geographical condition for Babylon. These rising signs were calculated not by trigonometric computation but by simple arithmetical progressions. They devised a simple arithmetical series, a linear formula, to calculate the average time for each of the twelve signs to rise[4] on the horizon for any given day. The Babylonians fit a pattern of ascension times to the ratio 3:2, and chose only one rising time (ρ) and a linear fixed increment of time to obtain the rising time of the next sign: ρ + increment. The rising time of third sign would be ρ + 2 * increment. And so on for the other three signs. They devised two simple patterns, both linear, known as "System A," or fixed increment, and "System B," or variable increment. Neugebauer believed that System A, the older of the two, was available at least by 300 B.C. In System A the equinoxes and solstices were located not at degree zero but at tenth degree, while in System B they were located at the eighth degree.

In ancient geography a locality was characterized not by geographical latitude but by the ratio of longest (M) to shortest daylight (m). *Clima* (κλίμα) or *climata* means a zone within which the longest daylight (M) can be considered constant. The Greeks recalculated the Babylonian system of rising times or oblique ascension (*anaphorai* in Greek) for Alexandria and for six other *climas*. *Anaphorikos*, the short treatise on rising times written by Hypsicles by mid-second century B.C., gave the rising times using System A for Alexandria, $M : m = 7 : 5$.[5] Once the rising sign or *anaphora* was known a system of Whole-Sign places could be launched. There is not further calculation needed. Actually before Ptolemy, there is no evidence of any astrologer using anything but the Whole-Sign system for delimiting the domains of life which every planet affected, writes Robert Hand.[6] Before discussing the distribution of the houses in the natal chart, the Greek words *moira* and *daimon* should be explored. Moira was not only linked to fate but was also the Greek term used to denominate degrees. Daimon was not only a term used to denominate houses eleventh and twelfth but also associated to the concepts of character and of the soul descending into the body at birth; therefore *daimon* could be linked to the rising sign.

Fate and Moira

Since Homer Moira, the goddess of fate and sometimes the goddess of death (*Iliad* 4.517, 18.119), was associated with fate and death. *Moira* meant one's portion in life, lot, or destiny. In the Homeric times, each man assumed the intervention of a higher power when his plans were modified or when misfortune overtook him; death was the certain lot (*moira*) for every human life. *Anaphorikos* divides the zodiacal circle into 360 equal degrees of arc called in Greek *moirai topikai* (μοίραι τοπικαί), in astronomical and geographical sense the term *moira* meant degree; as for time-degrees, Hypsicles divides the day (one revolution of the celestial sphere) into 360 equal sub-periods called *moirai kronikai* (μοίραι χρονικαί). The first degree of each sign was the *proto moira*. The *dodekatemoira*, explains Firmicus Maternus (Liber II, XIII), can be calculated for every planet adding that "whatever is hidden in the chart can be revealed by the duodecatemoira".[7] It can be argued that the zodiac being a circle made up of *moiras* can be considered as a circle of fate.

Death was not the only man's portion, there were other portions in life. As soon as each portion appears as the due and regular share, writes Nilsson, fatalism spreads over the whole of human life. Homer already set out upon this path. The idea of a universal "power" developed as men reflected upon the destinies of human life. As Nilsson notes, "for the different events in life have not each a separate *moira* as they have a separate *daimon*."[8]

The Daimon and the Rising Sign

The conception of the *daimon* was somehow linked to the idea of fate. The Greek *daimon* was an agent and a ruler of lots. In a fragment of Alcman (69) *daimon* has the meaning of the distribution of human lots. When translated to Latin the sense of "agent" was partially lost: in Rome, even though they had local agents or powers called "*lares*," "*penates*," and "*numen*," the chosen word was "genius."

A *daimon* represents a portion, adapted to the accidental manifestation of the moment, of the supranormal power recognized by man as phenomena unable to explain from his ordinary experience. Usener regarded the *daimon* as a momentary god, they had no real individuality, "that which suddenly appears before us as a dispensation from above".[9]

The term *daimon* was widely applied in Greek mythology. The idea of power, best known by the name of "mana," would be the very seed ground of religion itself. The Greek mind had a tendency to focus on the individual and the concrete, and even it did not preserve the idea of power, it gave a name to its manifestation: *daimon*. Besides the daemons associated to nature, primitive beliefs pictured powerful elements within the earth, so the title of daemon was given to a number of chthonic beings as well: the daemons of the dead and of the underworld.

According to Nilsson, *daimon* was merely a mode of expressing the belief that a certain effect was produced by a higher power. A *daimon* had no real individuality and, unlike a god, it acquired it only in the occasional manifestation of the divine power. The differentiation of the *daimones* depended not on religious phenomena but on Nature and of human life. A god is developed by a religious need and, through cult, into a characteristic individuality.

In Homer, the terms *theos*, *daimon* and *hero* are often interchanged. The most numerous passages in which something is ascribed to a *daimon* are those in which the *daimon* is the cause of bringing upon man something that is contrary to his will, purpose or expectations; in other passages a *daimon* is the cause of sudden inspiration; finally *daimon* also expresses fate or the destiny of man's life and, in a narrower sense, the doom of death.

By conceiving the soul of man as psyche, responsible for the breathing and the senses, and as daimon, responsible for man's destiny and surviving during incarnations, Empedocles conferred a new meaning to the *daimon*. The *daimon* had to know the lot of the soul, and became his allotter. That lot, and indirectly the *daimon*, would mold the character of each man. Herakleitus had a saying much in shape with that line of thought: a man's character is its *daimon*, which sometimes is translated as a man's character is his destiny.

As early as the fifth century B.C., a new belief emerged: the soul of the dead ascended to heaven. Actually the concept of the *daimon* was closely connected with the dead.[10] Empedocles uses the term *daimon* for the immortal soul which is cast out from heaven, descends into a man and passes through a cycle of "incarnations".[11] In the times of Pindar, a contemporary of Empedocles, there was a systematic body of religious doctrine known as Orphic. In those times the word *daimon* could be translated as spirit, meaning something incarnated in mortal bodies.[12]

Plato mentions a doctrine that the soul is imprisoned in the body as a punishment for some grave sin and calls it an Orphic theory. Xenocrates, Plato's pupil, considered the myth of imprisonment of the Titans in Tartarus as an allegory of the imprisonment of bad *daimones* in mortal bodies. Actually the idea of the soul confined in us originally as a *daimon*, which had committed an offense, had been about for more than one century. It is clearly stated in Empedocles (B 115) though he describes the incarnation in terms of exile rather than imprisonment, and he hints that there is not just one, but a series of incarnations.[13]

The appearance of the doctrine of transmigration of souls in Greece surely affected the concept of daimon. The Derveni Theogony was known as an Orphic theogony to an Ionian comentador of the early fourth century B.C. The oriental myth of the God of Time as the first progenitor and the theory of transmigration of souls both made their first appearance in Greek in Pherecydes of Syros, about 540 B.C. M. L. West notes that the account of transmigration resembles that of Empedocles which envisioned for the first time the four elements thoroughly blended by Love.[14]

A god is not necessarily nameless because he is not named or is usually addressed by a simple appellative. There are reasons to conceal it, like the fear that the enemy may work evil using the magic produced by uttering the name of the god, once he knows it. In a similar line of thought, it was ill-omened, remarks Farnell, to use the name of the deities of the nether world, because of their associations with dead, arousing euphemisms for the name of Hades, and the designation of the god and goddess of the lower world as "o Theos" and " Thea," which in the fifth century were "in vogue at Eleusis"[15]. That could explain the pairing of "Theos" with "Thea" in the ninth and the third house respectively. The third house is in the underworld (below the horizon).

The Four Centers

According to Ernst Cassirer, East, West, North, and South were not just mythical zones which served simply for orientation, word that comes from "Orient," but each had a specific significance of its own which Cassirer called an "inherent mythical life." In the *Isagoge* Geminus mentions (chapter II) a connection with the trine aspect in Babylonian astrology: a doctrine of the Chaldeans according to which the four wind directions are related to four triangles: north to Aries, Leo and Sagittarius, south to Capricorn, Taurus and Virgo, east to Libra, Aquarius and Gemini, west to Cancer, Scorpio and Pisces.[16]

Directions were associated with winds, writes Firmicus Maternus (Liber I, XII), linking the North wind with fire signs, the South wind with earth signs, the East wind with air signs, and the South-West wind with water signs. The directions, writes Cassirer, were taken as independent entities, as divine or demonic, friendly or hostile, holy or unholy characters. The East, the origin of light, is the source of life, whereas the West, the place of the setting of the Sun, is the place of death. Wherever we find the idea of the world of the dead as distinguished from the realm of the living, it is situated in the West of the world, concludes Cassirer[17]. Ovid (Metamorphoses XV) attributes to Pythagoras the idea that the four seasons of the year are the four ages of man. In the system of four angles the challenge is whether to put death at sunset or at midnight.[18]

Known in Greek as *kentra* (κέντρα), the four centers are the cardinal points of the chart: the rising (East), the setting (West), the upper culmination (South in northern hemisphere), and the lower culmination (North in northern hemisphere). Today the angles are the cusp of the cardinal houses; these four points correspond to the intersection of the ecliptic with the horizon and the meridian at any given moment. At the early times of the system of places the word "latitude" could not be taken as one of the spherical coordinates of the earth. The Greek name of each angle was astronomically descriptive: the rising point was called *Anatole* or *Horoscopos*, the setting *Dysis*, the upper culmination *Mesuranima*, and the lower culmination *Hypogeion* (or *Ypogeon*). In *L'Astrologie Grecque* Bouche Leclerq shows (p. 280) each of the four points of *dodekatropos* flanked by an *epanaphora* house on one side and by an a*ploklima* house on the other side. *Apoklima* is any declining house moving away from the angle. *Epanaphora* is any succedent house moving towards the angle. The system of twelve houses could be obtained by adding two houses to each center. Schmidt translated center as "pivot" and coined the phrase "angular triad" to describe the Hellenistic set of three houses[19] made up of one angular sign house (*pivot*), one *apoklima* house, and one *epanaphora* house. There were four angular triads, each centered around one of the four angles.

Most of the Greek names of the non-angular houses include non-astronomical terms like *daemon, tyche, arche, theos,* and *thea*. The second house is called *Aidou pulê* (αιδου μύλη), which means the gate of Hades; the third house is called *Thea* (φεά); the fifth house is called *Agathe tyche* (άγαθή τύχη); the sixth house is called *Kake Tyche* (κακή τύχη); the eighth house is called *Arche Thanaton* (άρχή φανατον); the ninth house is called Theos (θεός); the eleventh house is called *Agathos Daimon* (άγαθός δαίμων); the twelfth house is called *Kakos Daimon* (κακός δαίμων).[20] Since the angles have names of different nature than the rest of the houses, this might indicate that they were created differently, even though this does not mean that the system of houses began with the angles and later on the rest of houses were added.

The System of Eight Houses

Marcus Manilius, Vol. 2 808 ff, gives a long description of a system made up of eight houses, *octotopos*, stating that the spaces between the angles correspond to the four periods of human life[21]. According to Bouche LeClerq the only other astrologer to mention the *octotopos* is Firmicus Maternus (Liber 2, XIV) who may have used either Manilius or the same source as Manilius. At his discussion of the eight house system, Firmicus emphasizes the cardinal points and houses, arguing about the nature of the house: "in what sign, in whose terms" and adding to "note who is the ruler of the house itself, that is, of the sign: in what house it is placed; or in what kind of a sign it is"; from that description it must be noted first the importance of the cardinal point, and second Firmicus mentions one sign per house, while an eight house system would include more than one sign per house. He is actually speaking of a twelve whole sign house system cut to fit into an eight house system. Firmicus describes each of the houses of the *octotopos* as: "the House of Life is in the sign in which the ascendant is located; of Expectation of Inheritance and Wealth in the second house from the ascendant; of Brothers and Sisters in the third; of Parents in the fourth; of children in the fifth; of Health in the sixth; of a spouse in the seventh; of Death in the eighth"[22]. The *octotopos* of Firmicus does not seem to have had an evolution on its own. It is obtained simply by ruling out four houses of the *dodekatropos*, from house nine to house twelve both included. Thus the *octotopos* corresponds to houses one to eight of the *dodekatropos*, making the eighth house (death) the last one. It looks like the octotos is a derivate of the *dodekatropos*.

Pairing of Houses

Firmicus Maternus describes in the nativity (*Liber II*, chapter XVI) one set of four favorable houses to the ascendent: *Dea, Deus, Bona Fortuna* and *Bonus Daemon*, which are called by Greeks, respectively, *Thea, Theos, Agathe Tyche, Agathos Daimon*. These four houses are considered favorable because they "see" the ascendant either from 60 degrees or from 120 degrees away.[23]

Firmicus describes (*Liber II*, chapter XVII) the remaining four houses as feeble and debilitated because they are not aspected to the ascendant: "The first of these remaining four houses, however, which is located in the second house from the ascendant, is called the Gate of Hell, or the *Anafora* (rising up from the Underworld). The house which is diametrically opposite to this house, that is, the eighth from the ascendant, is called

Epicatafora (casting down into the underworld). The last of the four are those of *Mala Fortuna* and *Malus Daemon*." *Mala Fortuna*, called *Kake Tyche* by the Greeks, is located in the sixth house from the ascendant; *Malus Daemon*, the *Kako Daimon* of the Greeks, is the twelfth from the Ascendant.[24]

The pairing of *Agatho Daimon* with *Agathe Tyche* happened in Alexandria after the third century B.C. In the *dodekatropos*, the pairing happens in houses making good (*agatho*) aspect to the ascendant: *Agatho daimon* is placed in the eleventh house and *Agathe Tyche* in the opposite house, the fifth; as an evolution of the Erinyes, *Tyche* was considered chthonic and thus placed under the horizon. Another pair of opposite houses, not making good aspect to the ascendant and related to misfortune and loss (*kako*), is located next to the *agatho* houses: *Kako Daimon* in the twelfth house and *Kake Tyche* in the sixth. Another pair of opposite houses making good aspect to the ascendant is *Theos* in the ninth house and *Thea* in the third. The last pair of opposite houses is related to money and death; *ploutos* in Greek means wealth; the god of wealth (Pluto) was conflated with Hades (god of the dead); *thanatos* means death and *arche* implies origin, dissolution or return to the source: *Aidou pule* (gate of Hades) was assigned the second house, the first below the horizon (dark, night) and *Arche tanathon* was associated to the eighth house; they do not make good aspect to the ascendant.

Firmicus considered just one *Anafora*, the second house: the house next to rise after the ascendant. He also gave a sequence of houses (*Liber II*, chapter XVIII). The ascendant precedes the descendant, the *Medium Caelum* comes before *Immun Caelum*. The eleventh house (Agatho Daimon) comes before the fifth house (Agatha Tyche); the ninth house (Theos) before the third house (Thea). Then Firmicus writes, "Anafora, that is, the second place, is before Epicatafora," the eighth from the Ascendant, and Mala Fortuna (Kake Tyche), the sixth from the Ascendant, is before the Malus Daemon (Kako Daimon) twelfth from the Ascendant.[25]

The Eighth House

The Greek name of the eighth house was *Thanathon Arche*. *Tanathon* means death and *arche* means beginning, origin, and first principle, element. The first to use the word *arche* was Anaximander, as Aristotle says in Metaphysics (983 b 11). *Arche* was the original source of being, an originating cause or a starting point. Guthrie defined *arche* as "first, the original state out of which the manifold world has evolved and, secondly, the permanent ground of its being, or, as Aristotle would call it, the substratum".[26]

Aristotle used the word *arche* to describe the primary substance of the Milesians. For Thales the *arche* was water; for Anaximenes air and, like Anaximander, he assumed[27] that the *arche* was something divine. Diogenes of Apollonia took up in the fifth century the doctrine of Anaximenes that air was the *arche*. Most of the Presocratic world-systems proceed from *arche* to the infinite variety of nature by two stages: from the *arche* there evolved first the primary opposites or, in later systems, the four elements[28].

As *thanatos arche*, the eight house meant the death (*thanatos*) of the body as a compound of elements and their return to the original source (*arche*). The ninth house, God (*Theos*), could be interpreted as the (long distance) travel of the soul, after death, back to God. For the Greeks, God was most likely Zeus. Firmicus writes (*Liber II*, Chapter XIII) that "men would be immortal if the favorable influence of Jupiter," that is Zeus, "were never overcome in their charts. But since God the creator has made man in such a way that his physical substance is dissolved after a limited span of life, it is necessary to restrain Jupiter." In order for the compound of the body to be dissolved, continues Firmicus, "the dangerous and malevolent powers of the unfavorable planets must persist with increasing hostility."[29] As malevolent powers in charge of restraining Jupiter, Firmicus referred to Mars and Saturn.

The Fifth and Sixth Houses: Tyche

The earliest mention of *tyche* τύχη) occurred in Archilocus (c. 680-c. 645 B.C.). He attributed *tyche* all to the gods: *tyche* was a divine power, and man was incapable of fathoming the working of such power and was therefore uncertain of anything which the future had in store for him. This was also the tenor in Semonides, a roughly contemporary of Archilocus, concludes C. de Heer, adding that *tyche* "is the expression of this feeling of uncertainty, of the sense that men depends on the divine for whatever happens to him and that he cannot act to influence this,"[30] The scholar quotes A. A. Burks definition of *Tyche* as "the tangible fulfillment of divine disposition on earth in the shape of luck or catastrophe." When it comes to *tyche* one's personal merits play no part in it, rendering *tyche* very close to a "luck" propitiated by a divinity or by an agent of divine origin.

Rarely personified in Aeschylus (c. 525-455 B.C.), *tyche* means luck rather than fate. It may be good or evil, and may be associated occasionally with divinities. For the most part, *tyche* is the idea of chance as explanation of human vicissitudes and of events that cannot be foreseen or controlled by man.[31]

In Pindar (c. 522-c. 443 B.C.), the ancient Greek lyric poet from Thebes, *tyche* is not simply the tangible fulfillment of divine will, it is also a special aspect of the activity of the gods denoting the actual finding and obtaining, and the moment when it happens. According to Wilamowitz (Pindaros, 306) *tyche* is the dispensing power, which is unaccountable but on which everything depends. De Heer likens *tyche* as "a divine assistance given at a certain moment, but only then."[32]

In Sophocles (497-405 B.C.), *tyche* means also an external power that controls men's unhappiness and happiness. In Antigone, the king Creon suffers the effects of *tyche*: "*Tyche* rises and *tyche* humbles the lucky or the unlucky from day to day, and no man can prophesy to men concerning these things which are established" (1158-1160). When the king forbids the burial of Polyneices, Antigone decides to bury the body and the king sentences her to death. Then Tiresias warns the king: *Tyche* will play hard; Antigone will commit suicide and her suicide will trigger the suicide of your son (who was to wed Antigone), and the suicide your wife, after losing her only surviving son. For Sophocles *tyche* is a symbol of a living force which may be viewed in terms of ananke (necessity), as is necessary to bear the fortune that the gods send, "so death is itself is the gift of necessary fortune," which in stoic terminology was *fatalis necessitas* (*anagkaias tyches*). In the play, Tecmessa complains that "there is no harder evil among men than the fortune given by necessity," by which she meant her personal lot, the captivity forced on her by circumstance.[33] In *Greek Horoscopes* there are a three instances to *Agathe tyche* (ἀγαθέ τύχη); one of them is an invocation, and in the duplicate of the text No. 137b *Agathe tyche eutychei* (ἀγαθέ τύχη εὐτύχει) is written at the end.[34]

There is a connection of the Erinyes with Demeter, which supports Nillson's theory that Demeter was originally a daimon of the fields and crops, most likely a chthonic one. Dieterich notes a pre-Greek deity called Potnia which furnished the titles of Demeter and her daughter Persephone, the *Kore*, in Athens. The same occurred in Boeotia and on the peninsula of Mycale in Asia Minor. In Mycale too, they were associated with the Eleusinian Demeter, and were equated with the Erinyes through Demeter Erinys.[35]

Mentioned by Aeschylus in the fifth century, the cult of the Erinyes, or Erinys, was old. It emerged from the old Ge-

Demeter association and with similar deities. At Athens, the cult of the Semnae (Erinyes, Eumenides) was associated with the chthonic Pluto, Hermes, and Ge. The fact that the Erinyes were considered chthonic and since Tyche was a derivation or evolution from the Erinyes, that makes Tyche chthonic as well, that would explain her placement below the horizon.

The Eleventh House: Agatho Daimon

In the Theognidea daimon is a force which is beyond human understanding, the dispenser of riches or poverty, a hostile force which leads men to sin by blinding their judgment and causing them to act against their own interests, or any phenomena which is potentially adverse; man's life is felt to be under the control of a daimon which shapes his destiny in spite of himself.

The wish to be *eudaimon* is an appeal to the forces designated by *"daimon"* to be favorable or not to be hostile. Daimon is a force to which men can only appeal. The sense of personal guide is defined not earlier than in Plato's Phaedo[36]. In Pindar the daemons represent the divine in an intangible form encompassing all aspects to of human life. Those who achieve or who are *eudaimones* are the exceptional few who rise above the generality of mankind, whose life and success are proof of divine favour. To be *eudaimones* is the peak of human hopes and ambitions; victory is a personal achievement, but the gods are instrumental in its favour. If success leads to presumption, divine envy will cut it short. *Eudaimon* both expresses man's fundamental relationship with the gods and is proof of Pindar' pious humility towards the divine world.[37]

The goal of human existence is denoted and commended by *eudaimonia*. All Greeks, as mentioned by Aristotle in the *Nicomachean Ethics* (1095 a 17), are agreed on the word, though their interpretations may differ. Stobaeus (S.V.F. vol. III, 6, 7) writes that "They say that the end is *eudaimonein* (to have eudaimonia), for the sake of which all things are done [...] Zeno defined *eudaimonia* thus: *eudaimonia* is a smooth flowing of life. They say that *eudaimonia* is set up as a goal, the end being to attain *eudaimonia*, to do which is the same as *eudaimonein*".[38]

According to Zeno, *eudaimonia* depends on arête alone. Zeno says, writes Stobaeus (S.V.F. I, 47, 19), that "... of existents some are *agatha*, some are *kaka*, some indifferent. *Agatha* are such as the following: practical wisdom, self-control, justice, courage, and everything that is *arete* or partakes of *arete*. *Kaka* are such as the following: folly, license, injustice, cowardice, and everything that is *kakia* or partake of *kakia*. Indifferent are the following: life, death, fame, obscurity, pain, pleasure, wealth, poverty, disease, health and this of this nature".[39]

In the 1911 *Encyclopedia Britannica*, the definition of Agathodaemon refers, in Greek mythology, to the "good spirit" of cornfields and vineyards. At the end of each meal, it was the custom of the Greeks to drink a cup of pure wine in his honor (Aristophanes, Equites, p. 106). He was also regarded as the protecting spirit of the state and individuals. Often accompanied by *Agathe Tyche* (good fortune), in this aspect he may be compared with the Roman Genius and Bonus Eventus (Pliny, *Natural History* XXXVI, p. 23). In art, he is represented as a serpent or as a young man with a cornucopia and a bowl in one hand, and a poppy and ears of corn in the other. Prior the foundation of Alexandria, there is evidence *Agatho Daimon* as a serpent, but the evidence for his identification with the Egyptian Sai (anguiform of destiny) led to the opinion that it was *Sai* who gave its serpent form.[40]

The Alexander Romance implies the establishment of both a civic cult for a singular *Agatho Daimon* as special protector of Alexandria, and of private cults as protectors of individual homes and the city. It seems that both forms of cult had become established in Alexandria by the end of the 3rd

Century B.C. The public cult of *Agathos* Daimon is reflected in the *Oracle of the Potter*, dating from the 3rd to 2nd centuries B.C. Nevertheless, the vast majority of extant images of *Agathos Daimon* derive from Roman Egypt. Alexandria coins give the clearest indication of his high age: he is prominent on them between the reigns of Nero and Gallienus (A.C. 54-268) and experiences popularity in the Antonine period (A.C. 138-193). In the bulk of the extant images, mainly reliefs, terracottas, and coins, he is paired with *Agathe Tyche*. The frequency of *Agathos Daimon* appearances in the Greek Magical Papyri of the second to fifth century A.C. reflects not only his Hellenistic roots but his prominency during that period. His role, even before coming to Alexandria from Greece, was a bringer of good luck specifically as a promoter of trade success, and as power in connection to a specific place.[41]

The Agatho Daimon is an indicator of success which may have a certain similarity to the meaning of the Midheaven, yet in the Whole-Sign system, the Midheaven might not coincide with the tenth sign.

Conclusions

The adoption of the zodiac as twelve signs of fixed equal length of 30 degrees each allowed the Babylonians to calculate the length of the daylight as the time it tool for six constellations rise. Based on the relationship $M : m$ between the day of longest daylight M and the day of the shortest light m, they devised a linear formula for calculating the average time for each of the twelve signs to rise. Once the rising sign was known, the rest of the signs could be used as meaningful places creating a system of Whole-Sign houses. The Babylonian system was expanded by the Greeks to different zones (*climatas*). In those times, the *daimon* as fate and ruler of lots, *Tyche, Moira, Hades* and the *Arche* were added to different positions: *Tyche* and Hades were chthonic and placed below the horizon while the *daimon* and the arche were diurnal and appeared above the rising sign. *Agatho Daimon* was synonym of success and *Kako Daimon* of failure. *Tyche* was linked to *Agatho Daimon* and they were located in opposite places.

Endnotes

[1] Rochberg, Francesca, "Babylonian Horoscopes," *Transactions of the American Philosophical Society*, New Series, vol. 88, no. 1 (1998), 30.

[2] A. Sachs, "Babylonian Horoscopes," *Journal of Cuneiforn Studies*, vol. 6, no. 2 (Apr. 1952), 51-2.

[3] B. L.Van der Waerden, *Science Awakening II: The birth of astronomy* (Leyden: Nordhooff International Publishing, 1974), pp. 127-8.

[4] Neugebauer. *Ancient Mathematical Astronomy, vol. 2*, 727.

[5] Ibid, 728.

[6] Robert Hand, *Whole Sign Houses. The Oldest House System: An Ancient Method in Modern Application* (Las Vegas: Arhat, 2000).

[7] Firmicus, *Mathesis*, 42-3.

[8] Martin P. Nilsson, *A History of Greek Religion*, 2nd ed. (Oxford: Oxford University Press, 1967), 169-70.

[9] Ibid, 165.

[10] Georg Luck, *Arcana Mundi* (Baltimore: John Hopkins University, 1985), 210.

[11] Lewis Richard Farnell, *Greek Hero Cults and Ideas of Immortality. The Gifford Lectures Delivered in the University of St. Andrews in the year 1920*. Oxford University Press, London, 1970, 76.

[12] W. K. C. Guthrie, *A History of Greek Philosophy, vol. 2, The Presocratic Tradition from Parmenides to Democritus*, Cambridge, Cambridge University Press, 1965, p. 253.

[13] M. L. West, *The Orphic Poems* (Oxford: Clarendon Press, 1983), 22.

[14] Ibid, 108.

[15] Farnell, 83-4.

[16] Neugebauer, *Ancient Mathematical Astronomy, vol. 2*, 583.

[17] Ernst Cassirer, *The Philosophy of Symbolic forms, volume 2*, Yale University Press, Clinton, 10th printing, 1972, 98.

[18] Firmicus, *Mathesis*, 308.

[19] Schmidt and Black, *Peak Times and Patterns in the Life of Dane*

Rudhyar, p. 40. Discussed the angular triads more recently in *Definitions and Foundations*, 11.

[20] Auguste Bouché-LeClercq, *L'Astrologie Grecque*, Ernest Leroux Editeur, Paris, 1899, 280.

[21] Firmicus Maternus, translated from the Latin by Jean Rhys Bram, *Ancient Astrology Theory and Practice, The Mathesis of Firmicus Maternus* (Park Ridge: Noyes Press, 1975), 308.

[22] Firmicus, *Mathesis*, 44.

[23] Ibid, 47.

[24] Ibid, 47.

[25] Ibid, 47-8.

[26] W.K. C. Guthrie, *A History of Greek Philosophy, vol. 1, The Earlier Presocratics and the Pythagoreans* (Cambridge: Cambridge University Press, 1962), 57.

[27] Ibid, 77.

[28] Ibid, 273.

[29] Firmicus, *Mathesis*, 43.

[30] De Heer, *Makar, Eudaimon, Olbios, Eutiche, A Study of the Semantic Field Fenoting Happiness in Ancient Greek to the End of the 5th Century B.C.* (Amsterdam: Adolf M. Hakkert Publisher, 1969), 45.

[31] Williams Chase Greene. *Moira, Fate, Good and Evil in Greek Thought* (New York: Harper Torchbooks, 1963), 105-6.

[32] De Heer, 47.

[33] Greene, 146.

[34] Otto Neugebauer, H. B. Van Hoesen, *Greek Horoscopes* (Philadelphia: The American Philosophical Society, 1987), 163.

[35] Bernard Clive Dietrich, *Death, Fate and the Gods: The Development of a Religious Idea in Popular Belief and in Homer* (London: Athlone Press, 1965), 100,110.

[36] C. De Heer, 39.

[37] De Heer, 41-2.

[38] Adkings, *From the Many to the One*, 224.

[39] Ibid, 226.

[40] Daniel Odgen. *Drakon: Dragon Myth and Serpent Cult in the Greek and Roman Worlds*, Oxford University Press, 2013, 297.

[41] Odgen. *Drakon*, 305-9.

Vṛddhayavanajātaka by Mīnarāja

By Ronnie Gale Dreyer, M.A.

ABSTRACT: In this article, I provide a translation, commentary, and background information for the first 20 verses of the first chapter, "Division of Zodiacal Signs" in *Vṛddhayavanajātaka*, a classic Sanskrit text on Indian horoscopy. The text, which has never been fully translated into English, influenced many later classic texts on Indian astrology, which have been translated into English and are still utilized today as reference texts. *Vṛddhayavanajātaka* records a system of natal astrology that combines Hellenistic concepts such as the use of the zodiac with the *nakṣatras,* or lunar mansions, which was always used in India to divide the stars along the ecliptic. I review the development of natal astrology in India, the origins of this classic text, and the process by which we now have the definitive edition, which David Pingree compiled from numerous manuscripts. I also discuss the challenges and difficulties involved in translating old manuscripts that are often difficult to read, and which vary in their content. The translations and commentary here show how Hellenistic and Indian concepts combined to formulate the definitive iconography, symbolism, and meaning of the zodiac in Indian astrology.

Introduction

This article reflects work from an ongoing project exploring Mīnarāja's classic text *Vṛddhayavanajātaka* (Sanskrit for "great or old Greek astrology"), considered to be the earliest surviving Sanskrit text completely dedicated to *jātaka* ("natal astrology"), the study of the individual's fate and character based on the visible heavenly bodies at the exact moment of one's birth. Indian horoscopy falls under the broader category of *jyotiḥśāstra* ("science of the stars"), or *jyotiṣa* (Sanskrit for "stars" or "light"), the branch of learning that includes mathematics, astronomy, divination, and astrology.

Vṛddhayavanajātaka was originally dated by David Pingree[1] as having been written around 300-325 CE, which places the text toward the beginning of the Gupta Empire (320-550 CE), heralding what became known as India's cultural and intellectual "Golden Age." In addition to the emergence of some of the greatest works of literature, philosophy, art, architecture, drama, etc. that "defined classical Indian culture and society," the period in India between 300 BCE to 400 CE witnessed the establishment of the silk road and the expansion of maritime routes to the east.[2] It was during this heightened exchange between the East and West that *jātaka* emerged as a full-fledged mathematical and interpretive system, which synthesized Indian *nakṣatra*-based astrology with Hellenistic horoscopic techniques that emanated from the zodiac.

Background on Indian Astrology

Before the zodiac was implemented thus heralding the rise of horoscopy in India, the early lunar calendars originating around 2240-1760 BCE[3] marked off time with the *nakṣatras*. Commonly known to westerners as "lunar mansions," the *nakṣatras* were the 27 or 28 cluster of stars (depending on how they were used) that marked the path of the moon's 27.3 day cycle in its orbit around the earth. The *nakṣatras* were comprised only of visible stars that lie closest to the ecliptic, so that the moon would conjoin all of the stars in each group during its monthly journey.

The Moon's *nakṣatra* position was used, as it is in India today, to assign the best days for important events like starting a business, building a home, commencing a journey, getting married, naming a child, etc. They were also divided into four groups of seven—pertaining to East, South, West, and North—so that the best days to travel to a particular destination would correspond to the day when the Moon was in a *nakṣatra* that ruled that direction.

According to Pingree, the earliest surviving Sanskrit text on horoscopy is the *Yavanajātaka* ("Greek horoscopy"), a third-century metric version of a second-century work probably written in Alexandria and translated by Yavaneśvara ("Lord of the Greeks"), neither of which has ever been recovered. Sphujidhvaja, an Indian overlord of Greek descent, versified the text around 269/270 CE, and despite the fact that the manuscript he worked from was corrupted and had missing fragments, Pingree compiled, translated into English, and completely annotated the text, producing the *Yavanajātaka of Sphujidhvaja*,[4] which has become the definitive edition.[5]

Yavanajātaka, which, according to Pingree, preceded *Vṛddhayavanajātaka*, was the first text to show how Hellenistic concepts combined with Indian ones to form the basis of *jyotiṣa* as it is still practiced today. In addition to horary, electional, medical, and military astrology that was unique to India, *Yavanajātaka* incorporated the use of the twelve zodiac signs of thirty degrees each known as *rāśis* (Sanskrit for "heap").

For the first time, the concept of the *rāśicakra* ("horoscope" or literally "wheel of signs") was used to calculate the position of the planets, or *grahas* (Sanskrit for "seizers")—Sun, Moon, Mars, Mercury, Jupiter, Venus, and Saturn—whose relationship with one another at the moment of birth were used to determine the fate of the individual.[6]

Vṛddhayavanajātaka

With the appearance of *Vṛddhayavanajātaka*, the direction of Indian horoscopy changed once again, since this text only focused on natal astrology. *Vṛddhayavanajātaka* consists of 71 *adhyāyas* ("chapters"): Chapters 1-57 form the basic text, which includes defining planets, signs, houses, aspects, etc, planets in the signs and houses, planetary combinations, etc., Chapters 58-62 cover topics under the heading of *Strījātaka* ("women's astrology"), Chapter 63 covers *nakṣatras* for men, and Chapters 64-71 details omens. These last eight chapters are the only ones that do not deal directly with horoscopy.

Vṛddhayavanajātaka has numerous passages on natal astrology throughout the text that are similar—and in some instances almost identical--to passages on the same subject in *Yavanajātaka*. Although *Yavanajātaka* incorporates mundane, electional, and horary astrology, *Vṛddhayavanajātaka* sticks to horoscopy. The latter text is much longer, however, as it contains more in-depth information about horoscopy, including chapters on *nakṣatras* in the natal chart, women's astrology, and omens, all of which are missing from *Yavanajātaka*.

Translation Project

I first became interested in translating *Vṛddhayavanajātaka* when I had to decide on a topic for my Master's thesis from Columbia University in South Asian Languages and Cultures. I wanted either to work on astrological texts that had never been translated, or to revisit texts that had been given unsatisfactory translations. *Vṛddhayavanajātaka* fit perfectly into that category since even though it had been translated into Hindi, and perhaps other South Asian languages, it had never been fully translated into English. Classic texts on *jyotiṣa* that were no doubt influenced by *Vṛddhayavanajātaka*--including *Bṛhajjātaka* by Varāhamihira (550 CE), *Sārāvalī* by Kalyāṇavarrnan (around 800 CE), *Phaladīpikā* by Mantreśvara (around 16th century)—have been translated into English and are widely used as reference texts.

Valerie J. Roebuck, British author and scholar, translated some of the material contained in the first two chapters of *Vṛddhayavanajātaka* as the basis of her book *The Circle of Stars: An Introduction to Indian Astrology*.[7] Other than books that contain translations of the material in Chapters 58-62 on women's astrology (which I translated and analyzed for my MA thesis), Roebuck's book and Pingree's translation and commentary of similar passages in *Yavanajātaka* are the only two published works that I am aware of that contain English translations.

In conjunction with the Gaekwad's Oriental Series, a collection of Sanskrit texts that have been reproduced and published by the University of Baroda Press in Baroda, India, David Pingree planned a three-volume series in which he would produce a readable Sanskrit reproduction of *Vṛddhayavanajātaka* with a translation and commentary as he did with *Yavanajātaka*.

As opposed to the one or two manuscripts of *Yavanajātaka*, Pingree critically examined 16 different manuscripts of *Vṛddhayavanajātaka* that were of passable quality, and which ranged from copies of manuscripts to handwritten notebooks that were copied from manuscripts. Since these manuscripts have been copied over many times since the original texts were written, they often vary in words that are used. In other instances, the same word in two or more manuscripts may have a missing letter, making the word itself unrecognizable. In Sanskrit, if one vowel or consonant differs, it will change the word, and thus often the meaning of the entire sentence. Despite this, both sentences could still make sense, so Pingree had to make an educated guess in many instances as to what the original text may have been. He cited alternate words and phrases at the bottom of each page with the citation of its corresponding manuscript, which he labeled by letter. In this way, he laid out all possible options, so that the educated reader can come to his or her own conclusions.

Navigating through these problems, Pingree finally was able to edit his working manuscript to come up with what he considered to be a definitive edition. Volumes I and II, which were both published as Numbers 162 and 163 in the Gaekwad's Oriental Series in 1976, contain *adhyāyas* 1-39 and *adhyāyas* 40-71, respectively.[8] In Volume I, Pingree (just as he did in *Yavanajātaka*) wrote out the Sanskrit text using the Devanagari script in his own handwriting, but at certain points the printing process used to produce it make it difficult to read, with areas of text fading out in places. The second volume was typeset rather than handwritten, and is quite readable.

Pingree had expected to complete Volume III, in which the manuscripts he used for both volumes, along with others he examined, would be fully translated into English and annotated along with "an historical and technical introduction to Mīnarāja's work, editions of some shorter texts related to the *Vṛddhayavanajātaka*, and an index of verses."[9] This volume was never completed. Pingree's commentary, however, on *adhyāya*s 1-2 are among his personal papers at the American Philosophical Society, Philadelphia PA.

In approaching my own translation and commentary of *Vṛddhayavanajātaka*, I decided to start at the beginning even though this meant working from the somewhat flawed Volume I, which was a poor offset of Pingree's handwritten manuscript. Compounded with the problem of becoming familiar with Pingree's handwriting, was the task of trying to discern what belonged in the blank spaces where letters and words had faded out during printing. At times, I was able to figure out the Sanskrit word where a consonant or vowel was left out. In other instances, pure guess work was necessary. At times, even when I examined all of Pingree's possible choices, I was not always completely satisfied with the possible solution.

Despite these obstacles, I was able to transcribe the words, then translate, and then do research where needed to produce a preliminary translation and commentary for the first 20 verses of Chapter One. After I completed my translations, I compared them to Pingree's translations of the similar passages in *Yavanajātaka*, and to the translations in Roebuck's book *The Circle of Stars*. Sometimes my wording was quite similar to the wording used by either one or both scholars, since certain words and concepts are less variable than others. In other cases, my translations veered from theirs, and sometimes I concluded theirs were better, and at other times I left mine the way I originally conceived them. There were verses where I left out a word or words that I could not understand due to Pingree's handwriting, or that I could not translate because the terms were so archaic, but in those places the sentences were not reliant on those words.

Whenever necessary, I added commentary or background so that certain Sanskrit terms and concepts were more understandable. It was very common in Sanskrit literature, especially in *jyotiḥśāstra* texts, for the translator or editor to provide background information, or fill in the gaps in the text, which often followed the same style as scientific documentation in India.This specific style "required the scientist to depict his data, arguments, working and the results in capsule form, leaving out the details and rational, resulting in short pithy sentences, phrases, sentences or verses, with the result that the student was left in the dark. Commentaries came to the aid herein, especially those commentators who explained the words and were able to delve into the background which led to the enunciation of the *sūtra*s."[10]

The Text

Despite the unanticipated translation restrictions mentioned above, I have completed verses 1-20 of the first chapter entitled "The Division of Zodiacal Signs." These verses are the first of many different passages throughout the entire text that categorize the zodiacal signs according to everything from symbols to planetary rulers to dwelling places to body parts to vocations to colors. I begin by indenting the translation of the text, followed by commentary whenever necessary.

> 1. Praise to the shining Sun, who is [Brahma] the creator of the universe, Śiva, standing at its destruction, and to you [Viṣṇu] the imperishable who is in all things eternal, and contained in the Vedas in these three forms.

The first chapter begins as most Indian texts do, with a prayer and homage to one's guru or the deities one worships—in this case, the Sun God, who is also praised in the first paragraph in many classic *jyotiṣa* texts such as *Bṛhatsaṃhitā* and *Bṛhajjātaka* by Varāhamihira, *Sārāvalī* by Kalyāṇavarrnan, and *Phaladīpikā* by Mantreśvara. The Sun is worshipped in the forms of Brahma the creator, Viṣṇu the preserver, and Śiva the destroyer. It is obvious that Brahma and Viṣṇu create and maintain, but often people are under the impression that Śiva, who is worshipped in many different forms throughout India, is only recognized as the god of destruction. In reality, "Śiva is sometimes described as the god of destruction, part of the 'Hindu trinity' with Brahma as creator and Viṣṇu as sustainer, but for his devotees he is the supreme Lord who creates, maintains, and destroys the cosmos. He conceals his true nature from humanity, yet, at the same, time, can reveal his nature as an act of grace."[11]

> 2. By means of his own understanding, Mīnarāja skillfully reduced this science [astrology] that the ancient sage spoke to Maya long ago in 100,000 verses, to just 8000 verses.[12]

The "ancient sage" to which Mīnarāja refers is the Sun, whom he praised in the first verse, above, and who was said to have revealed knowledge to Maya. The architect of the demons, Maya, "the maker," should not be confused with *māyā*, the

Sanskrit word for illusion, often personified as a goddess.[13] When Mīnarāja refers to the ancient sage revealing astrological knowledge to Maya, he reaffirms that astrology is sacred. This verse also serves as one of only two verses in *Vṛddhayavanajātaka* that mention the author, Mīnarāja, at all, and since he is an enigma, it does give us some information about who he is. In addition to this second verse, the only other information about Mīnarāja may be culled from a verse that begins Chapter 67 on omens. Near the end of that verse, Mīnarāja again names himself, saying that he has carefully compiled and abridged teachings on omens that were spoken by Brahma long ago. In this verse, he calls himself a *Yavanādhirājaḥ* (Greek overlord), which was the basis of Pingree's reference to Mīnarāja as an Indian overlord of Greek descent from the kingdom of the Western Kṣatrapas. He may have lived in the late third-early fourth century CE, and likely came from the same social milieu as Sphujidhvaja and Yavaneśvara.[14]

3. The result of past actions of previous existences [*karma*] revealed in the horoscope is what the Creator has written on the forehead, just as a lamp reveals things in the dark shadows.

The third verse specifically states that the horoscope, or what is written or stamped one's forehead, reflects one's *karma*, (Sanskrit for "action"). Karma is to be understood as the result of past actions over previous cycles of reincarnation (*saṃsāra)*, with actions in this life determining whether there will be either another cycle of reincarnation or, instead, the salvation that comes through freedom from the present cycle. This verse about *karma*, which *Mīnarāja* placed early on in the third verse of Chapter One, shows the importance of his message—that the birth chart, if properly understood in terms of character strengths and weaknesses, destiny, and planetary cycles, will lay out how, or even if, it is possible to absolve past *karma* and find salvation. Actions not fulfilled by the end of this life will carry over into the next one. *Saṃsāra,* which literally means "passing through a succession of states," contributes to a non-judgmental approach to astrology, in which there is no good and evil but simply *karmas* that need to be experienced. In this way, the horoscope can be used as a tool in which to gain that knowledge in the current incarnation, ultimately achieving liberation from this cycle of rebirth.[15]

Description of Zodiacal Signs

The following verses numbered 4-15 consist of initial descriptions of the zodiacal signs. The Sanskrit word for a zodiacal sign is *rāśi,* literally Sanskrit for "heap," and refers to the heap or group of stars that make up the constellations from which the zodiacal signs are derived. While the constellations themselves are indeterminate in terms of scope and size, signs of the zodiac are thought of as twelve equal signs of 30 degrees each. (See Table I for list of English names of the signs and their Sanskrit equivalents.)

> 4. It is taught by the ancients that the first sign has the same form as a ram and is called the crown of the *kālapuruṣa* by the ancients The places are the trails of the she-goats and ewes, caves, mountains, thieves, fire, minerals, mines, gems.

Each sign description follows the same pattern consisting of: a) symbol (Aries as a ram, Taurus as a bull, etc.), b) parts of the body associated with the sign, and c) places and things that go hand in hand with the sign (mountains, caves, etc.).

The parts and regions of the body are listed according to how they appear in the *kālapuruṣa,* or cosmic man--an extremely important concept that requires an explanation. *Kālapuruṣa* literally means "time personified," and consists of two words--*kāla,* meaning time or the continuum of time, and *puruṣa,* which means man or human. With reference to the concept of

Table 1. The Signs of the Zodiac in English and Their Sanskrit Equivalents

1. Aries *Meṣa* (Ram)
2. Taurus *Vṛṣa* (Bull)
3. Gemini *Mithuna* (Couple)
4. Cancer *Kulīra* (Crab)
5. Leo *Siṃha* (Lion)
6. Virgo *Kanyā* (Maiden)
7. Libra *Tulā* (Scales)
8. Scorpio *Vṛścika* (Scorpion)
9. Sagittarius *Dhanu* (Archer)
10. Capricorn *Makara* (Crocodile with Deer Head)
11. Aquarius *Kumbha* (Water Pot)
12. Pisces *Mīna* (Fish)

Kālapuruṣa, however, *puruṣa* represents the archetypal man or "cosmic giant, the male person, or *puruṣa*, from the different parts of whose body the cosmos and society are formed."[16] This is, in other words, the cosmic man, the figure that links the parts of the body, from the head downward to the toes with the twelve signs, with Aries ruling the head, Taurus the neck, Gemini the arms, and so on down to Pisces ruling the feet. According to Dr. K.S. Charak

> "The term *kālapuruṣa* is often used in astrology. The concept of *kālapuruṣa* involves imagining a supernatural human form, which is spread over the whole zodiac. The various signs and divisions of the zodiac thus fall in the various parts of the body of the "*kālapuruṣa*," and therefore represent those parts."[17]

In the text there are times the word is abbreviated as *kāla*, and at other times, Mīnarāja equates *kālapuruṣa* with the concept of the lord, or the creator, which will become evident in the following translations.

5. It is understood that the second [sign] is personified as a bull. The region of the creator is the face and throat and neck. The places are forests, mountain peaks, herds of elephants and cows, farmers' homes and grounds.

Although the phrase "taught or it is said by the ancients or sages" is not repeated in each paragraph, it is understood that Mīnarāja learned these concepts from others, and then adapted them to make them his own.

6. The third [sign] is a woman and man holding a vīṇā and a club. The area [of the body] is the arms and shoulders of Prajāpati. Its domains are places of enjoyment, gambling, pleasurable activities, and where there are artisans, singers, and dancers.

This iconography of Gemini differs from that of the twins in modern western astrology. The Sanskrit word that is used for the third sign is *mithuna*, which literally means a pair, but not necessarily a pair of twins. In fact, the most common meaning of this term is of a couple who are bound by sexual union, and the description in this text attests to that.

The description of the sign is always, as it is here, delineated as a couple, a man holding a weapon, usually a club or mace (the Sanskrit word *gada* can mean both), standing next to a woman holding a *vīṇā*. The club is used as a weapon and, therefore, represents the masculine properties of heroism, bravery, and brute force. The *vīṇā*, often called the Indian lute, is a musical instrument that symbolizes the feminine qualities of devotion, creativity, and receptivity. As the wife of the creator God, Brahma, Sarasvatī, is identified with the goddess of speech (Vac) and inspires poetry, music, and learning.[18] She is iconographically depicted seated upon a lotus and playing the *vīṇā*, an instrument with a beautiful, pure timbre often used in religious ceremonies and rituals.

In his description of *mithuna*, Mīnarāja replaces the concept of *Kālapuruṣa* with Prajāpati, or the creator. Prajāpati, which literally means the lord of all creatures, is made up of two words, *prajā*, meaning "people" or "all creatures," and *patī*, meaning lord. In the Brahmanas, religious texts that appeared after the Vedas, Prajāpati, "the lord of creatures," is also an epithet of Brahmā, the creator-God, or of any of a class of primeval creators.[19]

7. The fourth sign of Cancer has the form of a crab that dwells in water, and its area of the body is the chest and breast. To it belongs water meadows, reservoirs, river banks, and the pleasure grounds of goddesses.

8. And it is said that the fifth is the lion on the mountain, the region of Prajāpatī is the heart. The domiciles of Leo are forests, rough ground, caverns, wooded dwellings, and mountains.

9. It is said that the sixth [sign] is the maiden in a boat on the water holding a lamp in her hand. The area of the body is the belly of the creator. The places are grasslands where artisans perform and practice their craft.

As is the case with the third sign of Gemini, the iconography of the sixth sign of Virgo veers from what we are accustomed to in the west. The term *kanyā* means maiden, or young girl. There are no depictions of the maiden with grain, the way she is often depicted here in the west, and she is instead pictured as described above on a boat with a lantern or torch in her hands, as if to imply that she is guiding the way.

10. [The seventh sign] is the man standing in the marketplace, placing his goods on the balancing scales. It is the region of the hips, abdomen, pelvis. Domains are customs house, cities, roads, and do-

mains of *vīṇās*, duties, and material goods.

11. And it is said that the eighth has the form of a scorpion in a pit. The region is the penis and anus of the lord. The places are hidden caves, stony cellars, places belonging to snakes and worms.

12. Sagittarius is the archer with the bottom half of a horse whose thighs are the domain of the creator of the world. Places are things that stand together and by themselves, domiciles of those skilled in archery or bearing arms, chariots and horses.

13. It is said that the tenth [sign] is the crocodile in the middle of water, with the front half, or top half or head of the deer. The place is the knees of the creator. Places are rivers, forests, form of lotuses or loveliness, or residences in which are seen the form of lotuses.

The iconography and symbol of Capricorn also veers from the western symbol, which depicts this sign as the mountain goat. Here we have the *makara*, a sea monster often depicted as a crocodile with the head of a deer. The deer may represent the same quality of the goat moving forward, while the crocodile is caught in the marsh, perhaps literally stuck in the mud. Another variation of the *makara* depicts the crocodile without the deer head.

14. It is said that the eleventh sign is a water pot on the shoulders of man being emptied and it is the lower leg. Its places are ponds, domiciles where they sell alcohol, gamble, and house women.

15. And the last sign is a pair of fish in water and is said to be the feet of the *Kālapuruṣa*. The places are dwellings of gods and Brahmins whose purpose is good deeds, places of pilgrimages, oceans, and clouds.

16. It was said that this world, comprised of the movable and immovable, has the nature of the sun and the moon. Its essence is seen in their rising and setting in the zodiacal belt (literally the circle of the stars or constellations)

17. The solar half (of the zodiac) is arranged beginning with *Maghā*; the other half, the lunar, arranged beginning with *Sarpa*. Arranged in order, the Sun gave the signs to the planets, the lunar half was in reverse order.

It is important to comment on verses 16 and 17 together, since here Mīnarāja divides the zodiac into the solar and lunar half. This means that Cancer and Leo, ruled by the Moon and the Sun, are the markers for the beginning of these two halves. The solar half begins with Leo, and moving clockwise, the signs that follow are Virgo, Libra, Scorpio, Sagittarius, and Capricorn. By the same token, the lunar half begins with Cancer, which is ruled by the Moon, and moving counterclockwise, the signs that follow are Gemini, Taurus, Aries, Pisces, and Aquarius.

Mīnarāja uses *Maghā* and *Sarpa*, the *nakṣatras* that begin and end at 0 Leo respectively, as the markers for the beginning of the solar and lunar half. As already stated in this article, the *nakṣatras*, or lunar mansions, were the primary means of dividing the sky long before the introduction of the zodiac, so using the lunar mansions as the markers for starting the solar and lunar half of the zodiac makes perfect sense. Once they were used for Indian horoscopy, they were divided into 27 *nakṣatras*, which consisted of 13 degrees 20 minutes. The 28th *nakṣatra* is still used for choosing the appropriate days for certain activities.

To this end, the solar half begins with *Maghā*, the first *nakṣatra* in Leo that spans 0-13 Leo 20, and the lunar half begins with *Sarpa* (Sanskrit for "snake," and more commonly called *Āśleṣā*), the last *nakṣatra* in Cancer that spans 16 Cancer 40-0 Leo. This is the first time this concept appears in a Sanskrit text since it combines the zodiacal signs, which originated in Hellenistic astrology, with the *nakṣatras*, uniquely Indian and used here for the first time in the context of natal astrology. Since *aśvinī* (0-13 Aries 20) was the starting point for both the zodiac and *nakṣatra* list, this meant zodiac and *nakṣatras* aligned and marked the merging of Greek horoscopy with Indian astrology.

> 18. According to their precise order, the sages assigned Mercury, Venus, Mars, Jupiter and Saturn to the signs.

The solar and lunar half maintain planetary rulers in the same order. The solar half begins with Leo, which is ruled by the Sun, and the signs that follow in clockwise order are Virgo, Libra, Scorpio, Sagittarius, and Capricorn, which are ruled respectively by Mercury, Venus, Mars, Jupiter, and Saturn. By the same token, the lunar half begins with Cancer, which is ruled by the Moon, and the signs that follow in counterclockwise order are Gemini, Taurus, Aries, Pisces, and Aquarius, which are also ruled by Mercury, Venus, Mars, Jupiter, and Saturn.

> 19. Of these signs, the odd-numbered signs are masculine, the even-numbered signs are feminine and the results are gotten in the same way. The odd-numbered signs have a nature that is cruel or harsh, and the even-numbered have a nature that is gentle or kind. They are all situated in order—movable, fixed, and dual—among the benefic and malefic according to their own nature.

Here Mīnarāja addresses the differences between the odd numbered signs—Aries, Gemini, Leo, Libra, Sagittarius, and Aquarius—and the even numbered signs—Taurus, Cancer, Virgo, Scorpio, Capricorn, and Pisces. The odd numbered are classified as harsh or cruel, and as a result, masculine, whereas the even numbered signs are classified as gentle or kind, thereby more appropriate for a woman to handle. This concept is also expressed in *Strījātaka* (women's astrology) in which the odd-sign Ascendants are not considered auspicious for a woman.

In the second part of the verse Mīnarāja addresses the modalities, or quadruplicities, in their order--movable, (cardinal), fixed, and mixed or dual (mutable). In terms of the modalities, the Sanskrit words for them provide a subtle contrast to western astrology. The Sanskrit word for the first set of modalities--Aries, Cancer, Libra, and Capricorn—is *cara*, which means moving forward, as opposed to the idea of cardinal, which means starting and initiating, but does not necessarily imply forward movement. The Sanskrit word for the second set of modalities—Taurus, Leo, Scorpio, and Aquarius—is *sthira*, which means fixed or steady, like the western counterpart. The greater difference is between what is translated as dual or mixed and the concept of mutability. To this end, the Sanskrit word for the third set of modalities—Gemini, Virgo, Sagittarius, and Pisces—is *dvisvabhava*, which literally means having two natures, with *dvi* meaning two and *svabhava*, meaning one's own essence, character, or nature. This is a bit different from the word mutable, which implies flexibility and adaptability.

> 20. Aries, Leo and Sagittarius rule the East, Taurus, Virgo, and Capricorn rule the South, Gemini, Libra, Aquarius rule the West, and Cancer, Scorpio, and Pisces rule the North.

In this verse, the triplicities are not linked to the elements of fire, earth, air, and water, as in Western astrology, but are instead linked to direction and their symbol. In Indian astrology, the elements, with the addition of "space," or "ether," align not with the signs but with the planets as follows: Mercury:

earth, Venus: water, Mars: fire, Jupiter: space, and Saturn: air.

The directions are always in the order of East, South, West, and North, moving clockwise around the chart. The first sign, Aries, is the East, the tenth sign, Capricorn, is the South, the seventh sign, Libra, is the West, and the fourth sign, Cancer is the North. In the same way that in western astrology, we assign three signs each to an element, in Indian astrology, we assign the same direction to the entire triplicity. Therefore, Aries, Leo, and Sagittarius rule the East, Taurus, Virgo, and Capricorn rule the South, Gemini, Libra, and Aquarius rule the West, and Cancer, Scorpio, and Pisces rule the North.

Conclusion

With these translations I have realized the great importance to be seen in the adoption of the zodiac in *jyotiḥśāstra*. Mīnarāja's presentation of the zodiac, rather than the planets, in the first chapter of his text (as was done in *Yavanajātaka*), attests to its importance in establishing Indian horoscopy and forming a union of Hellenistic and Indian techniques. It is quite possible that the zodiac may have been recognized and used in India before the writing of these texts, especially since, in addition to the Silk Road, there was documented trade between Babylonia, where the zodiac first developed, and certainly India was exposed to Hellenistic astrology following Alexander's conquest in the 4th century BCE. Despite this, the importance of the zodiac as a turning point in Indian astrology is shown by Mīnarāja's placement of it in the fourth verse of the first chapter, after the benediction and purpose of the text.

In closing, I would like to reiterate that these translations are preliminary and they still need to be refined, especially in light of the variations in the original manuscripts, and the poor quality of some of the text in the Gaekwad's Oriental Series edition of Volume I of *Vṛddhayavanajātaka*. I would like to thank AFA and AFAN for providing the research grant used for this article, and to Kenneth Irving who provided his editorial expertise.

Endnotes

[1] David Pingree became professor in the History of Mathematics Department at Brown University in 1971, and served as its chair from 1986 until his death in 2005. (The department closed in 2008.) He was recognized as foremost authority on the transmission of texts in the exact sciences from one culture to another. The David Pingree Collection in the John Hay Library at Brown University contains manuscripts that he collected throughout the world. Pingree's personal papers are stored at the American Philosophical Society in Philadelphia PA.

[2] Patrick Olivelle, ed., *Between the Empires: Society in India 300 BCE to 400 CE* (New York: Oxford University Press, 2006), v.

[3] Asko Parpola, *Deciphering the Indus Script* (Cambridge: Cambridge University Press, 1994), 204.

[4] See David Pingree, ed., *The Yavanajātaka of Sphujidhvaja.* 2 vols. (Cambridge MA: Harvard University Press, 1978).

[5] Most recently there has been a reassessment of possible dating of *Yavanajātaka* based on a translation of a resurfaced manuscript discovered in Nepal along with suggestions for possible redating of *Vṛddhayavanajātaka.* See Bill M. Mak, "The Last Chapter of Sphujidhvaja's *Yavanajātaka* Critically Edited with Notes", *SCIAMVS: Sources and Commentaries in Exact Science*, vol. 14 (December 2013), 59-148. See also Bill M. Mak, "The Date and Nature of Sphujidhvaja's *Yavanajātaka* Reconsidered in the Light of Some Newly Discovered Materials", *History of Science in South Asia*, vol. 1 (2013), 1-20. Updated information can be found at www.billmak.com.

[6] Some of the information about the development of astrology in India is adapted from my article "Women's Astrology in India" that was published in the AFA Research Journal, 2014.

[7] Valerie J. Roebuck, *The Circle of Stars: an Introduction to Indian Astrology,* (Rockport MA: Element Books, 1992).

[8] David Pingree, ed., *Vṛddhayavanajātaka of Mīnarāja.* 2 vols. (Baroda: Oriental Institute. Gaekwad's Oriental Series, vol. 162-163, 1976).

[9] Ibid. vii.
[10] K.V. Sarma, "Sanskrit and Science: A New Area of Study." in *Mathematics and Medicine in Sanskrit: Papers of the 12th World Sanskrit Conference held in Helsinki, Finland, 13- 18 July 2003,* Vol. 7, ed. Dominik Wujastyk. (Delhi: Motilal Banarsidass Publishers, 2009), 15.
[11] Gavin Flood, *An Introduction to Hinduism* (Cambridge: Cambridge University Press, 1996) 151
[12] Since Mīnarāja says there are 8000 verses, but clearly there are not, it is possible that Pingree's assessment that these were really half verses holds true. Originally Pingree used that agreement with *Yavanajātaka* and it might apply here as well. See *The Yavanajātaka of Sphujidhvaja,* Vol. I,3.
[13] Wendy Doniger O'Flaherty, *Hindu Myths* (London: Penguin Books, 1975) 348.
[14] David Pingree, *From Astral Omens to Astrology from Babylon to Bikaner,* (Rome: Istituto Italiano Per L'Africa E L'Oriente, 1997) 34.
[15] Nicholas Campion and Ronnie Gale Dreyer, "Indian Astrology," in *Religious Transformation in Modern Asia,* ed. David W. Kim (Leiden: Brill, 2015), 175.
[16] Gavin Flood, *An Introduction to Hinduism* (Cambridge: Cambridge University Press, 1996) 48.
[17] K.S. Charak, *Essentials of Medical Astrology* (New Delhi: Vision Wordtronic, 1994) 46-47.
[18] Gavin Flood, *An Introduction to Hinduism,* 182-183.
[19] Wendy Doniger O'Flaherty, *Hindu Myths,* 350.

History of the Astrological Technique of Solar Arc Directions

By Peter Gadek, M.S.

ABSTRACT: Every time a new "system" is proposed, it is important to identify and understand where it came from and how it works. This includes questions about history of the method, intentions of method creators, philosophical interpretations that the method can offer, or the situations when the method should be used at. These are the questions that I always ask when I learn a new method, and the same questions came to me when the solar arc direction method was introduced to me for the first time. Unfortunately, no one was able to tell me much about the origins of the method. I was told that the method derived from Ptolemy's *Tetrabiblos*. However, this was not enough to satisfy my personal curiosity. Method is simple and powerful, but the unanswered questions remained: When? How? Who? Why? Last year I decided I would explore the subject on my own. It has been a fascinating journey. It is clear that solar arc directions evolved out of primary directions. Both systems seem to share the same principle: one degree for one year. Still, they are very different. Primary directions are based on the earth's primary motion (around her own axis); one degree here relates to right ascension. Solar arc directions are based on the earth's secondary motion (around the Sun); one degree here relates to celestial longitude. The mathematical foundation of both methods is drastically different. Also very much different is the way in which these methods are used—the application of two very different astrological methodologies. But how was it that some astrologers or researchers made an effort to develop this new, simple, and practical technique? Who were they? When did they live? What was their motivation? What was the process of evolution? This article is an attempt to answer all these fundamental questions.

Introduction

The basic concept of the technique of solar arc direction is probably as old as the known history of astrology. It appears that this technique evolved from the primary directions technique. The purpose of this discussion is to trace the origins of the system of solar arc directions and outline how the technique developed.

Review of Main Predictive Techniques

1. Primary directions are called this because they are based on the earth's primary motion, namely its rotation around its own polar axis, which takes place on the plane of the celestial equator.

2. Secondary progressions are called this because the technique is based on the earth's secondary motion, its annual orbit around the Sun, which takes place on the plane of the Ecliptic. It is generally accepted that this technique was developed by Placidus de Titis in the 17th century, although some sources say that this technique was known before the time of Placidus. Placidus introduced this technique as an auxil-

iary system to primary directions, which he called secondary directions—currently called secondary progressions. The current practice of combining the primary directions of the angles with the secondary directions of the planets was originated by Alan Leo.

3. Solar arc directions were developed mostly in 19th century. This technique will be further clarified in this discussion.

4. Solar returns are sometimes called solar revolutions. This is a very ancient technique. The planetary arrangement is analyzed for the moment when the Sun (in its apparent motion along the ecliptic) returns to the exact degree of celestial longitude that it occupied at the moment of native's birth. This technique will not be included in this discussion.

5. Annual profection is a system of symbolic directions. This technique has been in use since classical antiquity. This was the widespread time-lord technique that was used during the Hellenistic period of astrology, and was used together with primary directions.

6. Transits. This is another technique has been known since antiquity. Ptolemy gives importance to the transits of the planets through the signs of the significators, using aspects by sign. Renaissance and modern authors give transits to directions the role of triggering events.

7. Ingresses. This technique presents the configuration of the heavens at the time of a solar, lunar or planetary entry into a zodiacal sign. The Sun's ingress into the sign of Aries is considered especially important in mundane astrology.

Primary Directions vs. Solar Arc Directions

The concept of directions is at least as old as Ptolemy. This technique was described in the *Tetrabiblos,* and further developed over the centuries. The technique of Primary Directions is built on this basic foundation, namely that the actual motion of the heavens in the hours following birth is bringing the planets and other points to significant places in the natal chart, and thus shows the unfolding events in years to come. In this technique one degree of such motion (primary motion—measured on the equatorial plane in right ascension) corresponds to one year of life.

As the earth turns on its axis, it completes a full circle (360 degree rotation) in 24 hours (1440 minutes). One degree of primary motion therefore equals about 4 minutes of clock time (1440/360 = 4). This one degree of primary motion is symbolically equated with one year or life, so that every hour after birth covers 15 years of life events. The directions formed to the natal chart within six hours of birth will then correspond to 90 years of life.

Every direction has two elements. The first element is considered more passive in determining the area of life concerned—this is the *significator*. Ptolemy, and many astrologers throughout the centuries after him, used only five significators: Ascendant, Midheaven, Sun, Moon, and Lot of Fortune. The second element is considered more active in determining the nature of the event—this is *promissor*. The traditional promissors are usually the original five planets (now seven), the major aspects, and sometimes the fixed stars. The promissor being carried by the east-to-west primary motion to the natal place of the significator constitutes a direct (right) motion. The significator being carried by the same motion to the place of the promissor constitutes a converse direction.

As an example let us consider the situation when sky carries one planet (for example the Sun) in its diurnal motion (clockwise) towards another planet that is stationary (for example Moon). Then we say that Sun is being directed to Moon—where Sun is the promissor (causes action) and Moon is the significator (target of action). This is the case of *direct primary directions*. Jean Baptist Morin assumes that in some situations the stationary planet (ex. Moon) can act causatively on moving planet (ex. Sun)—within the same scheme and the same motion (clockwise). The motion stays the same but actions of Sun and Moon are reversed. This would constitute *converse primary directions*.

To obtain accurate and reliable results (predictions), this method requires an accurate time of birth, within one minute (or less). It also requires an understanding of spherical geometry/trigonometry, as well as precise calculations. In the pre-computer era this was a major issue, since for this method the calculations were very demanding on astrologers. Because of the issues with calculations, by the beginning of the 20th century primary directions were largely abandoned as a predictive tool. At this time astrologers began to favor the use of transits, progressions and solar returns.

In the 19th century another astrological predictive technique also started to emerge: this was the increasing use of solar arc directions. This system gradually became a viable alternative to other predictive methods, such as secondary progressions or primary directions. Ease of use and effectiveness were the two major reasons that solar arc directions gained in popularity. This system is often used together with transits, with transiting planets acting as triggers for events.

This method is based on solar arc in longitude, referencing the position of the secondary progressed Sun. In solar arc directions, the Sun is first progressed (secondary progression), then the position of the natal Sun is subtracted from it. This number, or arc, is then added to all of the bodies and sensitive points of the natal chart. The new positions (the "arced" placements) are then compared to the natal placements, and exact aspects are noted.

With solar arc directions, the movement of *all* the planets and points is approximately one degree per year, since the secondary progression of the Sun is approximately one degree per year (with slight variations depending on the season of the year in which the subject is born). With an ephemeris it is easy for an astrologer to find the location of the Sun at the birth, and then count forward one day in the ephemeris for each year of life. This new position of the Sun (for the desired year) would represent the position of the progressed Sun. This is what makes the system of solar arc directions so easy to use, and it quickly became a useful tool in astrological practice.

Solar Arc Directions Methods

There are several methods, called "keys," used to calculate the solar arc for any given moment of life:

1. The Ptolemy Key. A quick calculation of one degree equals one year of life. This method is suitable for very general work.

2. The Cardano Key. This is based on the Sun's mean daily arc of 59' 11". It is more accurate than the Ptolemy key method. This system is based on the projection of 360 degrees of ecliptic into the time length of the year (365.00 days). 360 degrees/365.00 days = 59' 11" per day.

3. The Naibod Key. This key is based on Sun's mean daily arc of 59' 08". It is more accurate than either the Ptolemy key or the Cardano key. It is based on the projection of 360 degrees of ecliptic into the time length of the year (365.25 days). So, therefore, 360 degrees/365.25 days = 59' 08" per day.

4. The Individual Solar Arc (True Solar Arc). This is the most exact and the most reliable system for critical timing. The Sun's speed in its daily motion through the sky ranges from between 57' 05" and 1° 01' 10", depending upon the time of the year. The highest speed is near the time of the winter solstice; the lowest speed is near the time of the summer solstice (true for the northern hemisphere, and reversed for southern hemisphere). This is because the trajectory of the Earth in her motion around the Sun is elliptical, not circular.

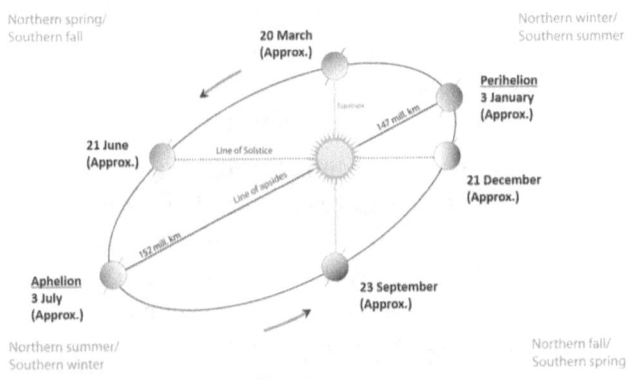

The Earth annual orbit around the Sun

Summer half of the cycle (20 March – 23 Sept) → 187 ½ days
Winter half of the cycle (23 Sept – 20 March) → 178 ½ days

5. Radix Directions. This is a variation of individual/true solar arc directions. The Midheaven, Sun and planets all move forward at the rate of the Naibod Key (0° 59' 8" per year, the sun's mean diurnal motion). However, the Moon is moved forward at the rate of 13° 11' per year, which is the Moon's mean diurnal motion (known as the "minor arc"). This system was developed by Sepharial and later further popularized by Vivian Robson.

Directions Over the Centuries

Hellenistic Astrology

Primary directions have been the major predictive technique in astrology for the better part of the last two millennia. Until the 17th century primary directions were known as simply directions. In the 17th century the secondary directions were introduced (now known as progressions). So, then the qualifier "primary" needed to be added to differentiate the original directions from the new ones.

The first traces of this technique come from Hellenistic astrologer Balbillus (1st century CE). However, these are only paraphrases. They suggest the use of directions since 1st century BCE. The first known author who demonstrates the examples of directions is Dorotheus of Sydon (1st century CE), in his work *Carmen Astrologicum* (Pentateuch). Other passages about directions have survived only in Arabic translations.

For Dorotheus, the ascendant is the main significator of life. He makes notes of planetary aspects and of the unequal divisions of the signs. He also makes notes of planets crossing the horizon and the intervals of these events. Based on this he produces the delineation, where the nature of the planet is given a meaning in relation to a specific period of time in the native's life.

Noting the rising of zodiacal degrees over the eastern horizon or Ascendant was the earliest form of direction technique. Soon, however, astrologers began to direct points to significators other than the Ascendant. Then the distance between the two points was converted into the time. The number of degrees of equatorial rising was converted into the number of years within the sign. However, each zodiacal sign requires a different amount of time to rise, culminate, or set. This meant the procedure did not reflect the actual situation in the sky. Examples of this simplified method can be found in the writings of Vettius Valens (2nd century CE) or Paulus Alexandrinus (4th century CE). They assumed—incorrectly—that each sign had its own uniform rising speed.

Claudius Ptolemy was the one who opposed this idea. He proposed (in *Tetrabiblos*) that for the direction that is made to Midheaven, the time of the direction should be evaluated by the degrees of right ascension. For the objects located between the horizon and meridian, the other intermediate method should be applied (oblique ascension).

Ptolemy was a natural philosopher and not a practicing astrologer. His primary concern was to provide the natural explanations for astrological procedures. Because of this, Ptolemy did not place much emphasis on astrological interpretations. For Ptolemy, as well as others of his time, directions were usually used to determine the length of life of the native. Some other major life events could also be prognosticated with this technique. It was Ptolemy who limited the number of significators (hylegiacal points) to five: Ascendant, Midheaven, Sun, Moon, and Lot of Fortune. He explained the method in several examples in his work *Tetrabiblos* in chapter III-10 "Length of Life," and chapter IV-10, "Of the Division of Times."

The Western Roman Empire fell in the 5th century. With the fall of Rome, the Empire's Greek scientific heritage (including astrology) disappeared in Western Europe. This heritage was partially preserved by the Byzantine Empire, and later absorbed by the Arab Caliphates. Arabic astrology emerged over the period of few centuries (8th-11th) during the Middle Ages. Omar Tiberiades (9th century) in his *Three Books of Nativities* describes both methods of directing: using the method of the rising times of the signs, and the method of Ptolemy. It appears that he favored the first method. The method of rising times of the signs was also favored by Sahl bin Bishr (9th century) in his book *On Times*.

In the 10th century Alcabitus gave a detailed description of the Ptolemaic method in his book *Introduction to the Art of Judgments of the Stars*. He does not mention the method of rising times; neither did Al-Biruni (11th century).

Late Middle Ages and Renaissance Astrology

The 11th and 12th centuries were the time of the Crusader Wars. The Eastern civilization at that time (late Middle Ages) surpassed that of Western civilization. The influence of the Crusades upon the intellectual development of Europe cannot be overestimated. Above all, it liberalized the minds of the crusaders. The knowledge of the science and learning of the East gained by the crusaders through their experiences greatly stimulated the Latin intellect. This helped to awaken in Western Europe the mental activity that resulted finally in the great intellectual outburst known as the period of the Renaissance. The crusades opened up a new intellectual world.

During medieval times in Western Europe the Hellenistic cultural, philosophical, and science-related heritage was mostly aborted. This was also true in relation to the astrological sciences. Arabs helped to preserve this knowledge by translating Hellenistic masters into Arabic, as well as other masters—from Persia and India. They were also introducing their own ideas, practices and theories.

The Crusades lasted approximately two centuries, and during this time created favorable conditions for all kind of exchanges between the West and the East, including intellectual exchange. This was the time when the science-related writings were translated from Arabic to Latin. Ironically, this allowed the West to reconnect with its own cultural roots, with the help of writings and other influences that came from the East. So this was the path for astrological knowledge to find its way back to Europe.

Guido Bonatti seemed to be one of the first astrologers who benefitted from these intellectual contacts with the East. His work, *Liber Astronomiae*, brought back the ancient Hellenistic techniques, translated back from the Arabic. The translations from Greek printed writings came later, and Bonatti's (16th century) descriptions of directions are based mostly on writings of Omar Tiberiades, who resurrected both methods: Dorothean as well as Ptolemaic. Authors from the 14th to 16th centuries, however, seem to favor the Ptolemaic method of directions.

Johan Muller (Regiomontanus) was one of the most influential mathematicians, astronomers and astrologers of the 15th century. He proposed a new interpretation of the Ptolemaic method, and his system won a great recognition throughout the Europe. It actually became the "standard" method for the calculation of primary directions. His method was later adopted by Morinus and William Lilly. However, about two centuries later it was proven that his method was not astronomically correct.

Jean Baptiste Morin de Villefranche (Morinus) has been known as a reformer of astrology. He lived in France in the first half of the 17th century. In his work *Astrologia Gallica* he made an effort to restore the intellectual position of astrology by proving the adherence of astrology to the natural sciences. At that time astrology was losing ground in Europe, and the Age of Reason and Enlightenment was advancing. Morinus adopted the Regiomontanus method of primary directions. He created a system of predictive techniques, with the primary directions being the most important component.

Placido de Titi (Placidus) contributed a tremendous amount to the development of the Primary Directions method. He was an Olivetan monk and professor of mathematics, physics and astronomy at the University of Pavia (17th century Italy). He was determined to base astrology on Aristotelian natural philosophy, and purge it of anything too symbolic. He is known for being the creator of the "new" predictive system, based on the primary directions. His procedure of calculations for directions restored the semi-arc method of direction, which had been largely abandoned in favor of the position-circle method. His approach to primary directions was astronomically correct. His system was based on Ptolemy's writings, but we need to remember that Ptolemy was not a practicing astrologer and his descriptions of the method are not very detailed.

Placidus created a system that was a balance between the writings of Ptolemy and his own inventions, that being his secondary directions and progressions. These were intended to support the main technique of primary directions. Placidus' secondary directions are now known as secondary progressions, while his original secondary progressions are now forgotten. It is believed that Placidus' methods were the interpretations of Ptolemaic descriptions of yearly and monthly profections. Placidus also introduced some other innovations, such as minor aspects and mundane aspects. The house system that he introduced had been in use earlier, with the earliest known evidence dating back to the 12th century.

The 17th century was a time of decline for astrology on the European continent. However, at the same time astrology began to grow and blossom in England. William Lilly was the main figure here. His astrological methods are explained in the master-work of his life, *Christian Astrology*. He based his predictions mainly on primary directions (the Regiomontanus method of calculations). Two of his students also became well known astrologers in their own right: John Gadbury and Henry Coley. Both of these astrologers adopted the Regiomontanus method of primary directions. Coley in his work *Clavis Astrologiae Elimata* explained the details of spherical geometry and used logarithms for calculations in astrology.

18th and 19th Centuries

Astrology in England in the 18th century had mostly vanished. It lived among the lower classes, mostly in almanacs. Still, the beginning of the 18th century brought one astrologer who continued the tradition of Ptolemaic primary directions: John Partridge. What is interesting is that Partridge calculated directions using the method of Placidus. He was the first one in England—and the only astrologer of his time—who adopted the Placidus approach of the Ptolemaic tradition.

Another prolific astrologer in England showed up at the end of 18th century: John Worsdale. Like Partridge, he based his approach on Ptolemaic tradition with the Placidus method of calculation, as well as other Placidus innovations such as minor aspects and mundane aspects.

The 19th century brought a popularization of astrology to England. However, the techniques were often simplified, and thus became somewhat distorted. A simplified version of Placidus was accepted by many authors and became the standard of the time.

There is one astrologer worthy of mention here: Alfred John Pearce. He was very dedicated to the traditional techniques and rigorous mathematical procedures (that accurately reflected the planetary motions) of the Ptolemaic and Placidean schools. He accepted no compromise. His *Text-Book of Astrology* was first published as a combined edition in London in 1911. It included the author's individual books on genethliacal astrology, mundane astrology, astro-meteorology, medical astrology, and elections. This classic work is filled with numerous examples and its original publication was praised by astrologers throughout the 20th century. Book 1 of this work lays out in detail the method of primary directions.

Pearce declined the offer to join the Society of Astrological Research, which was an organization that was dominated by theosophically-inclined astrologers such as Sepharial (Dr. Walter Gorn Old) and Alan Leo. Eventually Sepharial became disenchanted with Theosophy and the esoteric astrology of Alan Leo. Sepharial was, in fact, a much better astrologer than Alan Leo.

At the turn of 20th century British astrology had become radically simplified and connected to theosophy and occultism, mostly due to the efforts of Alan Leo. From this point in time, the use of primary directions declined. This was true both in England and on the European continent. This trend did not begin to reverse itself until the end of the 20th century. This was primarily due to the fact that there were a number of initiatives (Project Hindsight is an example) that focused on modern translations of the works of the old masters and revival of the knowledge that seemed to be lost.

The Emergence of the Technique of Solar Arc Directions

Johannes Kepler (1571-1630)

Johannes Kepler was a German mathematician, astronomer, and astrologer. A key figure in the 17th century scientific revolution, he is best known for his laws of planetary motion, based on his works *Astronomia Nova*, *Harmonices Mundi*, and *Epitome of Copernican Astronomy*. These works also provided some of the foundations for Isaac Newton's theory of universal gravitation.

During his career, Kepler was a mathematics teacher at a seminary school in Graz, Austria, where he became an associate of Prince Hans Ulrich von Eggenberg. Later he became an assistant to astronomer Tycho Brahe, and eventually the imperial mathematician to Emperor Rudolf II and his two successors. He was also a mathematics teacher in Linz, Austria, and an adviser to General Wallenstein. Additionally, he did fundamental work in the field of optics and invented an improved version of the refracting telescope, based in part on the telescope discoveries of his contemporary Galileo Galilei.

Johannes Kepler recognized that planets moved with variable speeds in elliptical orbits around the sun—Kepler's Laws of Planetary Motion. In the field of astrology he turned his attention to chronology and "harmony," the numerological relationships among music, mathematics and the physical world, and their astrological consequences. By assuming the earth to possess a soul (a property he would later invoke to explain how the sun causes the motion of planets), he established a speculative system connecting astrological aspects and astronomical distances to weather and other earthly phenomena.

One of the results was the creation of some of the minor astrological aspects in use today.

He is said to have considered that the number of days after birth that the Sun would take to reach the position of a natal planet, was equivalent to the number of years in the native's life that would elapse before the planet's indicated influence would manifest itself. This is a reference contemporaneous with the work of Maginus and Naibod, and prepared the way for the development of secondary progressions and eventually pure solar arc theory. James Holden in his *A History of Horoscopic Astrology* did suggest that Kepler may have originated secondary progressions, but he did not provide any solid source for this conclusion (p. 173).

According to contemporary astrologer and researcher Dr. Martin Gansten, the earliest suggestion of the technique of solar arc directions comes from Kepler. Jean-Baptiste Morin, known better astrologically as Morinus, discusses it and rejects it in *Astrologia Gallica*:

> "Kepler ... wants then, if it is required to find where a direction of the Sun and Moon extends to 30 years after birth, to take from the ephemerides the places of the Sun at noon on the day of the nativity and then on the 30th day after the nativity, and subtract the former from the latter, and there will remain the arc of the ecliptic, which, added to the radical places of the Sun and the Moon, will show where the directions of the Sun and the Moon extend to in the ecliptic in that 30th year." (v. 22, p. 79)

Morin cites Kepler's opinion that the solar arc be added to the radical places of the Sun and the Moon. This is clearly not secondary directions/progressions. (Planets other than the luminaries are not mentioned because they were not considered significators. Placidus is similarly concerned with the secondary movement—directions—of the luminaries.) It appears that this was the first attempt (historically noted) of solar arc directions evolving out of primary directions.

Morin criticized Kepler's system because it was a "symbolic" approach. Almost everything Morin did had its basis in nature, as stated in *Astrologia Gallica*. Through nature Morin defended astrology's validity in the face of the rising tide of skepticism from the Age of Enlightenment.

It is a known fact that Kepler needed to cast charts for clients to make his living. During this lifetime he calculated several thousands of charts. Considering that all the calculations were delivered manually and that primary directions were his main predictive technique, this must have been an immense effort just to prepare charts for his clients. And his laborious calculations were known for their precision. Under these circumstances it would be very natural that he would like to make the calculation process more efficient; especially in relation to chart rectification. It seems very natural that he would need a technique like solar arc directions as a preliminary technique in chart rectification. Primary directions would remain the main tool to confirm the birth time, as well as the main predictive tool.

William Joseph Simmonite (1809-1863)

Simmonite was undoubtedly the most influential astrological publicist of the early Victorian era. For most of his life he lived in Sheffield, England, where he was a professor of medicine and mathematics, and a prominent herbalist at Bethel Academy. From 1852 until his death he worked from his home at St. George's Square in Sheffield. At that time, astrometeorology shared forums and audiences with phrenology, mesmerists, scientific demonstrations, and instrumental exhibitions, most of which participated in the Victorian market for scientific amusement. However, astrology was illegal and its practitioners were in danger of persecution and imprisonment. Simmonite refused personal interviews following the prosecution of a colleague, and ran his practice by correspondence to avoid entrapment. This is further explained by his brother Henry, who was sentenced to prison for a month in 1862. Henry was charged with obtaining money under false pretenses for fortune telling. At the time William was living with Henry in Sheffield, and together they kept a "legal" drug shop.

Simmonite was known for his broad education; he knew fluently eight languages. Having educational background this extensive it is very likely that he studied the original (French) editions of Morin's *Astrologia Gallica*. In the 19th century this work was still not available in English.

Simmonite's works lay out very clearly the mathematical and astronomical foundations very much needed in astrology. Simmonite was the author of two major astrological works. One of them, *Horary Astrology,* was very much appreciated by fellow astrologers. Luke Broughton stated that this book was of great value to him and he used it frequently. The other book, *The Complete Arcana of Astral Philosophy,* is the one of the most essential astrological textbooks of the 19th century. This book laid out and organized this subject for practical astrological usage. His emphasis throughout was on primary directions, but secondaries are also mentioned. The *Arcan*a consists of two parts. Book 1 is focused on astrological foundations and delineations. Simmonite's descriptions for the general effects of directions seem to have been derived largely from those written by and initially presented by John Gadbury.

Book 2's focus is on astrological (astronomical/mathematical) calculations. His method combines "Spherical geometry, Spherical trigonometry, Astronomical problems, and the use of logarithms—inseparably connected therewith." Book 2 (pp. 187-242), guides a student on the subject of basic calculation techniques. The remaining part of the book, through page 306, demonstrates the techniques that directly pertain to primary directions. The final part of the book (more than 100 pages) consists of mathematical and astronomical tables that made the book very practical for students.

William Simmonite advocated the true solar arc approach in directing planets. He presents the procedure of converting the arc of directions into the time on the example in his work *Arcana* on page 276. This was in relation to primary directions method.

However, this approach can be applied to both methods of directing: primary directions and solar arc directions. Noel Tyl says in his book *Synthesis and Counseling in Astrology*:

> "Simmonite advocated using the actual motion of the Sun in progression after the birth date (the Secondary Progressed Sun measurement) as the individual's projected symbolic time factor. There would be no problem with slow or fast Sun; that factor would be included in the actual motion of the Sun. The measure would capture exactly the individual's measure of time and development." (p. 206)

Vivian Robson notes in his book, *A Students' Text-Book of Astrology*:

> "Simmonite's Method. The Sun's actual daily motion after birth represents one year of life. In other words the increase in the Sun's R.A. from noon on the day of birth to noon on the next day is the measure for the first year; that from noon on the first day after birth to noon on the second is the measure for the second year and so on. A variety of this method is to employ the Sun's actual daily motion in R.A. on the day of birth as a constant measure for the whole of life." (p. 218)

Vivian Robson confirms that the Simmonite method was based on the equatorial coordinate system so it pertained to the earth's primary motion (around its own axis). In primary directions the method is one degree of planetary motion across the daily sky (promissor in diurnal motion) is equivalent to one year of life.

Book 1 of Simmonite's *Arcana* does not discuss the techniques of solar arc directions or their delineations. Book 2, about calculations, demonstrates the calculations needed for directing. However, all the calculations are delivered in the equatorial coordinate system (right ascension and declination). In conclusion, we need to state that the method of solar arc directions was not mentioned in the *Arcana*.

Despite this fact, there is still good probability that Robson knew the method. And while he may not have invented the method, he was probably a major contributor—having Kepler as the initiator of the process.

Certain fragments of Robson's work indicate that he could have known and used the technique of solar arc directions for the purpose of rectification.

Knowing the complexity of primary directions calculations, and necessity of evaluation of multiple instances of directions, any rectification process with this method would be extremely time consuming in the pre-computer era. Using the solar arc directions in preliminary stages of rectifications would greatly simplify the process because it would help to narrow down the range of birth time.

Further details of this hypothesis are discussed in the conclusions section of this paper.

Luke Dennis Broughton (1828-1899)

Luke Dennis Broughton was born in England in Leeds. He came from a family of well-known astrologers and his paternal grandfather was a disciple of Nicholas Culpeper. It is thought that he came to America in 1854 when he was 26-years-old.

It is very likely that he knew William Simmonite personally, as well as his writings, before coming to the U.S. There are several reasons that bring me to this conclusion.

While in England he lived in Leeds, which is only 35 miles away from Simmonite's town, Sheffield. We know that when he came to America he was already well educated astrologer. We also know about his interest in medicine. After settling down in Philadelphia he studied natural medicine and graduated from Eclectic Medical College. Considering that there were very few astrologers in England in the mid-19th century, and even fewer astrologers being doctors of medicine, I came to the hypothetical conclusion that Broughton could have known Simmonite, or even been Simmonite's student in the field of astrology and medicine (p. 395):

> "Mr. Holdworth afterwards took lessons in astrology from my brother, and they became fast friends. He also brought a number of other students, and they formed an 'Astrological Society,' and Mr. Holdworth drew up the rules and by-laws for it. This astrological society was not the only society of the kind in the northern part of England. There was another one that my cousin William Broughton, W. J. Simmonite, Mr. Haywood, and a number of others whose names I have forgotten were members of. I believe they met once a week."

And one more fragment demonstrating the respect that Simmonite earned in England among contemporary astrologers and other well educated people (p. 396):

> "Mr. Holdworth, in some of his calculations had Mr. W. J. Simmonite, who had an academy in Sheffield, England, assist him. Mr. Simmonite, I think, was

the most learned and gentlemanly astrologer that England ever knew. He spoke, wrote, and taught eight different languages; besides being a thorough scholar and mathematician. He published a number of astrological works."

Broughton was the first astrologer in America to use horoscopes of famous Americans to teach and illustrate astrology.

In Philadelphia he established his practice of homeopathic medicine. In 1863 after an anti-astrology law was adopted, he transferred his medical and astrological activities to New York City. Following the Civil War, he rented lecture space and gave regular lectures on astrology. These lectures had a significant success, and eventually Broughton opened an astrological office. In addition to providing private consultations, he also began to teach, with significant results: the majority of the well-known American astrologers of the early 20th century were his students. He wrote several books and was known for providing astrological literature, especially the technical information necessary for the calculation of astrological charts. Broughton actively defended the rights of astrologers, and repeatedly acted as a witness in court cases where astrologers were arrested for "fortune-telling." The most notable of these cases was in 1886, when he defended a Mr. Romaine who was sentenced to 18 months in prison for practicing as an astrologer.

Broughton was a teacher to thousands of students. Astrology's spread and popularization in the United States is primarily due to his efforts. He correctly predicted the date of his own death on September 22, 1899 and made final arrangements and concluded his business on the day before in New York City. When Broughton died, he left his astrological practice to his daughter. She had overseen the publication of his most important book, *The Elements of Astrology*, in 1898, the last year of his life, and later carried on his work.

This book (*The Elements of Astrology*) contains a description of the technique that the author called primary directions, but judging by provided details it was actually the technique of solar arc directions (p. 170):

> "In addition to those aspects, there are what are termed Primary Directions, which we have to notice. These are reckoned by every degree in the longitude of the planets, as being equal to one year in the child's life. For isntance, Uranus is 4 degrees from a square of Mercury's place, therefore, at 4 years of age it would be an evil period for that child, and there being an evil secondary direction that came up for that year, it would intensify that secondary evil direction. Those primary directions are reckoned both by what are termed Direct, and also what are termed Converse Directions, that is, they are both noticed when the planets are applying to the aspect, and also when they are leaving any aspect. For instance, Jupiter is one degree past a square of the Moon, and by converse directions, it would be an evil period for the child at one year of age, as Jupiter will come to a square of the Moon, the co-significator, by converse directions, it being very near one degree from that aspect."

Note that he says: ". . . every degree in the longitude of the planets, as being equal to one year in child's life." Uranus is forming a four-degree square to Mercury, thus it is expected to complete the exact square in four years. This can only be obtained by using solar arc directions. Luke Broughton points directly to Simmonite as the source of his astrological knowledge (p. XI):

> "But probably one of the most learned astrologers that has given attention to the subject since Lilly's time, was Joseph W. Simmonite, of Sheffield, Eng-

land. His 'Arcana of Astral Philosophy' is an exceedingly good work, and it has been republished by the Occult Publishing Company of Boston. Dr. Simmonite simplified the long calculations and made many improvements. His Horary Astrology I kept on my desk for reference for over 30 years. His book on Revolutions is one of the best that has ever been published, and his Botanic Practice of Medicine is also an excellent little volume; I carried it in my pocket for years, and committed to memory his descriptions of diseases. Dr. Simmonite published for many years an almanac called the 'Meteorologist' and yearly Ephemeris; also a monthly periodical called the 'Messenger.'"

The "long calculations" Broughton refers to are usually associated with primary directions, and here he states that Simmonite simplified them. We know that Simmonite simplified the Placidean primary directions method, and organized it in a way that is easy to understand and follow. On the other hand, there is possibility that these simplifications and improvements could relate to solar arc directions—if we assume that the solar arc directions method was an auxiliary method used by Simmonite.

Dr. Heber Smith (1842-1914)

Dr. Smith was a thorough professional who was recognized, admired, and respected by everyone who knew him. He was a president of the Massachusetts Homeopathic Society, and was known as an educator, diagnostician, and family physician. He was also well known for his medical publications; he was one of the original faculty members of the Boston University School of Medicine, which was founded in 1873.

Dr. Smith had studied Sanskrit and the Eastern religions, and used his astrology as a diagnostic tool, although his patients never knew about his astrological expertise. It is believed that most of Smith's astrological knowledge was learned from Luke Broughton, including the technique of solar arc directions. Both Broughton and Smith lived in Philadelphia at the same time, at least until 1863.

It is certain that Smith knew the technique of solar arc directions. Smith demonstrated this during an astrological session that he gave to Evangeline Adams in approximately 1887. The time of birth that she gave Smith was 7:00 a.m. He rectified her chart to be a birth time of 8:30 a.m. The confirmation question he asked her was whether she broke her leg at age nine. Evangeline later confirmed the date of this event with her mother—that she was nine when she broke her leg. Her father's diary also later verified the 8:30 a.m. birth time. Thus solar arc directions was one of the techniques that Smith used for rectification as well as for life predictions.

Evangeline Adams (1868-1932)

Evangeline Adams was a famous American astrologer who had many well-known celebrities as clients. The first American astrologer who made her living entirely from her astrological practice, she is remembered for making many accurate predictions such as the economic difficulties that finally led to the stock market crash of 1929, and predicting that America would be at war in the years 1942-1944.

In 1914, in New York, she was arrested for fortune telling. During her trial she demonstrated her excellent astrological skills and subsequently was acquitted of all wrongdoing. Many papers quoted the judge's decision that she "had raised astrology to the dignity of an exact science." Judge Freschi tested Evangeline's skills during the trial. He gave her the birth data of his own son, expecting her to interpret his son's chart. What he heard from Evangeline amazed him since she correctly identified that his son had died in a boating accident.

Evangeline proved to him that the science of astrology has nothing to do with fortune telling.

Evangleine wrote several astrology books in which she outlined the elements of astrological theory with examples. Based on her writing we can develop some idea about the astrological tools she used in her arsenal. These would include:

- Essential and accidental dignity.
- Transits of planets, especially external ones (her main method).
- Planetary day and hour for electional astrology.
- Minor aspects such as semisextiles and quintiles.
- A technique she called the "new horary" in which she rotated the client's natal chart to a Ascendant that was for the moment of astrological consultation (she called it the accidental Ascendant). This method was especially useful with clients who did not know their time of birth.
- Solar arc directions. Presumably this technique was useful with clients who knew their approximate time of birth (for example, middle of the day, middle of the night, morning, evening)
- She might have used secondary progressions because it was easy to find them with the use of an ephemeris. However, it is not certain that she trusted this method.
- She did *not* use primary directions.

These astrological tools were not the only things she used during her sessions with clients. She was also a very intuitive person, having Venus, Jupiter, and Chiron in a conjunction in Pisces in her twelfth house, her natal Ascendant in Pisces, and natal Jupiter trine Uranus in Cancer in the fourth house. Jupiter, elevated by essential dignity, rules both her Ascendant (Pisces) and Midheaven (Sagittarius). She had the ability to see the person on both an intuitive and psychological level.

It is also known that she knew and used the art of palmistry during her sessions.

Some authors (notably, her primary biographer Karen Christino) believe that Evangeline Adams must have known the technique of solar arc directions, although this is not directly mentioned in Evangeline's own writings. There are two good reasons to believe this was true.

The first reason comes from the fact that she was introduced to astrology and studied the subject under the guidance of Dr. Heber Smith. She had her first astrological consultation with Dr. Smith when she was 19-years-old. Soon after she began studying astrology with him, and we know that he was familiar with the technique. He proved this at that first consultation with Evangeline.

Dr. Smith told Evangeline: "You are not only a born astrologer, and should take up the study of science, but you should go a long way with it." She often borrowed books from Dr. Smith that explained the history and philosophy of astrology. Smith was the astrologer who taught Evangeline how to cast a chart. Later he introduced her to the art of the chart analysis, and also the art of chart comparison (synastry).

However, Dr. Smith was a busy man, and he was not able to dedicate as much time to teaching as either he or Evangeline would wish. He referred her to Catherine Thompson, who was at that time one of the most prominent astrologers in Boston. She was a well-educated, cultured, and sophisticated woman who had studied astrology with Dr. Luke Broughton. It is almost certain that she knew the technique of primary directions as well as solar arc directions. However, unlike Dr. Smith her astrological practice was more practical than philosophical. Her focus was on life cycles, business success, marriage, and children. She was the teacher who gave Evangeline most of her astrological knowledge, although Evangeline never admitted this directly.

The second reason it is likely Evangeline used the technique of solar arc directions is that this is the process she probably used in her own consultations. When consulting with a new client who knew his or her approximate birth time (for example, morning or evening) she would be able to deliver quick rectification of the chart with the use of the following methods:

- Evaluation of body type, and facial expression.
- The art of palmistry.
- Evaluation of a psychological profile through the interview process.
- Solar arc directions based on dates of critical life events.

These tools would let her find the sign of the Ascendant in the first step, then the second and third steps, and then the exact degree in the final step. These were the methods that her teacher Dr. Smith used (except palmistry).

It is a known fact that consultations that Evangeline gave to her clients were not very long, usually only 20-30 minutes. It is also known that she prepared the necessary charts during the actual consultation, spending only three to five minutes on this process. Thus it is likely that she used solar arc directions, the simple method that she learned from Dr. Smith. And for the same reasons it is unlikely that Evangeline used the method of primary directions, the method that was extremely time consuming and which also required a thorough rectification of the chart. It is a known fact that Evangeline's mathematical skills were good but not outstanding. It is also a confirmed fact that she used to own the books of authors such as Simmonite, Broughton, and Pearce. It is thus safe to assume that she studied these works and was familiar with astrological/astronomical methods and theories laid out by authors.

We would likely know much more about Evangeline's techniques if we had access to her personal papers and library, since Evangeline was in possession of the original writings of her teacher Dr. Heber Smith. This library, and her personal papers have survived and are believed to be currently in the private possession of Norman Winski, a Florida stock trader, financial analyst, and astrologer. The entire collection was offered for sale several years ago, but apparently had no single buyer. It is unknown at this time if her books remain as a collection or if they have been sold on an individual basis to rare book collectors.

Sepharial (Dr. Walter Gorn Old) (1864-1929)

Sepharial was an astrologer who lived in England. His book, *The Science of Foreknowledge*, was printed in 1918. In this book Sepharial first proposed the system of what he called radix directions. Little is known about what inspired him to develop this system, although it is very likely that the writings of William J. Simmonite were influential. Sepharial gives much credit to Antonio Francis de Bonattis, an Italian professor of mathematics (of Padua) who published (in 1687) a treatise espousing Placidus methods, including secondary progressions.

Sepharial, in his proposed radix system method, presents pure Naibod progressions, adding the mean increment of the Sun's motion to each planet and point in the horoscope, then arcing them forward this amount in relation to the age of the individual. His system is accompanied by the technique of taking the mean daily motion of the Moon (13°10') and applying this increment to all planets and points in the natal horoscope. Sepharial argued that a consistent method of directing must maintain the radical relations of the planets because the radix (horoscope of birth) is the epitome of the whole life.

Vivian Robson (1890-1942)

Robson was also a British astrologer. His book, *The Radix System*, was printed in 1930.

Robson further modernized and popularized the radix directions system that was originally proposed by Sepharial in 1918. Robson presented the radix system, using angles and house cusps directed by solar arc, along with secondary and minor progressions for the lights and planets. His book was not intended to be a revolutionary advance in astrological forecasting. Both Robson and Sepharial were attempting to supply a forecasting method simpler than primary directions, which had become too complicated for novices to calculate. However, Robson personally believed this new radix system was inferior to primary directions.

Charles Ernest Owen Carter (1887-1968)

Carter, another British astrologer, is generally considered to be one of the most important and influential astrologers of the 20th century. His lifetime commitment raised the profile of astrology through his 30-year presidency of the Astrological Lodge of London, as well as the creation of its quarterly journal, for which he was editor for more than three decades. In 1948 Carter was the co-founder and first principal of the London Faculty of Astrological Studies (FAS), an astrological teaching facility.

Carter served as the second president of the Astrological Lodge of the London Theosophical Society from 1922 to 1952. He carried on a legacy begun by Alan Leo, but unlike the flamboyant showman who preceded him, Carter's strengths lay in his keen intelligence, gentle wit, and stabilizing influence as both president of the Astrological Lodge and creator and editor of the Lodge's magazine, *The Astrologers' Quarterly*.

His book, *Symbolic Directions in Modern Astrology,* was published in 1929. Symbolic directions, as the term implies, are those that correspond to no known planetary movement. Among the various symbolic directions discussed in this book are:

- The one degree (often used in solar arc directions).
- The naronic, a ratio of 4/7ths, which Sepharial described as useful in defining the periods of depression and expansion in any life.
- The duodenary of 2.5 degrees (division of a sign by 12) known in India as the
- Dwadashamsa, which Carter says gives excellent results.
- The novenary, of 3 degrees 20 minutes, formed by dividing a sign by 9, which is known in India as the navamsa.
- The septenary, of 4-2/7 degrees, formed by dividing a sign by 7.

Disregarding the one degree system as common, and combining the duodenary and sub-duodenary, Carter counts these as four systems. Of them, he says,

> "Yet the Four Measures constitute a net through which few events will pass without proper directional authorization! On the other hand, they do not furnish such a crowd of directions as to make it a foregone conclusion that there must be one or more for every possible occurrence—a criticism that has been made (I think unjustly) against some systems.
>
> "Those who find the four measures too many to apply to all elements of the map are advised to use only the traditional significators, the Sun, Moon and Angles. These will amply suffice for all important events, but if the exact time of precipitation is required, then lunations, transits, and lunar secondaries should be used."

Carter then goes on to the fractional method, a variable system, and then further shows what use can be made of these systems in ordinary life. Charles E. O. Carter greatly contributed to the popularization of the solar arc directions.

Reinhold Ebertin (1901-1988)

Ebertin was a German astrologer and physician whose research led him to the development of a new scientific discipline that he called cosmobiology. Ebertin defined cosmobiology as the following:

> "Cosmobiology is a scientific discipline concerned with the possible correlation between the cosmos and organic life and the effects of cosmic rhythms and stellar motion on man, with all his potentials and dispositions, his character and the possible turns of fate; it also researches these correlation and effects as mirrored by earth's plant and animal life as a whole. In this endeavor, Cosmobiology utilizes modern-day methods of scientific research, such as statistics, analysis, and computer programming. It is of prime importance, however, in view of the scientific effort expended, not to overlook the macrocosmic and microcosmic interrelations incapable of measurement."

The Hamburg School of Astrology (Uranian astrology) used the solar arc technique as its measure for developmental time.

Cosmobiology evolved out of Uranian astrology; Trans-Neptunian planets were excluded, but most of the other techniques remained. Ebertin used cosmobiology as a tool in his medical practice. The efficiency of this new tool had been proven by Ebertin through his many years of thorough testing in the medical field.

In 1949 Ebertin published his work in a book entitled *The 90-Degree Dial in Practice*.

After many additions and improvements it was released again in 1972 under its current title, *Applied Cosmobiology*. The book, *Directions: Co-determinant of Fate* (published in 1976) is dedicated exclusively to the subject of practical use of solar arc directions. This book explains the methods, interpretation, use of solar arc directions, graphic ephemeris, and more. By using these techniques, through cosmobiology, astrology became a quicker and more useful tool. Thus, solar arc directions became one of the critical tools of the cosmobiologist. In the pre-computer era, Ebertin created an elegant system of plastic and paper wheels that allowed an outer ring of solar arcs to rotate around a natal horoscope and to display direct and indirect arcs measured quickly and easily. Supporters of this new astrological school contributed to the popularization of the solar arc directions technique in the shape that we know it today.

Conclusions

Overview

The technique of solar arc directions emerged as a result of a process rather than a single idea or invention. The system evolved out of primary directions, a concept expounded by Ptolemy, and further developed by Placidus.

The first traces of solar arc directions can be found, according to Morinus, in the writings of Johannes Kepler, who lived in the early 17th century. The next author who made a step in the process of developing solar arc directions was William J. Simmonite, who lived in the first half of the 19th century. So, for more than two centuries no one continued the work on this technique. Or possibly there was no demand for a new technique. But why?

Both systems are called directions: primary directions and solar arc directions. Both systems use the spectrum of all natal planets being moved in one direction by the same arc (same speed). Primary directions are measured along the celestial equator and are measured in right ascension; planets are directed clockwise by primary motion. Solar arc directions are measured along the ecliptic and are measured in celestial longitude; planets are directed counter-clockwise by secondary motion.

With primary directions the aspects formed to the natal chart within six hours of birth will then correspond to 90 years of life. By comparison, with solar arc directions the aspects formed to the natal chart within 90 days following the birth will then correspond to 90 years of life.

To obtain reliable results with primary directions requires a very precise time of birth—within one minute of clock time or better. The mathematical calculations are extremely complex and lengthy, and need to be delivered with high precision. Because the mathematical requirements are so demanding for primary directions, they were abandoned as a predictive tool in favor of transits, secondary progressions, and solar arc direction. Historically through the 17th century the profession of astrologer required a high skill level. Astrologers needed to be astronomers, mathematicians, natural philosophers, and physicians at the same time.

In the 18th century this situation changed. With the coming of the Age of Reason, followed by the Age of Industrialization, astrology had been removed from university studies in the 17th century because it was too "symbolic"; it was impossible to verify astrology in terms of mechanistic reason. Casting charts and preparing material for predictions was a very time-consuming process. It was usually done for monarchs, heads of state, and wealthy people. In the 18th century astrologers were no longer regarded as people of the arts and sciences, but rather as magicians and people of superstition. At that time most mathematically gifted people became physicists or astronomers. Astrology was left with only second-rate minds, at least in terms of mathematics.

The end of 18th century also brought two major revolutions: the French and the American. These revolutions began the process of democratization in the western world. Did this mean that the demand for astrological consultations disappeared? Not at all.

In France and Germany there were very few astrologers left who practiced the traditional art/science of astrology. In 19th century England a law was passed that claimed astrology was an act of magic (or fortune telling) and made astrological consultations punishable by law. A similar law was later adopted in the United States. In the 19th century, in these two countries, astrology was practiced mostly by physicians, who were using astrological knowledge for diagnostic purposes. Thus, the 19th century introduced an entirely different attitude toward astrology to the western world—in political, economic, cultural, and social terms.

People in 19th century society still desired astrological consultations; however, the demand was different. An astrologer could not allocate a great deal of time and effort to prepare for a personal consultation. The technique of primary direction was still known by few, but the need emerged for a simpler technique that would deliver the results of comparable accuracy. In the new 19th century reality, potential astrological clients did not always know their exact time of birth, so a new technique needed to be able to compensate for this issue. Solar arc directions could fulfill this need.

In the 20th century the technique was further developed and improved by others. Eventually, solar arc directions became one of the main predictive tools of contemporary astrologers.

Hypothesis on the Derivation of the Method of Solar Arc Directions

References to the development of this technique are scattered over several centuries; however, the following will provide clues for those who would seek to learn more:

- Jean Baptist Morin: *Astrologia Gallica,* Book 23, in his writings about Kepler.

- William Simmonite: *The Complete Arcana of Astral Philosophy.*
- Alfred John Pearce: *The Text-Book of Astrology.*
- Luke Broughton: *The Elements of Astrology.*

Considering the historical evidence, it would appear that there are two options as to why and how the technique of solar arc directions developed:

First Option: The technique of solar arc directions emerged as a result of misunderstanding the system of primary directions; this would have occurred in the second half of the 19th century. At that time there were very few astrologers who had the required depth of understanding of astronomy and mathematics, as well as astrology itself. Their students could have potentially misunderstood the subject, and consequently interpreted directions from prime movement (the Earth's rotation on its polar axis) as directions from secondary movement (the earth's annual revolution around the sun on the ecliptic). The key that was used looked the same: one degree was the equivalent for one year. However, one degree of right ascension is not the same as one degree of longitude. Still, solar arc directions have been in use for more than 100 years, and they have proven their value. So, while the method is not incorrect, it differs significantly from that of primary directions.

Second Option: Solar arc directions were deliberately created by renowned astrologers who possessed considerable knowledge of both astronomy and mathematics. The method was developed to facilitate the process of chart preparations prior to an astrological consultation, since all the calculations still needed to be done manually. Historically, the use of primary directions was the main predictive technique, but it required laborious calculations. The time and effort required was compounded in the case of a natal chart rectification. There was a need to simplify and improve, or find an alternative, to the system of primary directions. For complicated situations, the use of solar arc directions thus became an option of choice. It would appear that the use of solar arc directions was the first choice as a preliminary technique in a chart rectification. Primary directions would still remain the main tool of rectification, as well as the main predictive tool. If this path of reasoning is correct, it would appear that solar arc directions were not intended for use independently from primary directions, by either Kepler's or Simmonite's intention. This is probably the reason why neither astrologer (nor those who practiced in the 200 years between them) published information on this technique in the time period from Kepler to Simmonite.

Proliferation of the technique really appears to have begun with Luke Broughton. According to his own testimony, before he arrived in the U.S., there were perhaps 10 astrologers in the U.S. who knew how to cast a chart. Thus he became very active educating a new generation of astrologers. The most famous of his students include Dr. Heber Smith, Dr. William Chaney, and Catherine Thompson. These three educated yet another generation of astrologers.

I believe that solar arc directions were tested extensively at that time. First by Broughton, since he was seeing many clients. Later, by his best students, as the three listed above. In this way the use of solar arc directions gained favor, and it is how the method started to live its own life.

This option would appear to be far more convincing.

Second Option—Details: To take a closer look at the idea of having solar arc directions as a preliminary (short-cut) step for rectification with primary directions, we need to analyze the celestial mechanics.

Simmonite in his work *Arcana,* in his chapter about nativity rectification (pp. 281-282) says:

"Observe. The best directions by which to rectify

the estimated time of birth are those of M.C. to Mars or the Sun, the Sun to parallels of Mars or the angles, as their effects do generally answer very closely to the time of direction. Marriage, accident, and death of parents, are safe events by which to rectify."

Why did he choose to use the Midheaven? Why Sun or Mars? Consider the scheme of rising planets and culminating planets in terms of right ascension and ecliptic longitude. A planet that is actually rising on the horizon is not rising at the same time as its right ascension degree or its celestial longitude degree. The illustrations below explain the difference. There are two factors to be observed:

1. A planet's equatorial ascensional difference (OA - RA)

2. A planet's ecliptic ascensional difference (LNG - LR)

Both factors need to be addressed, making it difficult to do a quick conversion from longitude (solar arc directions) to oblique ascension (primary directions). This means that with a solar arc directions chart we *cannot* make a quick judgment about primary directions (without delivering some calculations).

A planet that is actually culminating on the Midheaven culminates at the same time as its right ascension degree, and almost at the same time as its ecliptic longitude degree. (See illustrations.) This means that once we have a solar arc direction chart we *can* make quick judgments about primary directions (without delivering some calculations). In conclusion, this makes the solar arc direction method useful in preliminary stages of a natal chart rectification.

The reading can be exact in the case when celestial equator arc and ecliptic arc are symmetrical on the sky. This symmetricity depends on two factors:

a. Time of day. Symmetricity will be observed in the middle

of the night and the middle of the day. Maximal asymmetricity will be observed in the morning and in the evening, near sunrise or sunset.

b. Latitude of the birth place. For low latitudes when the birth place is close to the equator) the variations of asymmetricity are low. For a chart that is perfectly symmetrical one will observe the same degree of the same modality sign on both the Midheaven and Ascendant. However, even if these arcs are not symmetrical, we still can make relatively good and quick judgment about primary directions (without some calculations) through the eyeballing technique.

Symmetricity

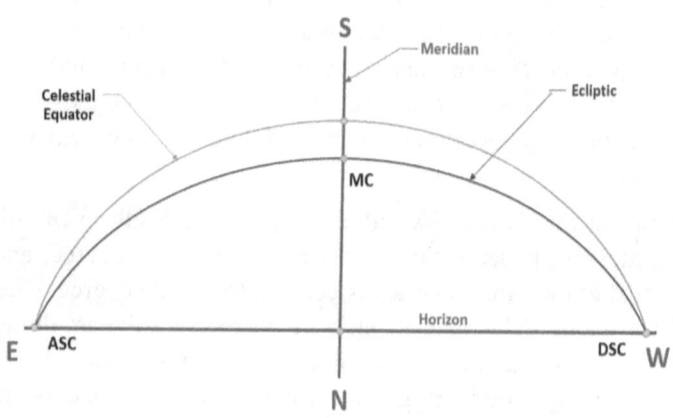

Planet Rising

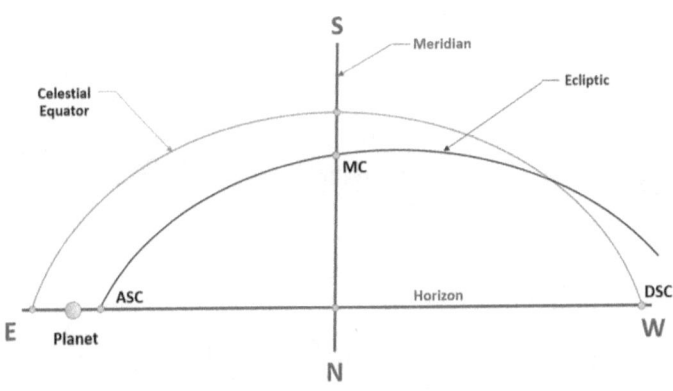

Planet Rising

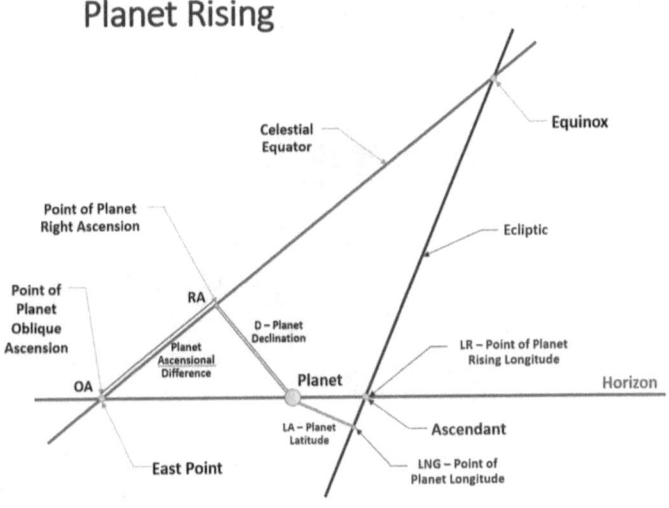

Planet Culminating

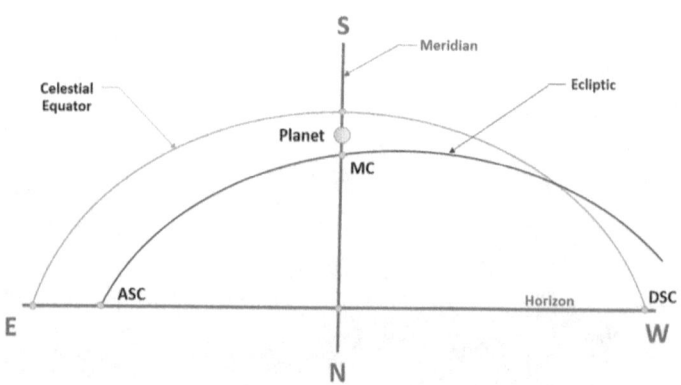

Planet Culminating

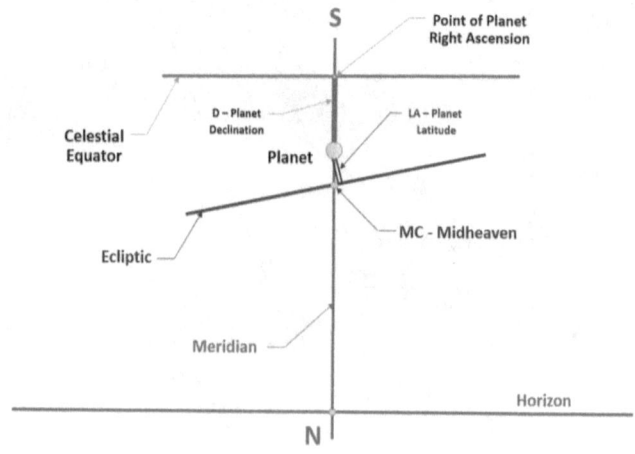

History of Solar Arc Directions

To begin the rectification we would need to start with Midheaven-IC axis and related symbolism.

The tenth house is a house of social status. It is about our place in work/career group and in society as a whole. It conveys authority. It is also about the promotions that we receive, any fame we may have. Vocation is important in this house. Through the tenth house we work on manifesting ourselves and the prestige and social status we gain by our career and vocation. It is also about parents (Midheaven-IC axis, fourth-tenth houses). These objectives can be accomplished with the help of solar energy or Martian energy.

The Sun represents the self, one's personality and ego, the spirit and what it is that makes the individual unique. It is our identity in relation to the world. The Sun also speaks to creative ability and the power of the individual to meet the challenges of everyday life.

Mars is the planet of action and assertiveness. Energy, passion, drive, and determination are the Mars key words. This planet commands people to stand up, be noticed, and get things done. It is about the power and confidence of expression of the individual. Under stressful conditions it can also mean, surgery, fever, or accidents.

For an astrologer who is to deliver a natal rectification it would be advisable to start with the events related to the tenth or fourth house (Midheaven-IC axis), especially if the natal Sun and/or Mars are not far from this axis. If this is the case then solar arc directions (and eyeballing directed positions) can be very helpful in a preliminary evaluation of the birth time of the native, with the final tuning being left to the method of primary directions.

Summary

The technique of solar arc directions appears to have been initiated by Kepler. His mathematical and astronomical abilities were exceptionally broad. Most likely, Kepler discussed the subject with his contemporaries. It is known fact that he corresponded regularly with Antonio Maginus discussing astronomical/mathematical subjects. While Kepler supported the Copernican heliocentric solar system, Maginus stayed with geocentric system. The matter was further discussed by other renowned astrologers after Kepler, such as Morin. Simmonite was the one who finally clarified and simplified the Placidean approach to primary directions; with solar arc directions being a part of the method. Although, solar arc directions were not mentioned in his *Arcana,* why would he not mention it? For all the generations of astrologers since Ptolemy, primary directions were the foundation, the core—it was the "real" thing, while the solar arc directions were "too symbolic." Or to rephrase it, primary directions offered the whole picture, while solar arc directions showed just the projection—yes a very important projection (Solar), but still "just" a projection.

If the solar perspective method is accepted, then probably the lunar perspective (projection) should be accepted as well. Solar arc directions are probably not suited to present lunar energies. It is still not clear as to other appropriate method(s), other than the secondary progressed Moon.

How much sense is there in creating lunar arc directions? The spectrum of natal planets maintains the natal aspects and rotates with the speed of the natal Moon. This is for fast changes, and would work like the minute hand of a cosmic clock (see Sepharial method).

Or having the spectrum of planets rotated with the speed of the progressed Moon, for lunar influence over the longer period of time; see *Forecasting Backward and Forward* by Bruce F. Hammerslough, p. 80.

The key factor to remember is that the solar arc direction method offers the solar perspective.

Purpose Of Directions, A Comparison

The purpose of solar arcs, at least as they are understood today, is not quite the same as the purpose of primary directions. Modern astrology places a great deal of emphasis on aspects in the natal chart. The use of solar arc directions keeps those aspects intact exactly as they are in the nativity. This is perfectly consistent once we accept the overriding importance of aspects. For example, if one believes that the Mercury-Jupiter square in the chart of a native describes much of his personality, then keeping that significant aspect intact throughout the life is important when doing predictions about the life.

Primary directions, on the other hand, show the kind of events that are most likely to occur in the life based on a natural planetary motion (allowing for converse directions as well). They show how the life unfolds. The nature of the planet is given a meaning in relation to specific period of time in native life. So although there are some similarities, we are really dealing with two different systems.

Two Schools/Approaches in Solar Arc Directions

There are two distinct approaches to solar arc directions. The first one is represented by the school of Sepharial/Robson/Carter. The other one is represented by Simmonite/Witte/Ebertin/Tyl. The former one uses the mean daily motion of the Sun (applied to the Moon and planets) while the latter uses the exact daily motion of the Sun which is specific to each nativity. Hence, Tyl emphasizes the difference in "slow" solar arc directions for people born in summer months and relatively "fast" solar arc directions for winter births. Thus, the solar arc Sun used by Tyl is identical to the movement of secondary progressed Sun.

The other difference is related to kinds of aspects (hard vs. soft). Astrologers representing Uranian astrology or cosmobiology or their followers tend to put focus on hard aspects only

(Witte/Ebertin/Tyl). They seem to adhere to the rule that only difficult life circumstances can change the native.

Astrologers of other schools observe all Ptolemaic aspects.

Final Statement

Every time a new "system" is proposed, it is important to identify and understand where it came from and how it works. This includes the questions about history of the method, intentions of method creators, philosophical interpretations that the method can offer, or the situations in which the method should be used.

These are the questions that I always ask when I learn a new method, and the same questions came to me when the solar arc directions method was introduced to me for the first time. Unfortunately, no one was able to tell me much about the origins of the method. I was told that the method derived from Ptolemy's *Tetrabiblos*. However, this was not enough to satisfy my personal curiosity. Method is simple and powerful, but the unanswered questions remained: When? How? Who? Why?

I decided I would explore the subject on my own. It has been a fascinating journey.

In the process I have reviewed many resources (books available to the public, both physical and online copies). Unfortunately, I was not able to find all the answers that I was seeking. Still, I am very glad that I was able to collect all the information I did pertaining historical development and present it in the form of one document. The hypothesis about method genealogy that I presented requires more research. I believe that some archive might contain documents that are more private in nature than published books, such as personal letters or private notes that come from William Simmonite, or Luke Broughton, or Heber Smith, or Catherine Thompson. Or possibly even from earlier authors, such as Kepler (this would be really a miracle if something could be found), or Maginus, or Morin. It is likely there are many more historical documents out there buried in archives waiting for explorers to find.

We know about one source: the library of Evangeline Adams that is currently owned by Norman Winski in Florida. This library used to contain writings of Dr. Heber Smith, and Smith used to study with Luke Broughton. Having access to this library would be the answer to a dream of many astrologers, but currently this library is not available to the public. In 2012, Norman Winski put his library up for sale. The list of items prepared by Mr. Winski does not contain any correspondence items or private notes of Heber Smith, or Luke Broughton, or William Simmonite. Private notes of Evangeline Adams are also not there.

However, there is a Web page dedicated to astrologers' memorials: http://www.solsticepoint.com/astrologersmemorial/. Memorial dedicated to Evangeline Adams contains a note by Norman Winski stating that he is in possession of Adams personal memorabilia such as family scrap books and correspondence. I have never contacted Norm Winski by myself. This is a potential path to be further explored by other researchers.

Acknowledgement

I would like to express my gratitude to my teacher Christine Arens for reviewing this article and for the support I received from her on my path of astrology.

Bibliography

Classical

Robert Blaschke, *Progressions* (Earthwalk School of Astrology, 1998).

Brau, Jean Louis, *Larousse Encyclopedia of Astrology* (New York: McGraw-Hill, 1980).

Luke D. Broughton, *The Elements of Astrology* (New York,

1906).
C. E. O. Carter, *Symbolic Directions in Modern Astrology* (Maryland: Astrology Classics, 2010).
____, *What Evangeline Adams Knew* (Stella Mira Books, 2004).
Henry Coley, *Clavis Astrologiae Elimata* (London, 1676), online edition available at http://www.skyscript.co.uk/clavis.html
Reinhold Ebertin, *Directions: Co-determinants of Fate* (AFA: Tempe, AZ, 1976, 2011).
John Gadbury, *Genethlialogia, or the Doctrine of Nativities* (London, 1658).
Bruce F. Hammerslough, *Forecasting Backward and Forward* (Minneapolis: Llewellyn Publications, 1994).
James H. Holden, *A History of Horoscopic Astrology* (Tempe, AZ: AFA, 2006).
Morin, Jean-Baptiste Morin, trans. James H. Holden, *Astrologia Gallica Book Twenty-Two: Directions* (Tempe, AZ: AFA, 2004).
Alfred J. Pearce, *The Text-Book of Astrology* (Tempe: AFA, 2006).
Claudius Ptolemy, ed and trans. F. E. Robbins, *Tetrabiblos* (Harvard University Press, 1940).
Vivian Robson, *A Student's Textbook of Astrology* (London, 1922).
____, *The Radix System* (London, 1930).
Sepharial, *Primary Directions* (Maryland: Astrology Classics, 2006).
____, *Science of Foreknowledge* (London, 1918).
William Simmonite, *Complete Arcana of Astral Philosphy* (London, 1890).

Contemporary Bibliography
Karen Christino, *Foreseeing the Future: Evangeline Adams and Astrology in America* (One Reed Publications, 2002).

Gansten, Martin B., *Astrology's Old Master Technique* (Wessex Astrologer, Bournemouth, 2009).

Deborah Houlding, "An Easy Introduction to Primary Directions" (www.skyscript.co.uk/easy-directions.html).

Charles A. Jayne, *Progressions and Directions* (Tempe: AFA, 2011).

Rumen Kolev, *Primary Directions I and II* (Placidus Research Center).

Anthony Louis, *Primary Directions in Astrology* (Kindle edition, 2013).

M. J. Makransky, *Primary Directions* (Dear Brutus Press, 1988).

Noel J. Tyl, *Prediction in Astrology* (Minneapolis: Llewellyn Publications, 1995).

____, *Solar Arcs* (Minneapolis: Llewellyn Publications, 2001).

____, *Synthesis and Counseling in Astrology* (Minneapolis: Llewellyn Publications, 1998).

Software

Morinus 6.2 astrology program (free software) by Robert Nagy

Stellarium 0.13.3 astronomy program (free oftware) by Stellarium Developers

Outer Planet Conjunctions and the ~1500 Year Climate Cycle

By Bruce Scofield, Ph.D.

ABSTRACT: A ~1500-year periodicity has been reported in paleoclimate proxy data and claims have been made that this rhythm persists through glacial and interglacial periods. It has been suggested that the periodicity is driven by solar cycles, though solar cycles longer than 200 years are not well-documented. Here this periodicity is investigated in the context of a 1542-year recurring series of conjunctions of Saturn, Uranus and Neptune. Correlations with solar irradiance, galactic cosmic ray flux, and global temperatures suggest that these conjunctions may drive a regular periodicity in climate regimes that are inherently unstable, but only punctuate stable climate regimes that are following longer orbital periodicities.

Keywords: Holocene, barycenter, BP (before present), IRD (ice rafted debris), THC (thermohaline circulation), solar irradiance, GCR (galactic cosmic ray) flux, TSI (total solar irradiance), proxy data, cosmogenic isotopes ^{10}Be and ^{14}C,

Introduction

In traditional Western astrology, both historical developments and climate events (i.e. droughts, floods and storm frequency) have long been associated with the conjunctions and cycles of Jupiter and Saturn, the two outermost planets known prior to the modern era. The ~20-year synodic cycle of Jupiter and Saturn was considered the primary rhythm of historical and climate trends while their recurrence cycles of 60 and 800 years were used to designate larger historical periods (Devore, 1947; Baigent et al, 1984). In the literature of astrology correlations between planetary conjunctions (and other geometrical alignments) and historical and meteorological events have been noted and described in publications, but this evidence is, with few exceptions, anecdotal and interpretations are subject to the depth of knowledge of astrologers who are, with extremely rare exceptions, not also professional historians or climatologists.

In modern Western astrology, cycles of history and climate have been also linked to the cycles of Uranus, Neptune and Pluto. Again, anecdotal evidence abounds, but serious studies and causal explanations are rare. It is even thought by many that a causal connection between planets and observed terrestrial effects simply does not exist, or if it does an unknown force or cosmic principle is somehow involved (Tarnas, 2006). This position, which is itself an unelaborated synchronicity hypothesis relying on interpretations of coincidence as primary evidence, is convenient as it immediately eliminates the need for technical scientific knowledge and the funding necessary to pursue the rigorous demands of quantifiable research. One alternative hypothesis, however, is that gravitational forces of the outer planets modulate either the Earth system directly or the sun which consequently affects the Earth in various ways. In this paper a potentially quantifiable hypothesis will be examined in the context of configurations of the Jovian planets (Jupiter, Saturn, Uranus and Neptune), particularly in regard to a mysterious ~1500-year periodicity found in climate proxy data.

Here I present and test against several datasets the following hypothesis: *heliocentric outer planet alignments, specifically conjunctions, force changes in solar irradiance and consequently terrestrial climate events and trends that influence historical trends.* First, a summary of known extra-terrestrial influences on climate will be reviewed followed by a discussion of possible mechanisms that link solar activity to climate conditions. Second, the case for the existence of a ~1500-year cycle will be reviewed and then discussed in regard to a series of regularly repeating triple conjunctions of Saturn, Uranus and Neptune that occur in 1542-year intervals. This triple conjunction cycle, and in some cases, a quadruple conjunction, will be investigated as a possible modulating factor of solar activity using several long paleoclimate records. In this investigation only the celestial longitudes of these planets will be considered.

Materials and Methods

Paleoclimate data and modern instrumental data from NOAA/ NGDC Paleoclimatology Program, Boulder CO, and the NASA Solar Data Analysis Center is used in this investigation of correlations between outer planet alignments and changes in solar irradiance. Before the era of instrumental data (~1650) the resolution of climatological data presents difficulties. Datasets from ice cores beyond 20 kyr BP have, at best, century resolution and consequently are not appropriate to investigations of discreet outer planet alignments. Meaningful correlations require at least decadal resolution and several have been used in this study. One of these is a Holocene reconstruction of sunspot number based on dendrochronologically dated radiocarbon concentrations. This 11,500-year dataset is an indicator of solar variability and has decadal resolution (Solanki, et al, 2005). In addition a 9,300-year dataset of total solar irradiation (TSI) based on cosmogenic radionuclide ^{10}Be from ice cores in Greenland and Antarctica, also decadal in resolution, has been used (Steinhilber, F., et al. 2009). Other datasets used include a 2,000-year dataset of Galactic cosmic ray (GCR) flux, another indicator of solar variability (Usoskin, I.G., et al., 2008), and a dataset of reconstructed TSI of annual resolution since 1610 (Lean, J., 2004). From 1984 to 2003 high resolution TSI data from the Earth Radiation Budget Satellite (ERBS) has been used.

The method of investigation in this study consists of graphic comparisons of planetary alignments against various datasets of solar variability. Although planetary conjunctions occur in cycles, in a linear sense they more accurately represent discreet points over time. Correlations with climate phenomena thus do not take a form suitable for standard correlation analysis except in regard to coincidence with turning points. Given the wide range of possible planetary alignments, including combinations of planets, degree of separation, location in celestial longitude or latitude, etc., only a very long, highly resolved, climate could produce enough data points for proper statistical evaluation. No such dataset exists and this study does not pretend to be anything other than a preliminary investigation into possible correlations that may be resolved when more accurate data becomes available.

Solar System Influences on Terrestrial Climate

Climatologists, chronobiologists and other scientists interested in solar system influences on various components of the Earth system (atmosphere, hydrosphere, lithosphere and biosphere) generally frame their subject matter terms of cycles. Well-known and well-documented climate and biological cycles driven by extra-terrestrial factors include the 11-year Schwabe sunspot cycle and also the 22-year Hale cycle that consists of two paired Schwabe sunspot cycles of opposite hemisphere solar magnetic fields (Hoyt and Schatten, 1997, Halberg, 2000). Over the course of these cycles solar irradiance varies about 1%, though more so in the UV portion of spectrum. Abundant evidence for these cycles is found in many climate records including those of temperature and rainfall. The amplitude of the Schwabe cycle itself varies and a roughly 80-100 year cycle of its amplitude, called the Gleissburg cycle, has been found in cosmogenic isotope data. An even longer cycle of roughly 180-210 years, with correlations also found in cosmogenic isotope data, is known as the Seuss or de Vries cycle. The length for these later two cycles varies considerably and their connections to actual climate measurements are not consistent and usually treated skeptically. Other alleged solar cycles, longer than the Seuss cycle, have been found in some climate data, but not consistently. A problem in linking a solar cycle with climate data is in regard to consistency over time. Climate processes linked to one of the solar cycles may last for decades but then disappear or suddenly switch to another rhythm. This later observation suggests that entrainment of climate processes is a fragile condition and that the climate system is constantly evolving around set points which themselves change.

The cause of the Schwabe and Hale cycles is explained in most references by the dynamo model in which the differential rotation of the sun stirring plasma in its interior modulates emerging magnetic fields in a cycle—which just happens to average 11.1 years. This model, while generally accepted, has some problems and is not considered definitive. An alternative and generally unpopular and heavily criticized model considers the gravitation effects of the planets on the angular momentum of the entire solar system causing the sun to orbit the barycenter, i.e. the center of mass of the solar system. A second alternative considers the direct tide-raising gravitational effects of the planets on the atmosphere of the sun as a modulating factors in solar irradiance. Details of each of these theories and the current status of the debate are not considered in this paper, but it should be noted that the planets can move the sun out of the center of mass of the solar system (the barycenter) by as much as one solar diameter. The sun thus orbits the center of mass of the solar system, and it does so in a pattern that has a period of roughly 178 years. (Fairbridge and Sanders, 1987; Landscheidt, 1987; Mackey, 2007) This effect is commonplace in the galaxy as a large number of exoplanets have been discovered through observations of stars being moved by the gravitational effects of unseen orbiting planetary bodies.

In addition to the variations of solar irradiation produced by solar cycles, astronomical effects on climate are also demonstrated by cycles produced by variations in the Earth's orbit around the Sun called "orbital" or "Milankovich" cycles (Hays, et al, 1976; Mayewski, 2002; Burroughs, 1992). The three primary variations, precession (~23 kyr), obliquity (~40 kyr) and ellipticity (~100 kyr), are driven by gravitation effects of the Moon and other planets, especially Jupiter, on the tilt and shape of the Earth's orbit. Such changes modulate the amount of solar irradiation reaching the Earth (particularly the northern hemisphere where more land mass is concentrated) and consequently the climate over long periods of time changes accordingly. The periodicity of ice ages have been found to concur with orbital cycles and over the past 800 kyr years the ~100 kyr ellipticity cycle has dominated. Before that the ~40 kyr obliquity cycle was dominant, this being another example of how the Earth system evolves and can switch from one periodicity to another.

Abundant evidence has produced confidence in short solar cycles and the long orbital cycles as important factors in climate cycles and changes. In both cases it is the variations of solar irradiance that is the ultimate causal factor, though the sequence of steps from irradiance to climate is complex and somewhat speculative. Several mechanisms have been proposed including direct radiative heating of the stratosphere which then redirects the general circulation in the troposphere. In the case of the shorter solar cycles data exists that suggest the planets are an important modulating factor, although the details have not been worked out to the extent that the field of climatology has come to embrace it (Fairbridge and Sanders, 1987). Landscheidt has proposed that intense solar storms can affect the spin rate of Earth which then affects general circulation (Landscheidt, 1987). Another mechanism posits that when solar irradiation is low and consequently Earth's magnetic field is weakened, an increase in galactic cosmic rays (GCR) leads to an increase troposphere cloud cover, increasing albedo (reflectance) and thereby cause cooling. (Svensmark and Friis Christensen, 1997) In the case of the orbital cycles, the alterations in gravitational forcing from the planets modulates ellipticity. Gravitational torques from the Sun and Moon modulate orbital tilt and precession. It is apparent that climate change can be driven by solar system dynamics and it is out of this correlation that certain historical events driven by climate occur and are then ascribed to planetary positions. The correlations between climate and human history are typically as follows: climate changes (i.e. drought, extreme cold, heat, floods, etc.) drive changing economic conditions that lead to migrations, population pressures, political and rulership changes, crowd control, and a wide range of human disasters.

A Possible 1500 Year Cycle

There is a large gap between the lengths of solar cycles and orbital cycles. What has not been established with any degree of certainty are millennial length cycles. Some cycles of solar activity longer than the Seuss cycle have in a few instances been found in climate proxy data, but not in a consistent way and are generally regarded skeptically. However,

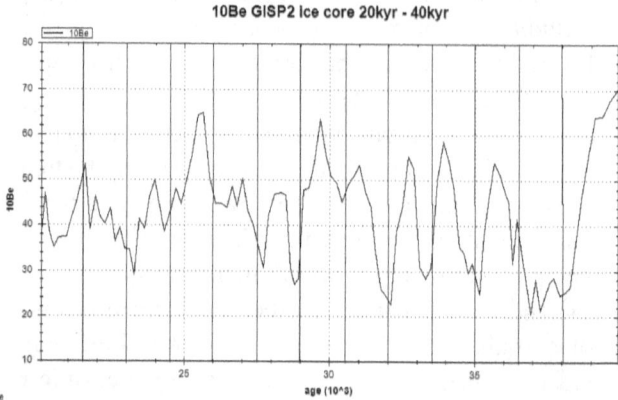

Figure 1. ^{10}Be concentration, an indirect measurement of solar activity, in the GISP2 ice core from 20 kyr to 40 kyr showing regular D-O cycles of rapid climate change spaced in most cases about 1500 years apart or a multiple of that length. Solid verticals lines space the data at 1500-year intervals. Note the strong regularity of the isotope signal between 30 kyr and 36 kyr. (Finkel, R.C., and K. Nishiizumi, 1997)

a cycle of rapid transitions between cold and warm periods of approximately 1500 years that occurred before human civilization began has been found in ice cores of the Greenland Ice Sheet Project (GISP2) (S. J. Johnson 1992; Dansgaard, 1993). Dansgaard-Oeschger (D-O) events, as these regular cycles are called, are found in oxygen isotope ratios used as a proxy for temperatures and are characterized by abrupt warmings of ~10 degrees. The recurrence time of D-O events do not appear to reflect a particularly stable cycle in the climate record except between 20 and 50 kyr before the present (BP) where the spacing is very regular and quite close to 1500 yr, though some of the periods in this section of the core are longer multiples of this figure, i.e. 3000 and 4500 yr. (Schultz, 2002).

Further evidence of a possible 1500-year cycle was found in a pattern of sediment grains from North Atlantic marine cores

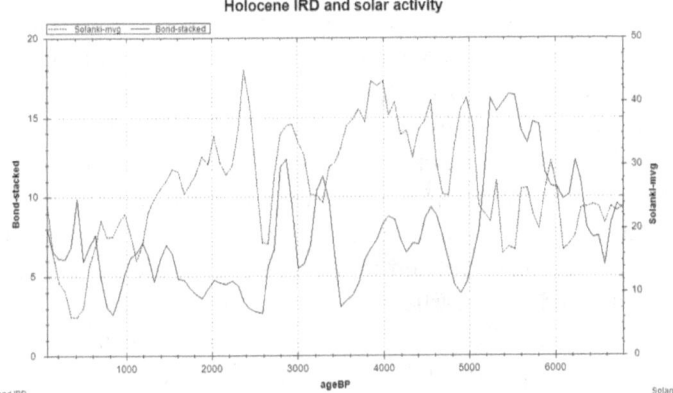

Figure 2. Solid line: Ice rafted debris (IRD) data based on sediments found in marine cores as a proxy for Holocene temperatures cycles. Higher percentage implies colder climates. (Bond et al, 1997). Dotted line: reconstruction of solar activity based on dendrochronology smoothed using a 20-point moving average (Solanki, 2005). A strong correlation which would be negative as high solar activity would correlated with lower IRD, is not found. The two datasets only show a weak negative correlation (r = -0.2237).

(Bond, et al., 1997). The authors of the paper hypothesized that the grains in the sediment layers correlated with periods when drift ice came as far south as the coring sites. Such increases in ice rafted debris (IRD) would then logically correlate with colder temperatures in the North Atlantic, making them a proxy of a cold climate in that region. Bond et al. concluded that the marine core records reflect an approximately 1500-year climate cycle in the North Atlantic that has been in operation not only during the Holocene, but also throughout the previous glaciation as evidenced by more regular D-O cycles found between 12 kyr and 50 kyr. Such cyclic continuity implies a forcing agent that apparently persists independent of the larger glacial or interglacial climate periodicities, which are driven by orbital parameters, i.e. Milankovitch cycles, and beyond the shorter solar cycles.

The Holocene component of the proposed cycle Bond et al. estimate averages 1374 years (+/− 502 years − a 36% variability). The glacial component of the cycle, which is argued to be the same as D-O rapid climate change events (sudden warmings followed by slow coolings − see below) that punctuated the last glaciation, averages 1470 years (+/− 532 years). Further, Bond et al. argued that the Little Ice Age (LIA− approximately 1550-1850) was not an isolated cooling event. It may have been related to a previous warming event several hundred years earlier, a period called either the Medieval Maximum, Medieval Warming Event, or Medieval Climate Anomaly (approximately 500-1200). From this perspective the LIA constitutes the cooling phase of a rapid climate change event that began with a warming in the Middle Ages. The primary difference between the ~1500-year climate cycles in the Holocene and the previous glaciation is then only one of amplitude. Both Holocene and glacial 1500-year cycles may therefore be responses to the same forcing mechanism which could be solar.

Bond et al. argued that the climate of the North Atlantic during the Holocene is not as stable as had been thought, but that it had undergone a number of climate reorganizations on millennial time scales. The paper also suggested that rapid climate change events have occurred during historical times and they may, should it turn out that the ~1500-year cycle is a true climate periodicity, serve as an index into the direction of natural, non anthropogenically-forced, climate change today. Evidence of a ~1500-year cycle is not limited to the North Atlantic region, it has also been found in Asia and Antarctica. Unfortunately, the idea of a 1500-year cycle was seized upon by climate change skeptics and held up as evidence against carbon dioxide driven warming. This appropriation of the ~1500 year cycle by politically-motivated writers quickly led to silence and divestment of the topic by the climatology establishment (Singer, 2006).

Mechanisms

Proposed mechanisms for the periodic nature of the ~1500-year cycle include oscillations of a natural and apparently highly sensitive internal ocean-atmosphere coupling – the thermohaline circulation (THC) of the North Atlantic that directly affects climate in Europe and indirectly many other parts of the world (Broecker, 1994, 2001). An internal cycle of surging ice sheets, the result of ice build-up, that drives a periodic calving of icebergs from Greenland that freshens the North Atlantic and shuts down THC has been also been proposed (van Kreveld et al, 2000). However, the more or less precise rhythm of the cycle strongly suggests some sort of external forcing driving the system. Bond et al. (1997, 2001) argue that the driver could be solar irradiance which is far more likely to produce a regular cycle length than one resulting from factors internal to the system. Evidence for solar forcing, determined from isotopic records of ^{10}Be from Greenland ice cores and ^{14}C from tree rings, do show sudden large amplitude increases consistent with solar minima, times when a weak solar wind is less effective in deflecting GCRs that generate these isotopes. Higher levels of these isotopes in climate records also correlate with increases in drift ice and therefore colder temperatures. It is thought that solar-induced climate signals that lead to ice melt could be amplified by resultant shifts in THC, causing major climate change in the North Atlantic as well as elsewhere.

Potential external forcing is not limited to solar variability. Tidal forcing has also been suggested as a climate change mechanism and an ~1800-year tidal cycle has been proposed to be driving millennial-length cycles. The mechanism proposed for this tidal cycle involves very high tides caused by the convergence of several lunar cycles that break up ice sheets leading to a cooling of sea surface temperatures (Keeling and Whorf, 2000). Tidal forcing may play a role in rapid

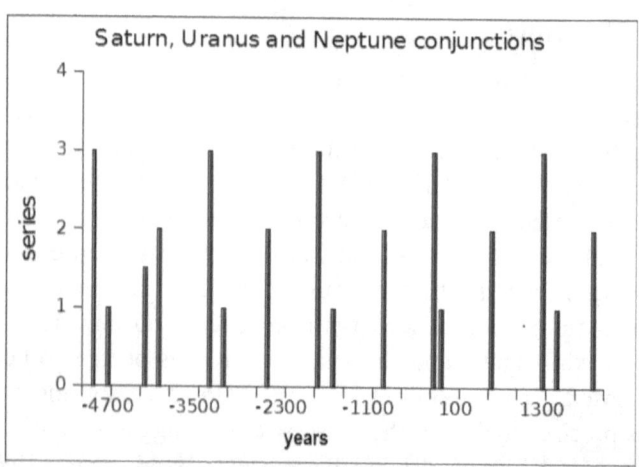

Figure 3. Conjunctions of Saturn, Uranus and Neptune over 7,000 years (within the limits of the calculating software – Solar Fire 8.1) displaying the regular ~1500-year periodicity of these conjunctions. The scale is CE dating. The height of the bar distinguishes between conjunctions of a specific series (see Table 1 below). Bars at 3 = series A, bars at 2 = series B and bars at 1 = series C. Bar at 1.5 = isolated conjunction.

climate change but it does not appear to correlate with Bond's data.

The case for the reality of a ~1500-year climate cycle in the North Atlantic is scientifically complex and the issue is far from resolved. Paleoclimate data is generally not well-resolved eliminating the possibility of closely matching planetary alignments with climate changes, which themselves take decades. Precise instrumental records only became available since about the mid-seventeenth century but millennial-length cycles cannot be seen in these datasets that are of 350 years at most. Some climate modeling studies suggest that a ~1500-year cycle could be produced by resonances of shorter cycles, for example 8 repeats of the 179-year orbit of the sun around the barycenter, what some regard as the Suess cycle (Landscheidt, 1997). 1500 years is, however, a length that is very close to a regularly repeating 1542-year cycle of Saturn, Uranus and Neptune conjunctions. These can been seen in Figure 3.

Planetary Modulation of Solar Activity

In this paper I am proposing that a punctuated solar influence on terrestrial climate sometimes establishes millennial-length climate cycles, including a ~1500-year cycle, and that this solar influence is driven by conjunctions of the outer planets. One possible mechanism posits gravitational effects of the outer planets on the sun's orbit around the barycenter that stimulate solar activity (including eruptions, i.e. flares and coronal mass ejections) which are then registered on the Earth as disruptions to the magnetosphere, upper atmosphere and possibly spin rate (Landsheidt, 1997). A pulse of direct radiative heating could cause a displacement of the upper atmosphere shifting air masses toward the poles causing retreat in the polar front and increased ice melt in the Arctic. The timing of such a blast is probably important and may be more effective when occurring at the northern hemisphere vernal equinox (Shindell et al., 2003). At the same time, higher levels of UV radiation in the stratosphere from an active sun may increase O_3 production creating a greenhouse effect. Once initiated by a sudden burst of solar activity and sustained by stratospheric UV, ice sheet or sea ice melt is accelerated and icebergs enter the northern seas and inject fresh water which lowers salinity and consequently slows THC. The time interval between the pulse of solar activity and lowered salinity may be as short as a decade or two. The consequent slowdown or stoppage of THC then results in a colder North Atlantic climate and within decades this change begins to be registered in other parts of the world bringing about changes in economic life (i.e. extreme winters and short growing seasons) and consequently historical events (i.e, social crises, migrations and, in response, forceful political solutions).

Because this solar signal is hypothesized to be driven by periodic planetary alignments, certain frequencies should be prominent in climate records. The question is then—does the paleoclimate record contains many signals resulting from planet-modulated solar activity, a few of which will emerge as dominant in a spectral signal because of their high degree of regularity and synchronicity with other cycles? The 179-year cycle of the sun around the center of mass of the solar system, which corresponds very closely to six cycles of Saturn and 15 of Jupiter, may be the foundation for the ~200-year rhythm (Seuss/de Vries cycle) found in climate records, though it is not clear why that particular resonance, six/fifteen, becomes so powerful (Fairbridge and Sanders, 1997). Other longer cycles may be based on multiples of this cycle (i.e. eight 179-year cycles equals 1432 years) or possibly other known solar cycles. Another possibility, though implausible if one considers gravity as the force involved with planetary modulation of the sun or Earth, is the recurrence cycle of Neptune and Pluto. This 492-year period contains two revolutions of Pluto and three of Neptune. Three of these amounts to a 1476-year period and have been associated with Huntington's Migration Cycle and Petry's Culture Cycle (Devore, 1962).

The regularly-spaced conjunctions of Saturn, Uranus and Neptune fall into several series, not all of which contribute to a single steady rhythm detectable in paleoclimate data. Further, conjunctions that also include Jupiter may produce a strong enough pulse of solar activity to shift climate in one region or another into a different state and distort any existing regular rhythm. So while an ~1500-year beat exists in conjunctions of Saturn, Uranus and Neptune, other types of alignments, i.e. oppositions, quadratures, etc., will have their own effects which, depending on current climate conditions, may or may not be amplified. In other words, a continuous cycle in the climate record of the length of the Saturn, Uranus, Neptune 1542-year cycle should probably not be expected, though this beat may entrain the climate system at some, but not all, times, eg. D-O cycles which occurred during a time of climate sensitivity. The point that a search for cycles may be misleading, will be considered later in this paper.

Table 1. Saturn-Uranus-Neptune Conjunction

Series A Year BP	Year CE	Min Orb	Mean Helio Long	Years from Previous
644	1306	1.3	223 13 Sc	1543
2187	-237	7.5	63.8 4 Ge	1540
3727	-1777	2.2	282 12 Cap	1544
5271	-3321	0.9	128.8 9 Le	
6813	-4863	4.2	333.7 4 Pi	
Series B				
+210	2169	8	320 20 Aq	(170)1540
+49	1999	7.5	277.4 7 Cap	1372
1324	636	5.2	165.6 16 Vi	1543
2867	-917	3.6	15.7 16 Ar	1543
4410	-2400	14.6	227 17 Sc	1542
5952	-4002	7.4	73.3 13 Ge	
Series C				
464	1486	23	217.5 18 Sc	1542
2006	-56	12.5	112.5 23 Can	1542
3548	-1598	14.1	322.9 23 Aq	1542
5092	-3142	20.3	174.3 24 Vi	1544
6634	-4684	13	16.5 17 Ar	1542

Isolated Saturn-Uranus-Neptune Conjunctions. Not in above series.

6133		14.3	26.8 27 Ar	

Table 2. Jupiter-Saturn-Uranus-Neptune Conjunctions

Year BP	Year CE	Min Orb	Mean Helio Long	Years from Previous
464	1486	23	217.5 18 Sc	179
644	1306	8.9	244 4 Sa	2225
2869	-919	22.5	2.2 2 Ar	179
3048	-1098	12.5	326.7 27 Aq	179
3227	-1277	23.2	288.9 20 Cap	319
3546	-1596	20.3	329.2 29 Aq	1547
5093	-3143	24.8	167.4 17 Vi	179
5272	-3322	5.9	123.2 3 Le	179
5451	-3501	20.5	82.6 23 Ge	498
5949	-3999	33.5	93.1 3 Can	

Tables 1 and 2 show the outer planet conjunctions to 7000 BP. One series of conjunctions of Saturn, Uranus and Neptune (Series B in Table 1) occurred at 1324, 2867, 4410, and 5952 B.P. (Common Era: 626, -917, -2460, and -4002) all very close to Bond's data. (Data from Solar Fire 5.1 software published by Astrolabe Software, Inc. Brewster, Massachusetts)

Apparent correlations between large planetary conjunctions and reconstructed sunspot number as an indication of solar irradiance are interesting, though in themselves they prove nothing. The first problem is the limitation of the proxy data. The reconstructed dataset used in Figures 4a and 4b is based on tree ring radiocarbon concentrations and is only of decadal resolution (Solanki, 2005). The full 11,500-year dataset, one of very few reconstructions to extend well beyond the modern period, does contain a peak frequency of 756 years (0.001322) which doubled is 1512 years, possibly a signal that in some way works to create the impression of a ~1500-year cycle. But it is unrealistic to focus on a particular year, or even decade with this data, only general trends can be observed. The rough correlations of Saturn, Uranus, Neptune conjunctions with re-

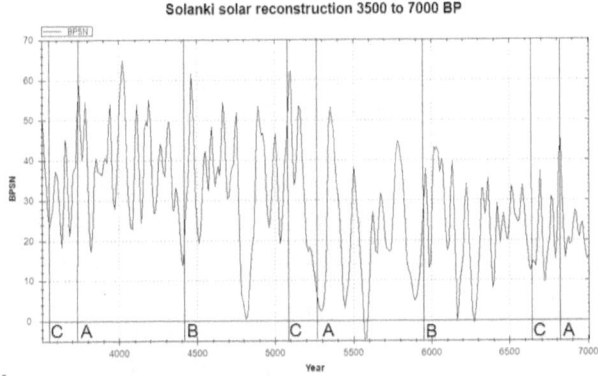

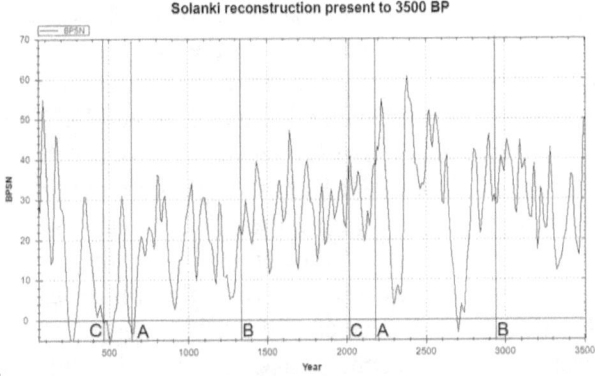

Figures 4a and 4b. The Saturn, Uranus, Neptune conjunction series in Table 1 are plotted against a dataset of reconstructed solar irradiance (Solanki, 2005). The scale is BP. The dataset, a reconstruction of the sunspot number, is based on dendrochronologically dated radiocarbon concentrations. What is noted in the graphs is the frequent proximity of change in direction of data with the conjunctions. In 4a, note the low ss number at ~4800 BP. A very close Ju, Sa Ne conjunction occrred at 4793 BP. Another close Ju, Sa, Ne conjunction occurred in 2747 BP, the time of a cool period known as the Homeric Minimum, shown in 4b as a ss low. The low sunspot numbers between roughly 200 and 600 BP mark the range of the Little Ice Age.

versal points in the reconstructed data may suggest that the conjunctions have some kind of an effect that does become a part of the climate record but with a range of decades. For example, Bond's IRD peaks recorded in marine cores roughly follow the Series B conjunctions of Saturn, Uranus, and Neptune by up to a hundred years or more (see Table 1). Given the possible mechanism involving THC outlined above, which takes decades to be effective, this is not an unreasonable correlation between signal and effect.

The Little Ice Age

The Little Ice Age (LIA) is generally dated as 1550-1850, though many argue that its beginnings should be pushed back to the 13th and 14th centuries. Bond and others have suggested that the LIA, in combination with the previous Medieval Warm Period (~950-1250), was a Holocene muted ~1500-year period, though in this instance the length would be roughly 900 years. The correlation of low sunspot numbers with colder temperatures during the LIA has suggested that variations in solar activity were driving these climate changes (Eddy, 1976). But there are other indicators of the cooling trend. In 1257 a massive volcanic eruption, possibly in Indonesia, occurred. This explosion injected 200 or more megatons of volcanic ash into the atmosphere making it 8 times larger than Krakatoa in 1883 and twice the size of Tambora in 1815. Volcanic sulfate records in ice cores show a large spike, an indication of a major eruption and consequent cooling due to the blocking of solar irradiation by volcanic aerosols. Other eruptions, one around 1280, over the next 40 years extended the cooling. These events effectively ended the medieval warm period. In 1303 and 1306-07 the Baltic Sea froze over twice, the first time in recorded history. From 1310 severe winters and cold, rainy summers were recorded. Mount Tarawera in New Zealand erupted around AD 1315 which coincided with The Great Famine of 1315-1317, the first of several major cri-

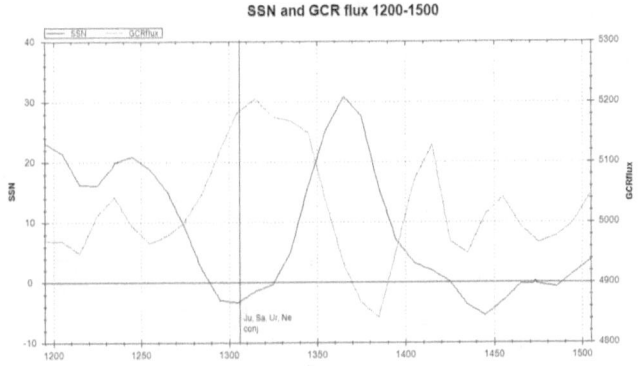

Figure 5. Here GCR flux, which inversely expresses the strength of the solar wind and is therefore a proxy of solar activity, is plotted against a reconstruction of sunspot number (Solkani 2005). GCR flux data is from 10Be, a cosmogenic nucleotide, found in the layers of the GISP2 ice cores (Usoskin, I.G., et al., 2008). The 1306 four-planet conjunction is located at a reversal point in both plots. Solar activity increased after that event. A Jupiter-Saturn conjunction located in a triangle with Uranus and Neptune (Ju,Sa = Ur/Ne) occurred in 1365 just before a second reversal in the data.

ses in Europe, including the Black Death (1346-1352), during which millions died.

In 1306 AD (644 BP) a close conjunction of the four Jovian planets occurred. Several climate records indicate changing weather conditions around that time, including the freezing of the Baltic Sea noted above. A high-resolution speleothem record from Oman indicates that the climate in Indian Ocean region began to seriously deteriorate by 1320, leading to a change in the monsoon pattern that the authors believe was reflective of the LIA in the North Atlantic region (Fleitmann et al., 2004). Figure 5 below plots two indicators of solar activity, SSN and GCR flux, both of which appear to be in a state of reversal near the time of the conjunction. Data from an ice core at the South Pole (Bard, E. et al., 2003) also shows a

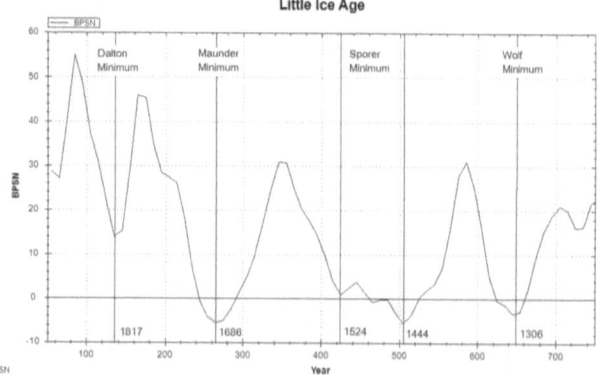

Figure 6. Little Ice Age cool periods indicated by low BP sunspot number. Names of minimums (cold periods) are indicated at top, vertical lines indicate CE dates of outer planet conjunctions. 1306 = Ju,Sa,Ur,Ne; 1444 = Ju,Sa,Ur; 1524 = Ju,Sa,Ne; 1686 = Ju,Sa opp Sa; 1817 = Ju,Ur,Ne.

rise in cosmogenic nuclide (^{10}Be and ^{14}C) production peaking around 1330 followed by a sudden decline, which suggests a quiet sun suddenly heating up. Resolution is decadal and a lag time of a decade or more must be taken into consideration. It is hypothesized here that this rare conjunction in 1306 produced a several year-long pulse of solar activity that moved the polar front north causing a general destabilization of the already cooling climate in Europe by increasing ice melt and consequent desalination, that, via THC, led to significant North Atlantic extreme weather and general cooling over a timespan of decades.

A factor in the decline of astrology was the prediction of a flood in February 1524 (426 BP) by a number of astrologers using the new media of print. These prognostications caused something of a panic and, when a flood failed to appear, did much to discredit astrology (Thorndike, 1941). Records at the time indicate that it was a very wet year in parts of Europe, however. The prognostication was based on a conjunction of

Jupiter and Saturn in the water sign Pisces, joined in February of that year by the Sun, Mercury, Venus and Mars. What was not known is that Neptune was also closely conjunct Jupiter and Saturn. This year of this conjunction is marked in Figure 6.

Discussion

If solar activity is the driver of a ~1500-year cycle, then the following scenario may apply. First, solar activity modulated by outer planet alignments occurs in strong, punctuated bursts that initially causes Northern Hemisphere heating and ice sheet or sea ice melting. The consequent lowering of North Atlantic salinity then operates as an amplifying mechanism causing cooling, forcing the region's climate across a threshold where it remains for several centuries. Some of these episodes occur at approximately 1500-year intervals because one specific type of outer planet conjunction cycle, that of Saturn, Uranus and Neptune, is close to this period. The severity of such a pulse of solar activity followed by a cooling is probably relative to the general climate conditions operative at the time, which are driven by orbital cycles, specifically precession. The more precise regularity of 1500-year periods between 20 and 40 kyr (see Figure 1) has been explained as stochastic resonance of a system at a bifurcation point. Prior to ~50 kyr global cooling was proceeding slowly, after ~20 kyr deglaciation was beginning. In between these points, the climate was suspended in a state between the two and was far more susceptible to weak external signals (Ganopolski and Rahmstorf, 2002). This would also explain why D-O events are more pronounced than weak Holocene warming and cooling events which can hardly be said to be a ~1500-year periodicity.

The observation here is that regularly paced 1542-year cycles of Saturn, Uranus and Neptune are not necessarily drivers of a cycle, or given the several series of conjunctions, drivers of several cycles of ~1500 years. Cyclic phenomena may arise

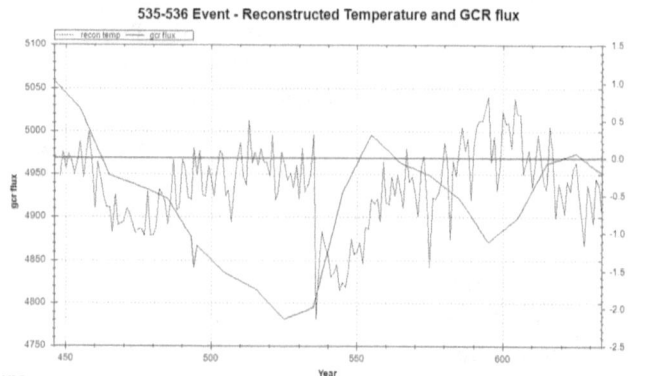

Figure 7. Here GCR flux is plotted relative to reconstructed temperatures (Christiansen Ljungqvist, 2012) centered around 535, the year of a Saturn Uranus conjunction closely opposite Neptune.

when the climate is highly sensitive, but otherwise the conjunctions may only bring about a change in solar activity that may or may not amplify the climate regime at the time. In addition, other effects may occur. For example, what is called the 535-536 CE event was the most severe episode of cooling worldwide in the past 2000 years and caused cold, drought, crop failures and famine in many parts of the world. The cause was probably the eruption of a volcano in tropics, possibly Krakatoa, indicated by high concentrations of sulfates in ice cores. What is interesting, however, is that the date is close to a shift in solar activity at that time as well (see Figure 7). In 535 a conjunction of Saturn and Uranus, both simultaneously opposite Neptune, occurred. It has been suggested that solar events may affect Earth spin rate which may trigger geological events (Landscheidt, 1997). The 535-536 event may illustrate how outer planet alignments act as triggers with effects that depend on climatic or geological conditions at the time.

In the hypothesis explored in this paper, major planetary conjunctions are thought to produce a short, pulse-like forcing factor driving rapid climate change that begins as heating and quickly becomes cooling, via THC, in the North Atlantic region. Second, the consistent 1542-year pulse of Saturn, Uranus and Neptune conjunctions may be amplified by the 1430-year 8th harmonic of the 179-year solar cycle or several other astronomical variables including high frequency extensions of precession, soli-lunar cycles, and rotation and revolution periods (Kelsey, et al., 2015). A close examination of the most recent conjunction may prove useful in moving toward an understanding of this hypothetical mechanism of climate modulation. During 1988-1989, a Saturn, Uranus, Neptune conjunction formed, with the minimum orb occurring in the spring of 1989. The average solar constant for the year was not unusual and this period marked the height of the current solar cycle, i.e. more sunspots were forming and the sun was consequently more active. However, one of the largest coronal mass ejections in recent times occurred in March of 1989. In late 1989 to early 1990 Jupiter opposed this conjunction making this a relatively rare outer planet configuration.

Figure 8 is a graph of TSI from satellite data for the years 1987-1991 that also depicts the sum of the heliocentric angular differences in longitude between the four outer planets Jupiter, Saturn, Uranus and Neptune for the five years 1987 to 1991. While a sharp drop in TSI does coincide with the lowest planetary distance figures, the curves are otherwise only weakly matched. The data was calculated as follows. Because the configuration formed in 1989-1990 was a conjunction of Saturn, Uranus and Neptune with Jupiter in opposition 180 degrees away during August and September 1989, the second harmonic of the angles was used which brings Jupiter into the same range as the other three. This was done by locating all bodies (in this case only Jupiter) moving between the vernal equinox and the autumnal equinox (first degrees of tropical signs Aries and Libra) as they normally would be, from 0 degrees to 180 degrees. Planets moving between the autumnal equinox to the vernal equinox were likewise located

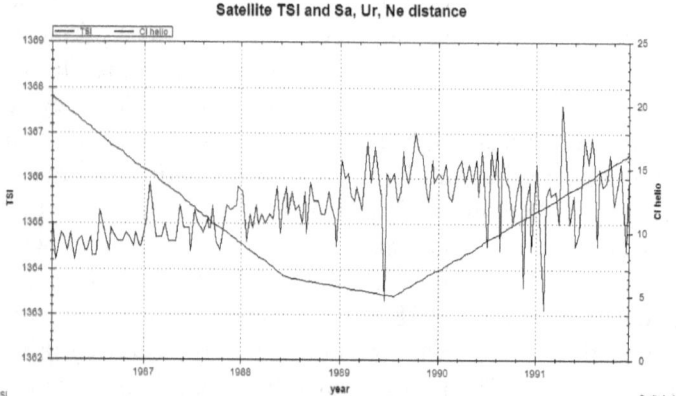

Figure 8. TSI data from the Earth Radiation Budget Satellite plotted against total angular separation distance between Saturn, Uranus and Neptune. The lowest figure for inter-planetary distance coincides with a sudden drop in TSI in June of 1989. Using the above data, a 20-point moving average of TSI correlated with CI displays a weak negative correlation: r = -.356.

between 0 and 180 degrees. This procedure allows an opposition between planets to appear numerically as if it were a conjunction. After adjusting the degrees of longitudes of the four planets, the difference in degree between each pair were calculated 10-day intervals during the five year period. There are six differences: Jupiter-Saturn, Jupiter-Uranus, Jupiter-Neptune, Saturn-Uranus, Saturn-Neptune, Uranus-Neptune. The differences in degrees of longitude for each quarter were then averaged to yield the figures in the graph below which reaches the lowest value, the point at which all four bodies came closest to each other, in late 1989. This methodology is a variant of the cyclic index of Barbault (Baigent, Campion and Harvey, 1984).

The above data is suggestive that the planetary hypothesis could be further tested by correlation analysis in modern, highly resolved data. A long paleoclimate dataset with annual resolution would, however, be the ideal solution to the problem of supporting or falsifying the hypothesis. With correlations and a possible mechanism, the final problem in elucidating the hypothesis is in regard to the long chain of events between solar activity and climate modulation. For example, the hypothesis assumes that increased solar activity drives a warming of a highly sensitive polar region in the northern hemisphere. Should highly resolved climate data show that the opposite occurs, that is planetary conjunctions lower solar activity or that the North Atlantic shows no response, this aspect of the hypothesis would need serious revision. Each portion of the hypothesis offers opportunities for study. Ultimately though, it is the establishment of high resolution paleoclimate data that will be most effective in falsification or validation.

References

Alley, R. B. et al., Making Sense of Millennial-Scale Climate Change. 385-394. In. Clark, Peter U., Robert S. Webb, Lloyd D. Keigwin, Eds. *Mechanisms of global Climate Change at Millennial Time Scales*, (Washington D.C.: American Geophysical Union, 1999).

Baigent, M., N. Campion and C. Harvey, *Mundane Astrology*. Wellingboro: The Aquarian Press, 1983).

Bard, E. et al., Reconstructed Solar Irradiance Data, IGBP PAGES/World Data Center for Paleoclimatology Data Contribution Series #2003-006 (Boulder, Colorado: NOAA/NGDC Paleoclimatology Program, 2003).

Bond, Gerard, William Showers, Maziet Cheseby, Rusty Lotti, Peter Almasi, Peter deMenocal, Paul Priore, Heidi Cullen, Irka Hajdas, Georges Bonani, "A Pervasive Millennial-Scale Cycle in North Atlantic Holocene and Glacial Climates," *Science*, 278 (1997), 1257-1266.

Bond, Gerard, Bernd Kromer, Juerg Beer, Raimund Muscheler, Michael N. Evans, William Showers, Sharon hoffmann, Rusty Lotti-Bond, Irka hajdas, Georges Bonani, "Persistent Solar Influence on North Atlantic Climate During the Holocene," *Scienceexpress*. November (2001).

Broecker, Wallace S., "Massive iceberg discharges as triggers for global climate change," *Nature*, 372 (1994), 421-424.

Broecker, Wallace S., "Glaciers That Speak in Tongues," *Natural History*. Oct./Nov (2001).

Burroughs, William James., *Weather Cycles: Real or Imaginary* (Cambridge University Press, 1992).

Christiansen, B. and F.C. Ljungqvist. 2012. "Northern Hemisphere 2000 Year Multiproxy Temperature Reconstruction," IGBP PAGES/World Data Center for Paleoclimatology Data Contribution Series # 2012-049. NOAA/NCDC Paleoclimatology Program, Boulder Colorado (2012).

Dansgaard, W., S.J. Johnsen, H.B. Clausen, D. Dahl-Jensen, N.S. Gundestrup, C.U. Hammer, C.S. Hvidberg, J.P. Steffensen, A.E. Sveinbjornsdottir, J. Jouzel, and G. Bond, "Evidence for General Instability of Past Climate from a 250-kyr Ice-core Record," *Nature*, 364 (1993), 218-220.

De Vore, Nicholas, *Encyclopedia of Astrology* (New York: Philosophical Library, 1947).

Eddy, J.A., "The Maunder Minimum," *Science* 18 June 1976: Vol. 192. no. 4245 (1976), 1189-1202.

Fairbridge, Rhodes W. and John Sanders, "The Sun's Orbit, A.D. 750-2050: Basis for a New Perception on Planetary Dynamics and Sun-Moon Linkages," *Climate: History, Periodicity and Predictability*. Ed. M.R. Rampino, J. Sanders, W.S. Newman and L.K. Konigsson, 446-471 (New York: Van Nostrand Reinhold, 1987).

Finkel, R.C., and K. Nishiizumi, "Beryllium 10 Concentrations in the Greenland Ice Sheet Project 2 Ice Core from 3-40 ka.," *Journal of Geophysical Research*, 102:26699-26706 (1997).

Fleitmann, Dominik, and Sstephen J. Burns, Ulrich Neff, Manfred Mudelsee, Augusto Mangini, and Albert Matter, "Palaeoclimatic Interpretation of High-resolution Oxygen

Isotope profiels Derived from Annually Laminated Speleothems from Southern Oman" *Quaternary Science Reviews* 23 (2004), 935-945.

Ganopolski, Andrey, and Stefan Rahmstorf, "Abrupt Glacial Climate Changes Due to Stochastic Resonance," *Physical Review Letters,* 88, No. 3 (2002).

Halberg F., "Historical encounters between geophysics and biomedicine leading to the Cornélissen-series and Chronoastrobiology," Schröder W, ed. *Long- and Short-Term Variability in Sun's History and Global Change* (Bremen: Science Edition, 2002), 271-301.

Hays, J. D.; Imbrie, J.; Shackleton, N. J., "Variations in the Earth's Orbit: Pacemaker of the Ice Ages," *Science* 194 (4270) (1976), 1121–1132.

Hoyt, Douglass V. and Kenneth H. Schatten, *The Role of the Sun in Climate Change* (Oxford University Press, 1997).

Issar, Arie S., *Climate Changes During the Holocene and Their Impact on Hydrological Systems* (Cambridge University Press, 2003).

Johnsen. S. J., H. B. Clausen, W. Dansgaard, K. Fuhrer, N. Gundestrup, C. U. Hammer, P. Iversen, J. Jouzel, B. Stauffer, and J.P. Steffensen, "Irregular Glacial Interstadials Recorded in a New Greenland Ice Core," *Nature*, 359 (1992), 311-313.

Keeling, Charles D. and Timothy P. Whorf, "The 1,800-year Oceanic Tidal Cycle: A Possible Cause of Rapid Climate Change," *PNAS*, 97 (2000), No. 8.

Kelsey, A. M., Menk, F. W., and Moss, P. T., "An Astronomical Correspondence to the 1470 Year Cycle of Abrupt Climate Change," *Clim. Past Discuss.*, 11 (2015), 4895-4915, doi:10.5194/cpd-11-4895-2015.

Landscheidt, Theodor, "Long-Range Forecasts of Solar Cycles and Climate Change," *Climate: History, Periodicity and Predictability*. Ed. M.R. Rampino, J. Sanders, W.S. Newman and L.K. Konigsson (New York: Van Nostrand

Reinhold (1987).

Lean, J., "Solar Irradiance Reconstruction. IGBP PAGES/ World Data Center for Paleoclimatology Data Contribution Series # 2004-035," NOAA/NGDC Paleoclimatology Program, Boulder Colorado (2004).

Mackey, Richard, "Rhodes Fairbridge and the Idea that the Solar System Regulates the Earth's Climate," *Journal of Coastal Research* (2007) 955-968.

Mayewski, Paul Andrew, and Frank White, *The Ice Chronicles: The Quest to Understand Global Climate Change* (Hanover, and London: University Press of New England, 2002).

Moberg, A, D.M. Sonechkin, K. Holmgren, N.M. Datsenko, and W. Karlén, "Highly Variable Northern Hemisphere Temperatures Reconstructed from Low- and High-Resolution Proxy Data," *Nature*, 433 (2005), No. 7026, 613-617.

Niggemann, S., Mangini, A., Mudelsee, M., Richter, D.K., and Wurth, G., "Sub-Milankovitch Climatic Cycles in Holocene Stalagmites from Sauerland, Germany," *Earth and Planetary Science Letters,* 216 (2003), 539-547.

Overpeck, Jonathan T., "Century to Millennial Scale Climate Variability during the Late Quaternary, " *Global Changes of the Past*, ed. Raymond S. Bradley (UCAR, 1989).

Rahmstorf Stefan, "Timing of Abrupt Climate Change: A Precise Clock," *Geophysical Research Letters*, 30 (2003), No. 10. 9.

Shindell, Drew; D Rind, N Balachandran, J Lean, P Lonergan, "Solar cycle Variability, Ozone, and Climate," *Science*, 284 (1999), 305-308

Singer, Siegfried Fred; Avery, Dennis T., *Unstoppable Global Warming: Every 1,500 Years* (Rowman & Littlefield, 2006).

Svensmark, Henrik and Eigil Friis-Christensen, "Variations of Cosmic Ray Flux and Global Cloud Coverage—a Missing Link in Solar-climate Relationships," *Journal of Atmo-*

spheric and Solar-Terrestrial Physics, vol. 59 (1997), no. 11, 1225-1232.

Seymour, P.A.H., M. Willmont, and A. Turner, "Sunspots, Planetary Alignments and Solar Magnetism: a Progress Review," Vistas in Astronomy: 35 (1992), 39-71.

Schulz, Michael, "On the 1470-year Pacing of Dansgaard-Oeschger Warm Events," Paleoceanography, 17, No.4 (2002), 1-9.

Schulz, Michael and Andre Paul, "How Important is the Glacial 1470-year Cycle During the Holocene?" http://www.bjerknes.uib.no/events/Hafslo/Schulz.pdf.

Solanki, S.K., et al., "11,000 Year Sunspot Number Reconstruction," IGBP PAGES/World Data Center for Paleoclimatology Data Contribution Series #2005-015. NOAA/NGDC Paleoclimatology Program, Boulder Colorado.

Steinhilber, F., et al., "Holocene Total Solar Irradiance Reconstruction," IGBP PAGES/World Data Center for Paleoclimatology Data Contribution Series #2009-133. NOAA/NCDC Paleoclimatology Program, Boulder Colorado.

Tarnas, Richard, Cosmos and Psyche. (New York: Plume, 2006).

Thorndike, Lynn, History of Magic and Experimental Science, Vol. V (New York: Columbia, 1941).

Usoskin, I.G., et al., "2,000 Year Cosmic Ray Induced Ionization (CRII) Rate Reconstruction," IGBP PAGES/World Data Center for Paleoclimatology Data Contribution Series # 2008-029. NOAA/NCDC Paleoclimatology Program, Boulder Colorado.

van Kreveld, S., M. Samthein, H. Erlenkeuser, P. Grootes, S. Jung, M.J. Nadeau, U. Pflaumann, A. Voelker, "Potential Links Between Surging Ice Sheets, Circulation Changes, and the Dansgaard-Oeschger Cycles in the Irminger Sea," 60-18 kyr. Paleoceanography, 15:4 (2000), 425-442.

Adolescent Behavior and Lunar Phase

By Alex Trenoweth, M.A.

ABSTRACT: This paper is the result of an investigation into adolescent behavior and lunar phase. The data used is from an anonymous United Kingdom school whose behavior policy stipulated that teachers record incidents of poor behavior on an educational application. These data entries are then analyzed by an information and technology professional who in turn prepares data reports for relevant teachers. On casual analysis by the researcher, the data showed that pupil behavior was worse at the New Moon than at the Full Moon, as expected by communal reinforcement. Further analysis showed that poor behavior peaked when the New Moon was at higher latitudes rather than low latitudes, when eclipses happen and when astrologers might expect poor behavior. There is no gender divide, which might be expected by astrologers. This is also in direct contradiction to the results of studies on human behavior, many of which show that there is no significant correlation between lunar phases and accidents, suicides, and crime rates. Studies on sleep cycles show that humans experience a loss of sleep during the Full Moon and therefore sleep better during the New Moon phase. Adolescents who experience a disturbed sleep pattern are better rested during the New

Moon and therefore have more energy to misbehave. Teachers may also have more energy to record poor behavior during the New Moon. The implications of these findings could be used to improve school behavior strategies in the education of adolescents by targeting times when intervention is most needed. The results suggest there is a need for further study over a longer period of time.

Introduction and Rationale for this Research

The many investigations into the lunar effect on human behavior have yielded mixed results. In this study, research focused on investigating whether a lunar effect could be found in adolescent behavior by analyzing the four major phases of the Moon and counting the number of incident sheets filed for poor behavior. The latitude of the Moon was also investigated to see if the Moon's proximity to the earth might account for differences.

The researcher has been a teacher of adolescent pupils (ages 11-18) for sixteen years. In her role in educational management there was responsibility for preparing reports based on records noting poor behavior. There had been many casual comments from teachers (and others) who assume that pupils tend to behave in a more rowdy manner during the Full Moon phase. These assumptions seemed to be based on communal reinforcement about the Full Moon. Is there an element of truth to this assumption? The researcher also had an interest in investigating the findings of other studies on accidents, suicides, and crimes based on phases of the Moon.

On the researcher's casual observation, based on cursory examination of data entries made by teachers reporting poor behavior, there seemed to be indication of a contradiction between cultural assumptions about the Full Moon and reality. The researcher, being an astrologer, wished to organize the data in such a way as to investigate if there could be a correlation between phases of the Moon and an increase/decrease in poor behavior.

More complete preliminary data calculated by a designated information and technology specialist who has no interest in astrology also seemed to show that poor behavior peaked at the New Moon. Again, this was in complete contradiction to the assumptions made about human behavior and the Full Moon. What could account for this contradiction? And could there be a difference in the number of incident sheets recorded by gender?

The researcher was aware that the circadian cycles of sleep differ between adolescents and adults. It is well known there is more human activity during the Full and New Moons based solely on the number of religious observations occurring during these times. There needed to be further research on whether or not an adolescent was likely to experience sleeping disruptions during the different phases of the Moon.

The sheer number of investigations and studies into the effects of the Moon on human behavior that show insignificant results suggests there is a need to differentiate different phases based on lunar latitude and proximity to the nodal axis. The Moon does not remain in an equal distance from the earth so perhaps different latitudes of the Moon could account for the contradiction.

Cycles of the Moon, including latitude, are predictable and therefore such correlations could be useful in organizing behavior management strategies in secondary schools.

Methodology

Data was collected from an educational application called Capita SIMS. All staff members can access this information stored on all pupils (date of birth, parental contacts, academic progress, attendance, behavior, achievements, ethnic and religious origins, timetables, etc.). The potential database for this project was massive (more than 20,000 entries) and so to make it more manageable was reduced to a single academic year (September 2012-July 2013) with 8,000 entries. A second academic year, September 2009-July 2010, was added as a means of comparison. The effects were to be compared by percentage and further results assessed through an investigation into the latitude of the Moon.

The effects of a high latitude Moon were also considered (high node versus low node, i.e. whether syzygy near or far from the nodal axis => large or small lunar latitude). So this investigation focused on two different lunar monthly cycles: Moon phase of 29 days and the nodal (nutation) cycle of 27 days. The celestial latitude of the Moon increases north and south of the ecliptic each month and then reaches zero latitude when it crosses over the ecliptic. This happens twice a month, and the Moon is then conjunct its node. For the purposes of this study, no distinction was made between the North and South Nodes, just as the researcher made no distinction between north and south celestial latitude. Lunar latitude is totally separate from lunar phase, except that they come together when eclipses occur.

The school has a clear behavior policy with guidelines on what constitutes poor behavior and how such behavior should be recorded on the SIMS application. There is no analysis on whether the incident sheets are recorded in line with school policy. It is assumed that if the school is using the data, then it must be in line with its own policy.

This data is used by the school to produce reports in order to offer a bespoke education to all pupils, which is in line with government regulations. Intervention strategies are determined from the reports. This can often mean that pupils who have no academic or behavioral concerns are ignored. For the preliminary research, the reports used were calculated and distributed by a designated information and technology professional each half term. For the behavior reports, there was a distinction made between the different types of behavior, the age, gender of the pupil, and the date the behavior entry was made by members of staff. The graphs produced were generated by the school but were available to me (and others) as a member of the leadership team. All I had to do was copy and paste the results for the preliminary research. The strength of this data was that personal bias was removed.

The latitude of the Moon had to be added to the data by the astrologer after the preliminary reports had been separated by lunar phases. Again, there is no personal bias in this.

There was no consideration of age or type of behavior. Only gender and date of issue for the reports were taken into consideration. The numbers of incident sheets were then divided according to dates and calculated to determine at which phase of the Moon the behavior occurred. There is a small margin of human error.

To investigate whether gender could show a correlation between behavior and lunar phases, the behavior of boys (who have far higher incidents of poor behavior overall) and girls was separated.

At the time of data collection, the astrologer was in a position of management in charge of monitoring the behavior of one year group. Because of this position, the researcher had access to and an interest in the data outside of astrological interests. It was only after she left the post that it was realized that there might be enough information to analyze whether the lunar phases had an effect on behavior.

It must be noted the data from this school is completely anonymous. In its current form and the way the data is collated, it would be unrecognizable to the manner in which it is distributed to teachers at the school.

Literary Review

Astrologers tend to see the Full Moon as a time of high energy. For example, Molly Hall, who is called an "astrology expert" on astrology.about.com writes: "Many people feel the energetic buzz of the Full Moon. What's cool to note is that it always means the Sun and Moon are in opposite zodiac signs. It's a super-charged time, but also one of balance. The solar yang and the lunar yin are in harmony."[1] Of the New Moon, she writes: "When the Moon is new, the luminaries—the Sun and Moon—are aligned in the same zodiac sign. That makes it a charged time with concentrated energies of that sign. A New Moon is a symbolic point of attention, and a symbolic portal for new beginnings."[2]

While it would be erroneous to expect every astrologer to interpret New and Full Moons in exactly the same way (particularly with such colloquial language), one may be hard pressed to find an astrologer who doesn't attribute *any* significant to the major lunations. Despite this, there seems to be some expectation in correlating the New and Full Moon phases and human behavior based on the astrological model. Further, although falling far short of academic standards, this astrologer's views on the effects on the lunar phases and behavior demonstrates communal reinforcement in astrology.

The Full Moon has long been linked to crime, suicide, mental illness, disasters, accidents, birthrates, fertility, and other things such as lycanthropy.[3] As has been pointed out by Arkovitz and Lillienfield (2009), there has been little evidence to back up any claims that the Full Moon has a detrimental effect on human behavior. Further, the idea of difficulties happening during the Full Moon seems to be perpetuated by communal reinforcement.[4]

However, not all studies have concluded that the lunar phases have nothing to do with tragic events on earth. A. L. Lieber's (1978) study on aggressive behavior in Dade County, Florida involved gathering data from police files on aggravated assaults, medical examiner reports on suicides and fatal accidents, and hospital records on psychiatry referrals from emergency room visits; all showed lunar correlations with variance on lunar phase. Homicide and aggravated assault clustered around the New and Full Moons. Correlations between the suicide curve with both fatal traffic accidents and aggravated assault suggests a component of self-destruction.[5]

Other studies have shown similar results by taking into account that fatal accidents were more likely to occur when there is a New or Full Moon *and* the accident happens at the weekend.[6] It would seem that other variables occurring only at the weekend of New and Full Moons affected the outcome of the study.

Owen et al (1998) concluded that: "No significant relationship was found between total violence and aggression or level of violence and aggression and any phase of the moon."[7] Further, other studies (Little et al, 1987; Durm et al, 1986) have failed to demonstrate any relationship between lunar phase and disruptive behavior in mental hospitals.[8]

The communal reinforcement of the effects of the Full Moon on behavior have persisted throughout various stages of history. For example, in *Othello*, Shakespeare wrote of the Moon at lower latitude: "It is the very error of the moon. She comes more near the earth than she was wont. And makes men mad."[9] Even earlier, Aristotle (384 BC) and Pliny the Elder (circa AD 23) suggested that the moist nature of the brain meant that it was subject to lunar influences. However, astronomer Larry Sessions of Astronomy Essentials points out that although so-called "super moons" (perigee-syzygy), have an effect on perigean tides, the actual effect of the lunar pull on humans would be minimal.[10]

Further, this has not stopped organizations using the cycles of the Moon to prevent crime. For example, in 2007, several police departments in the United Kingdom even added officers on Full Noon nights in an effort to cope with presumed higher crime rates.[11] The article does not indicate if this has been effective in crime prevention.

It would seem that it would be difficult to find a reliable and/or significant correlation between the lunar phases and adolescent behavior.

In comparing the number of behavior reports, one obvious influencing factor between the genders in adolescence could relate to the menstrual cycle. A 1986 study found that among 826 female volunteers, aged between 16 and 25 years (with a normal menstrual cycle), "a large proportion of menstruations occurred around the New Moon (28.3%), while at other times during the lunar month the proportion of menstruations occurring ranged between 8.5 and 12.6%; the difference was significant ($p<0.01$)."[12]

A study conducted in Canada in 1973, found that females were significantly ($p<.05$) more likely to self inflict injuries by poisoning during the first quarter cycle of the Moon and less likely to do so at the third quarter of the lunar cycle. The study also found that males did not show lunar periodicity ($p<.025$). Overall, the study found that "a significant correlation between periods in which a large number of self inflicted injuries occurred and the apogees and perigees of the Moon, was found ($p<.005$)."[13]

However, a 1985 investigation on a lunar-aggression hypothesis and the number of aggressive penalties awarded over the course of a season for an all-male ice hockey team found: "Interpersonal aggression was found to be unrelated to either the synodic or anomalistic cycles, a result consistent with recent reviews of lunar research."[14]

It would seem, based on literature, that girls may be more susceptible to the lunar effect than boys.

Perhaps one of the reasons the Moon has little effect on human behavior can be attributed to the fact that 21st century humans are more unaware of the cycles of the Moon; today's artificial lighting was not prevalent 150 years ago. But even without physical observation, could there still be a lunar effect on humans?

A possible answer to this question seems to be dependent on the effects of sleep deprivation. Ro "o" sli, et al (2006), found that people slept a mean of 19 minutes less on nights with a Full Moon compared with a New Moon.[15] More recent studies by Cajochen, et al (2013), have shown that the phase of the Moon affects the human sleep cycle. "We have evidence that the distance to the nearest full-moon phase significantly influences human sleep and evening melatonin levels when measured under strictly controlled laboratory conditions, where factors such as light and personal moon perception can be excluded."[16]

Award-winning sleep expert Mary Carskadon has found that sleep patterns in adolescence vary greatly, causing sleep deprivation. She indicates that "the effects of inadequate sleep are more than mere annoyances: they affect our mood and how we perform at school, work, and home and behind the wheel. Lost sleep also accumulates over time; the more "sleep debt " an individual incurs, the greater the negative consequences." (Carskadon and Dement, 1981; Wolfson and Carskadon, 1998).[17]

Twenty minutes may not seem like a lot of lost sleeping time, but this is particularly important to adolescent behavior as that age group already suffers from a disturbed circadian cycle. A survey by Wolfson and Carskadon of 3,120 high school students across four public high schools (self-reported) indicated that their total sleep time increased by up to one hour at the weekends but decreased by 40-50 minutes during the school week. While this survey did not take into account the phases of the Moon, it demonstrates how the sensitive circadian cycle is prone to disturbances. And thus could be affected by the light of the Full Moon according to Ro "o" sli, et al.

It would appear that more sleep may mean that pupils have more energy to get into trouble. It could also mean that teachers have more energy to record poor behavior.

Results

Data: 8,000 school punishments from an East London Secondary School

Administered: September 2012-July 2013

Weekday pattern: Fewer detentions given on Fridays

The investigation: Can adolescent behavior be influenced by lunar phase?

Method: The data was divided arbitrarily into four segments, each of more or less 2,000 (A, B, C, and D) for analysis. This was done for the convenience of analyzing the data and has no particular significance. As explained, lunar quarters were measured by Sun-Moon angle, centered on the Full and New moons, 0-180 degrees. The diagram shows the eight sectors of the circle which are implied by such a fourfold division.

Three axes or dimensions were investigated: 1) Full Moon versus New; 2) boy-girl; 3) high node versus low node (i.e. whether syzygy was near or far from the node axis, => large or small lunar latitude). (Syzygy means the line joining Full and New positions in the ecliptic.) There was no time of day information for when the events happened, so the Sun-Moon angle is only accurate within several degrees. All the data was *sorted by* Sun-moon angle 0-360 degrees and thereby grouped into the four sectors.

Results: Total number of discipline cases over one academic year, grouped by lunar quarter

	A	B	C	D
New Moon	575	533	545	568
1st Quarter	451	430	514	495
Full Moon	483	478	473	477
3rd Quarter	487	560	467	408
NM/FM diff.	19%	24%	15%	19% => 16% overall
Totals	1996	2001	1999	1948

Summary: New Moon quarters scored more than Full Moon quarters. They also scored 16 percent more than the rest of the month combined.

Waxing versus waning Moon: Referring to the diagram, the waxing Moon is the two-week period of 0-180 degrees, followed by the two-week waning period of 180-360 degrees. During the waxing period the Moon is seen to be growing in the sky, and then decaying as it wanes. No difference was found in the data.

Boys only: At least three-quarters of data is from males. Selecting only the dates when punishment or discipline was administered to boys, and again arbitrarily grouping them into four parts for data-analysis, then grouping by Sun-Moon angle:

	A	B	C	D
New Moon	473	409	415	410
1st Quarter	366	330	386	377
Full Moon	377	360	346	361
3rd Quarter	399	436	346	320
NM/FM diff.	+25%	+14%	+20%	14% => 18% overall
Total	1615	1535	1493	1468

There was a slightly smaller difference found for girls, but overall this gender effect was not significant.

Moon furthest from ecliptic in celestial latitude (This happens when the Moon is at 90 degrees to the lunar node axis.): Twice yearly, as explained earlier, syzygy will coincide with the lunar node axis at the eclipse seasons. Around these months of the year, New Moons will occur close to the ecliptic, i.e., they will be of low celestial latitude. Three months later, they will be far from it. At the time of the study, eclipse seasons were falling in May and November.

The researcher selected for a large lunar latitude at syzygy (Full and New Moon), such that the angle between Sun and nodal axis was greater than 60 degrees. Twice each year, the Sun moves 60-120 degrees away from the nodal axis, i.e. from either of the lunar nodes. Then the researcher selected about *one-third* of the data. For this selection-process the *Sun-node angle* was measured.

	A	B	C	D
New Moon	188	201	122	221
1st Quarter	161	135	86	137
Full Moon	99	109	204	133
3rd Quarter	100	132	161	119
Total	548	577	673	610
NM/FM diff.	90%	84%	-40%	66% => 34% overall

This extra-large effect is for that one-third of the year when the New Moon happens at high latitude, i.e. far from the ecliptic. It is a counter-intuitive result; one could expect the low-latitude New Moons (when eclipses happen) to be more influential.

This node effect, however, needs testing over at least a 10-year period. The results presented here are offered as being suggestive and worthy of further study.

The 2009 (September 2009-July 2010) sample was smaller, just 1,299 cases:

The results are as follows:

New Moon	370
1st Quarter	330
Full Moon	259
3rd Quarter	340
Total	1299
NM/FM diff.	43%

The lack of behavior reports filed on Fridays could be because the school operated its whole school detentions on this day of the week. Perhaps teachers did not file reports because they knew pupils would be in detention on that day. However, ignoring poor behavior was certainly not a part of the behavior policy. Further, it could be that teachers did not record poor behavior until after the weekend (although this would not affect the actual day the behavior occurred).

Discussion

The results for 2012-2013 are counter-intuitive to communal reinforcement and previous studies that focused on the lunar phases: more behavior reports are filed in the New Moon phase. With >34% difference between the New and Full lunar phases, this result is significant.

This is in contradiction to Arkovitz and Lillienfield (2009), Little et al, 1987; Durm et al, 1986 and Owen et al who indicated there was little evidence to support a lunar effect. However, these researchers did not study adolescents.

With Law's research into the menstrual cycle and the lunar phases, it was found that more women menstruated at the New Moon. It was expected that this might have an affect on adolescent females. Further research by the Ossenkopps showed women were more likely to self-harm at the New Moon, which may indicate that female adolescents are more prone to poor behavior at the New Moon. However, a significant result was not found when the data was separated by gender: girls did not appear affected by the New Moon any more than at the Full Moon. Boys, however, did show >18% more behavior reports at the New Moon than at the Full Moon.

Further, when latitude was taken into consideration, it was found that behavior is significantly worse when the New Moon is at a higher latitude (the Moon farthest away from the earth), suggesting higher latitude New Moons being more influential than others. This pattern was replicated from the 2009 data (although the total number of entries was few, owing to lower enrolment).

These cycles are predictable and if teachers are open to them, strategic interventions can be put into place to cope with the fallout of behavior. What isn't clear about the results is whether it is the pupils who are in trouble or the teachers being more sensitive to pupil behavior.

The studies on sleep indicate that the circadian cycles of humans are more likely to be affected with less sleep at the Full Moon than at the New Moon. Simply, adolescents are better rested at the New Moon. It follows that they might have more energy to get into trouble.

Further studies could investigate the types of behavior exhibited and the consequences of the behaviors to gain a fuller picture.

It is also clear from the research of Mary Carskadon that adolescents are more affected by a lack of sleep than adults. Again, more research needs to be done to determine the effects of a lack of sleep according to age.

It would also be fascinating to investigate religious observations such as Ramadan to determine if there is an impact on children of a specific demographic. There is also scope to investigate whether poverty has an effect on the circadian cycle and therefore on behavior.

Conclusion and Recommendations

Pupil behavior is significantly worse at the New Moon in higher latitudes. It seems remarkable to me that the this kind of research into the effects of the lunar phases on pupil behavior has not been taken into account before, especially when the data results show significantly show that the New Moon is when pupils and teachers appear to have more energy.

This information can be used so productively to enhance pupil learning by capitalizing on their peak energy levels at the New Moon at higher latitudes that so clearly need to be appropriately utilized and channeled.

Much more research needs to be done to work with the circadian cycles of adolescence. For example, is there a difference between the circadian patterns of key stage three pupils and key stage four pupils? If so, can the schools adjust timetables accordingly to benefit the pupils? With the potential for significant results, this is worth further research.

Working with the natural cycles of the lunar phases seems such an easy win in education. However, in order for this to work, educators would have to be willing to draw their own conclusions about these effects, which have so long been a part of folklore.

Endnotes

[1] Hall, Molly, "The New Moon" Website at: http://astrology.about.com/od/foundations/p/FullMoon.htm. Accessed November 2015

[2] Hall, Molly, "The Full Moon," http://astrology.about.com/od/foundations/p/NewMoon.htm, accessed November 2015.

[3] Carroll, Robert Todd, *The Skeptic's Dictionary*, "Full Moon and Lunar Effects," http://skepdic.com/fullmoon.html, accessed November 2015.

[4] Arkowitz, Hal and Lilienfield, Scott O., Scientific American, Feb. 2009, "Lunacy and the Full Moon: Does a Full Moon

Really Trigger Strange Behavior,"http://www.scientificamerican.com/article/lunacy-and-the-full-moon, accessed November 2015.

[5]Lieber, A. L. "Human Aggression and the Synodic Lunar Cycle," https://www.ncjrs.gov/App/Publications/abstract.aspx?ID=49286, accessed November 2015.

[6]Rotton, James and Kelly Ivan W., "Much Ado about the Full Moon: A Meta-analysis of Lunar-Lunacy Research" *Psychological Bulletin*, Vol. 97, No. 2, pages 286-306.

[7]Owen, Cathy; Tarantello, Concetta, Jones; Michael, Tennant, Christopher, "Lunar Cycles and Violent Behaviour," http://anp.sagepub.com/content/32/4/496.abstract, accessed November 2015.

[8]Howard, J.M, http://pb.rcpsych.org/content/pbrcpsych/13/7/383.full.pdf.

[9]Shakespeare, William, *Othello*, Act V, scene 2.

[10]Sessions, Larry, "Does the Supermoon have a Supper Effect On Us," http://earthsky.org/space/does-the-supermoon-have-a-super-effect-on-us, accessed December 2015.

[11]BBC News, June 5, 2007, "Crackdown on Lunar-fuelled Crime," http://news.bbc.co.uk/2/hi/uk_news/england/southern_counties/6723911.stm.

[12]Law, S. P., 1986, "The Regulation of Menstrual Cycle and its Relationship to the Moon," *Acta Obstetricia et Gynecologica Scandinavica*, 65:45-48.

[13]Ossenkopp, K. P. and Ossenkopp, Margitta D, "Self Inflicted Injuries and the Lunar Cycle: a Preliminary Report," Journal of Interdisciplinary Cycle Research, Vol. 4, No. 4, 1973, http://www.tandfonline.com/doi/abs/10.1080/09291017309359396, website accessed December 2015.

[14]Russell, Gordon W.; de Graaf, Jane P., "Lunar Cycles and Human Aggression: A Replication," *Social Behavior and Personality: an International Journal*, Vol. 13, No. 2, 1985, 143-146.

[15] Ro "o" sli, M., Ju oni, P., Braun-Fahrlä nder, C., Brinkhof, M.W.G., Low, N., and Egger, M., "Sleepless Night, the Moon is Bright: Longitudinal Study of Lunar Phase and Sleep," *J. Sleep Res*, 15, 149-153.

[16] Cajochen, Christian, Altanay-Ekici, Songul, Munch, Mirjam, Frey, Sylvia, Knoblaunch, Wirz-Justice, Anna, "Evidence that the Lunar Cycle Influences Human Sleep," *Current Biology*, 23, 1485-1488, August 5, 2013, http://dx.doi.org/10.1016/j.cub.2013.06.029.

[17] Graham, Mary, ed., "Sleep Needs, Patterns and Difficulties of Adolescents," summary of a workshop, http://www.nap.edu/read/9941/chapter/2, accessed November 2015.

Bibliography

Arkowitz, Hal and Lilienfield, Scott O., "Lunacy and the Full Moon: Does a full moon really trigger strange behavior," *Scientific American*, Feb. 2009, http://www.scientificamerican.com/article/lunacy-and-the-full-moon/ Website access November 2015

BBC News, June 5, 2007, "Crackdown on lunar-fuelled crime" http://news.bbc.co.uk/2/hi/uk_news/england/southern_counties/6723911.stm.

Cajochen, Christian, Altanay-Ekici, Songul, Munch, Mirjam, Frey, Sylvia, Knoblaunch, Wirz-Justice, Anna, Current Biology 23, 1485-1488, August 5, 2013 a2013 Evidence that the Lunar Cycle Influences Human Sleep Elsevier Ltd http://dx.doi.org/10.1016/j.cub.2013.06.029

Carroll, Robert Todd, "Full Moon and Lunar Effects, *The Skeptic's Dictionary*, website accessed November 2015, http://skepdic.com/fullmoon.html.

Graham, Mary (editor), "Sleep Needs, Patterns and Difficulties of Adolescents," summary of a Workshop, website available online at: http://www.nap.edu/read/9941/chapter/2, accessed November 2015.

Hall, Molly, http://astrology.about.com/od/foundations/p/

FullMoon.htm. accessed November 2015.

———, "The Full Moon," http://astrology.about.com/od/foundations/p/NewMoon.htm, accessed November 2015.

Howard, J.M, "Letter to the Editor," http://pb.rcpsych.org/content/pbrcpsych/13/7/383.full.pdf, accessed November 2015.

Law, S. P., "The Regulation of Menstrual Cycle and its Relationship to the Moon," *Acta Obstetricia et Gynecologica Scandinavica*, 65 (1986): 45-48. http://onlinelibrary.wiley.com/doi/10.3109/00016348609158228/abstract, accessed December 2015.

Lieber, A. L., "Human Aggression and the Synodic Lunar Cycle," https://www.ncjrs.gov/App/Publications/abstract.aspx?ID=49286 , accessed November 2015.

Ossenkopp, K.P. and Ossenkopp, Margitta D, "Self inflicted Injuries and the Lunar Cycle a Preliminary Report," *Journal of Interdisciplinary Cycle Research*, Vol. 4, No. 4 (1973), http://www.tandfonline.com/doi/abs/10.1080/09291017309359396, accessed December 2015.

Owen, Cathy; Tarantello, Concetta, Jones; Michael, Tennant, Christopher "Lunar Cycles and Violent Behaviour," http://anp.sagepub.com/content/32/4/496.abstract, accessed November 2015.

Rotton, James and Kelly Ivan W, "Much Ado about the Full Moon: A Meta-analysis of Lunar-Lunacy Research," *Psychological Bulletin*, Vol. 97, No. 2, 286-306.

Ro "o" sli, M., Ju oni, P., Braun-Fahrlä nder, C., Brinkhof, M.W.G., Low, N., and Egger, M., 2006, "Sleepless Night, the Moon is Bright: Longitudinal Study of Lunar Phase and Sleep," *J. Sleep Res. 15*, 149-153.

Russell, Gordon W.; de Graaf, Jane P., "Lunar Cycles and Human Aggression: A Replication," *Social Behavior and Personality: an International Journal*, Vol. 13 (1985), No. 2, 143-146.

Sessions, Larry, "Does the Supermoon have a Supper Effect On Us?" http://earthsky.org/space/does-the-supermoon-have-a-super-effect-on-us, accessed December 2015.

Shakespeare, William, *Othello*, Act V, scene 2.

The Ukraine Crisis

By Lutz Rathke

ABSTRACT: Long before the year 1989, the close coincidence of conjunctions between Saturn and Neptune in 1989, Uranus and Neptune in 1993 was interpreted by an astrologer to indicate the end of communist rule in the Soviet Union and East European states within the years 1989-1993. In particular the first of the three conjunctions in 1989 was understood to refer to the Soviet Union, and the exact conjunction horoscope has since her disappearance functioned as mundane radical chart for almost all former Soviet republics including Russia and Ukraine, to be computed for the different capital cities. The Ukraine crisis began in late 2013 when Pluto was going to transit the 1989 positions of Saturn and Neptune. This is a general way to apply mundane astrology with no need for birth or proclamation data.

In late 1989, Soviet rule in eastern Europe collapsed, and in late 1992, Soviet rule in the Soviet Union collapsed. Communism and socialism were no longer a major issue in worldwide ideological principals; the main conflict switched to antagonism between Islam and countries adherent to European ideology, including China and India.

The end of communism's rule in most countries, the continuing rule of the Communist Party in some (China, Cuba, North Korea, Vietnam), and its upcoming in a few new countries (Zimbabwe, Venezuela) all have their astrological origin in three consecutive conjunctions between Neptune and Saturn in 1989, followed rapidly by three consecutive conjunctions of Neptune and Uranus in 1993.

In the horoscopes of the first and of the third conjunction of Saturn and Neptune in 1989, Uranus is approaching these planets, whereas in the second conjunction, with Saturn and Neptune both retrograde, and Uranus as well, their respective actual relationship was inverse. The three conjunction horoscopes have in common that Saturn was always in his domicile, the conjunction always took place in 11 Capricorn, and all three planets remained all the time in between in Capricorn.

If a 20th century astrologer had known well ahead that the *Saturn-Neptune aspect cycle used to refer to the political left, in particular to communism, i.e. to any feeling of allegiance to a supranational rule above the state government, while the Saturn-Uranus cycle had to do with national independence, nationalism, and the like*, the astrologer would have pointed out that the conjunction of Saturn and Neptune so close to a conjunction of Neptune with Uranus should indicate a major change with regard to the political left, with revolutionary (counter-revolutionary) events marking a possible end of Communist rule in some or many countries. There was such an astrologer: before the mid-1950s, André Barbault in France predicted the collapse of bolshevism and communist rule in the years 1989-1993, based on his understanding that Stalin's death had happened under the rule of the Saturn-Neptune conjunction in 1953 and that many if not all important events in the history of the political left were in correlation with aspects between Saturn and Neptune.

The Uranus-Neptune aspect cycle refers to the principal ideological conflict dominating world politics, and every 170 years, when new consecutive conjunctions of Uranus and Neptune are due, the matter of the principal world conflict changes, other main antagonists come up, and it is about something not before experienced.

In short, the period of the Uranus-Neptune cycle is 170 years. Its main topic is an ideological principal conflict dominating the whole world.

Until 1993 (or rather until Uranus entered the zodiac sign where he would finish his new, threefold, conjunction with Neptune, i.e. 1988-89), this conflict was about the antagonism of capitalism versus communism or civil republicanism versus socialism (since 1820 when Uranus and Neptune had completed their former conjunction). Before it was about Enlightenment versus Christian faith (since 1650), preceded by the conflict of Protestantism versus the Roman Catholic Church (since 1480).

Each two subsequent conjunctions—rather, each series of usually three conjunctions within a year or less—take place in the same zodiacal sign, and the zodiacal degree of the series advances by about 15 degrees, placing two series of conjunctions within the same sign, the next two series of conjunctions both in the subsequent sign, and so on. A pair of series of conjunctions within one sign is followed by the next pair in the next sign.

Thus there is a relationship between each two 170 years' eras of ideological conflicts, followed by two others with their own continuous topical relationship: first, the heretics (Waldensians, Hussites) versus the Catholic Church; next, Protestantism versus the same church; then the next two eras featuring Enlightenment versus Christian religions; and followed by socialism versus bourgeoisie (which was in the beginning on the side of the monarchies, but with constitutions and parlia-

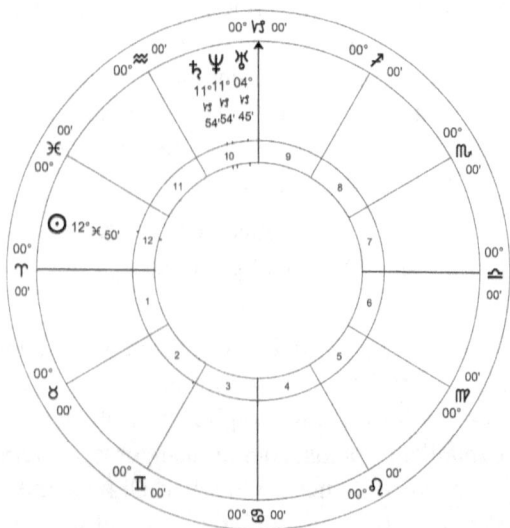

March 3, 1989. Sun in Pisces. Saturn conjunction Neptune with Uranus in their back and all moving forward.

ments; however, after the Uranus-Neptune opposition democracies, i.e. constitutions and parliaments with elections of and term-limits for heads of state were favored).

Meaning of the Three Saturn-Neptune Conjunctions

In 1989, there were three exact conjunctions of Saturn and Neptune, all in 11 Capricorn, all in the presence of Uranus, which had already come close to Neptune. At the first and third conjunctions these three planets were moving forward, and at the second conjunction all three of them were retrograde. This means that at the first and third conjunctions, Uranus was to advance sooner or later to all positions then held by Saturn and Neptune. This is what I call Uranus being in the back of the two planets in conjunction. At the second conjunction, however, Saturn and Neptune were in the back of Uranus. To be in someone else's back means an advantage and the promise to be able to overcome the other, with limits to the

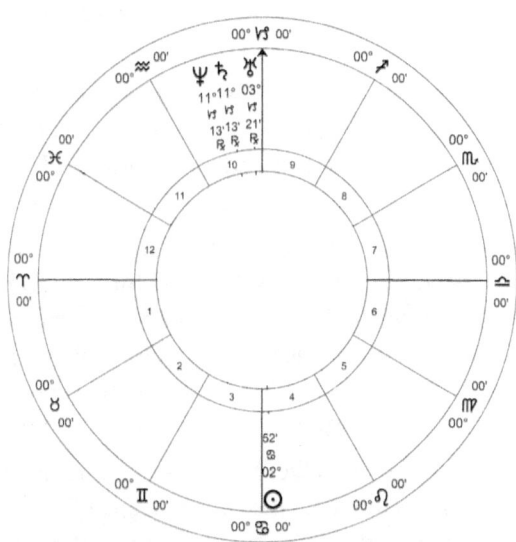

June 24, 1989. Sun in Cancer. Saturn conjunction Neptune in the back of Uranus, all moving retrograde.

November 13, 1989. Sun in Scorpio. Saturn conjunction Neptune with Uranus in their back, all moving forward.

extent of such a victory if the overcome planet is in domicile, whereas the overcoming planet is not.

The Sun in the first Saturn-Neptune conjunction horoscope of 1989 is in Pisces, in the second (Saturn, Neptune, Uranus, all retrograde) one in Cancer, and in the third and last one in Scorpio.

So the first conjunction was focused on the center (Sun) of the political (Saturn) left (Neptune, Pisces)—in fact, on the main country of communism, i.e. the Soviet Union—and it brought about a revolutionary change (Uranus), although not really replacing all the old men of the State (Saturn in his domicile too strong to be entirely overthrown), nor all old structures.

The second conjunction referred to communist regimes founded by home-grown people (Sun in Cancer)—communist governments that had not been forced upon the country by foreign will and foreign military power. And it promised those governments a successful suppression of a rebellion against the Communist Party's monopoly of power (Saturn retrograde in the back of Uranus retrograde). In the end, the rebellions would fail and the regimes would persist. (This conjunction was also applicable to communist Yugoslavia.)

The third conjunction applied to states that had come (in total or in part, as in Germany) under Communist Party rule by military occupation (Sun in Scorpio), not out of their own actions. This was perfectly true with all the Warsaw Pact partners of the Soviet Union, as well as with the three small Baltic states that had been annexed by force as an immediate consequence of the Hitler-Stalin Pact.

This three-way interpretation owes its basics to André Barbault, but is my own and goes beyond what he had predicted. I first expressed the basic idea of it, inspired by André Barbault's fundamental predictions, in a lecture delivered at a meeting of Uranian astrologers at Munich in the late 1980s.

As the three-way interpretation of the three conjunction horoscopes soon proved true, with the horary charts and transits at many significant steps in the course of the three sequences of events (for simplification purposes, attributed just to Russia, China, and Eastern Europe) in strong synastry with the respective conjunction chart, it became clear to me that the three conjunction horoscopes not only applied to the actual events but also to the mundane radical horoscopes of the resulting political units, i.e. in particular the remaining and emerging independent states, continuously adherent to socialism (second conjunction) or formerly socialist (third conjunction) or formerly soviet (first conjunction), and of their fates to come.

Therefore, the first conjunction horoscope is the mundane radical horoscope for twelve states: Russia, Ukraine, Belarus, Moldova, Armenia, Georgia, Azerbaidjan, Tajikistan, Kazakhstan, Turkmenistan, Kyrgyzstan, and Uzbekistan, computed for their respective capital cities in 1989.

The second conjunction is the mundane radical horoscope for the People's Republic of China, Vietnam, North Korea, and Cuba, and may also apply to the socialist regimes of Zimbabwe and Venezuela, which have since been established.

The third conjunction is the mundane radical horoscope for Poland, Hungary, Czechoslovakia (soon falling apart into Czechia and Slovakia), Bulgaria, Romania, Albania, and three Baltic states (Estonia, Latvia, Lithuania) that had become Soviet republics near the end of World War II, and later when the Warsaw Pact states became communist, although formally remaining independent people's republics.

Mundane Radical Horoscopes in Comparison with Horary Radical Charts

Mundane radical charts have big practical advantages compared with horary radical charts based on events (birth of important persons, proclamations, entries into force, openings and closings):

1. The time is always precise to the second because the chart is calculated for a celestial event, i.e. the moment of an exact aspect between two planets or of the ingress of a planet.

2. To know the appropriate mundane event, and thus the chart to calculate, a merely approximate date of what it is supposed to refer to is entirely sufficient. This means that for all historical data a meaningful chart can be cast and compared with many charts with regard to similar events, thus increasing one's knowledge base remarkably beyond what is possible based on actual dates of events on earth.

Of course it is crucial to learn what kind of mundane horoscope is related to what kind of events on earth and how to interpret a mundane horoscope in spite of its general, earth-wide character with definite regard to a particular geographic area and to a few countries.

And it may pose difficulty in cases such as the post-Soviet and the post-communist eastern European states if one single set of planetary positions and aspects should be common to all mundane radical horoscopes for all the post-Soviet and post-communist states established since World War II.

This difficulty is in part avoided by the geographical distances between the capitals, allowing very different house cusps. In addition, every planet represents one of the states concerned.

Planets Representing Political Powers

In the first of the three Saturn-Neptune conjunctions in 1989, it is obviously Russia (former Soviet Union) that is the principal and by far the biggest and most powerful state; it is represented by the Sun. As the Sun is in Pisces, its ruler Neptune can also be a significator of Russia.

Which planet represents Ukraine? More precisely, which planet represented Ukraine at the time when the Soviet Union

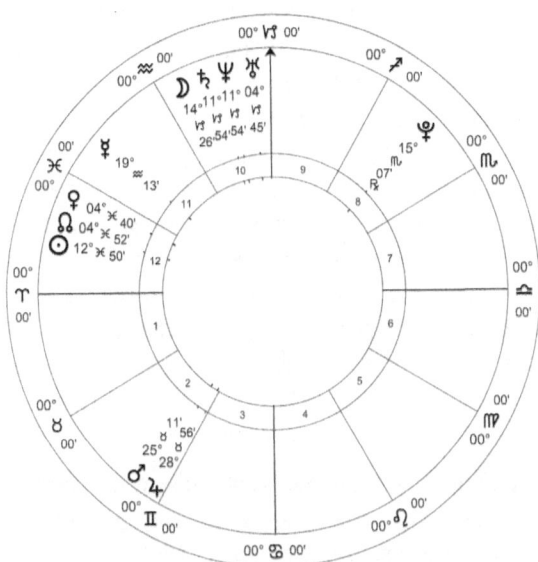

March 3, 1989, geocentrically at 10:46 a.m. GMT. First exact conjunction of Saturn and Neptune in 11 Capricorn

broke apart and the Soviet republics became independent? No doubt, Ukraine was Pluto and therefore continues to be Pluto. Pluto is the planet of atomic power, and at the time of their independence, Russia and Ukraine were the only two post-soviet powers in possession of atomic weaponry. Although Ukraine soon ceased this status, the independent republic had started under the rule of this mundane radical horoscope while being a power of nuclear arms.

For these reasons, Russia is the Sun power and Ukraine is the Pluto power among the post-Soviet countries. In addition, Russia is Neptunian because the Sun is in Pisces, and Ukraine is Martian because of the Mars rulership of Scorpio.

Pluto in 15 Scorpio and Saturn in 11 Capricorn are the only two domiciled planets of that horoscope. So when one of the two most powerful planets is transiting the only other most powerful planet by passing through 11 Capricorn, we cannot fail to assume that the post-Soviet states are having a highly unusual time and their joint history might undergo a significant change. And we understand from the beginning that it is about Ukraine, its acute situation and twists and turns (Pluto moving forward and back), regarding Russia (Neptune, as well as this conjunction altogether), and perhaps involving a third post-Soviet republic, represented by Saturn in his domicile Capricorn—of course much less affected by Pluto's transit than Neptune in Capricorn. This third republic seems to be Belarus, which has indeed acted a bit as a mediator and much as a host for talks between the powers and factions involved (Agreement of Minsk, capital of Belarus). Saturn in Capricorn depicts the Belarus government quite well.

However, Pluto's transit to Neptune's weak radical position coincides with Neptune's current stay of 13 years in his own domicile, Pisces. Only long after Pluto has departed and stopped transiting the radical Neptune position will Neptune leave Pisces, his domicile. So the weakening of Russia (Neptune) by the Ukraine (Pluto) conflict is unlikely, and Russia's course looks rather gainful, as Neptune has transited Venus and the ascending lunar Node. Venus and the Node are in a very close conjunction. Does this Node represent the Crimean Peninsula? And does Venus represent the now secessionist Russian-speaking East Ukrainian regions that seek to be integrated into the Russian Federation?

The Initial Trigger

The initial trigger was the Ukraine government's denial of a comprehensive treaty with the European Union, which had just been negotiated and its signing already scheduled.

The significance we attribute to that Saturn-Neptune conjunction with regard to the post-Soviet countries in general and to the Ukraine crisis might be suspected to be mere arbitrary coincidence without evidence.

March 3, 1989. Topocentric, 10:46:44 a.m. GMT, Kiev, Saint Sophia Cathedral. First exact conjunction of Saturn and Neptune, in 11 Capricorn 55.

As there is not a data set of several Soviet Unions and their collapses in history, but just one case, we have to set statistics aside. Of course there have now and again been collapses of empires, but astrology would deny that those empires were all under the rule of Saturn-Neptune. Collapses of different extent and courses of events and circumstances would have to be defined as comparable enough to allow the use of statistics. Astrology's focus, however, is on individuality, and it is a tricky question as to how much several cases, i.e. of an empire's collapse, are sufficiently comparable to apply statistics.

The only way to gather evidence regarding the validity of a horoscope is to search for other significant events. Events peculiar to this one case should correspond to constellations of the horoscope in a highly suggestive, if not convincing manner. Such events are, for instance, the initial trigger of the crisis, the way the government was finally overthrown, the new government's loss of control in parts of the country, and the loss of the Crimean Peninsula to Russia.

Looking at the Saturn-Neptune conjunction horoscope cast for Kiev, note its Ascendant in 20 Cancer 44 and read from the November 2013 ephemeris that Jupiter almost completed a transit to the Ascendant, but refrained by becoming retrograde in 20 Cancer 31, thus postponing the perfection of this transit for more than half a year.

Jupiter refrained from completing a transit to the Ascendant, and the Ukrainian government refrained from signing a treaty.

This *almost* transit corresponds convincingly with what happened: After a comprehensive treaty with the European Union had been negotiated and the date of signing set, the Ukrainian parliament disapproved several related legal measures that would have been necessary or instrumental to the treaty between Ukraine and the European Union. The majority for the disapproval came from President Yanoukovitch's party, while the opposition demanded the acceptance of the treaty. Right after the decision of the Ukrainian parliament, first the prime minister, then President Yanoukovitch announced their intention to postpone Ukraine's agreement to the treaty that would have brought Ukraine much closer to the European Union, to the detriment of its relations with Russia and the other post-Soviet countries.

On Friday, November 21, 2013, eight days before the treaty was to be signed, the Ukrainian parliament refused to approve it and the president refrained from signing it, certainly under pressure from the Russian government and with regard to the disastrous financial situation of the country and its dependence on Russian goodwill and support. The *almost* approval and *almost* signature perfectly matched to the *almost* transit of Jupiter, to whose topics belong legal and judicial actions, conceding and obtaining privileges and of course international affairs.

Jupiter turned retrograde on November 6, and was about to leave the degree of his stationary retrograde point, when on November 21, the Ukrainian government declined to sign the treaty. Venus, planet of agreements, treaties, diplomacy (rulership of Libra) and last but not least, money (rulership of Taurus), entered Capricorn the day before Jupiter's retrogradation began, on November 5. Capricorn, where Pluto was and whose transit to the Saturn-Neptune conjunction of 1989 marked that year and the following (2013 and 2014) as important ones in the history of the post-Soviet countries, Russia (Neptune) and in particular of Ukraine (Pluto). Venus was set to undergo a period of retrogradation in Capricorn, meaning that a period of unsuccessful diplomacy, failing mediation, and receding peace was to be unleashed.

The coincidence of the Venus ingress with Jupiter's retrogradation linked their meanings; the ingress in the sign of Pluto's transit linked both to Pluto, the generally slowest of the three. Thus, the decision not to sign the treaty, unsuccessful diplomacy, and violence served to ignite a crisis of Ukraine with regard to Russia and the post-Soviet countries.

Saturn-Pluto: Challenge or Change of Power

This understanding of the astrological mechanics underlying what happened in November 2013 inspires us to pay attention to the celestial coincidences of ingresses, changes of direction, and the presence of another planet in the same sign. So it cannot be meaningless that Pluto began his way forward from the end of his annual retrogradation on September 20, 2013, in sextile and mutual reception with Saturn in Scorpio, promising a challenge and possibly a change of power for a head of state or government before Pluto's next retrogradation. Aspects between Saturn and Pluto determine which governments might be challenged and/or replaced.

Of course there is no period without a change of power occurring somewhere. However, it is Pluto's transit to the Saturn-Neptune conjunction of 1989, and sextile with Saturn that relates to this in a post-Soviet country, either Russia (Neptune to be transited) or Ukraine (transiting Pluto).

Pluto completed an aspect, a sextile, with the Sun of the 1989 Saturn-Neptune conjunction on February 19, 2014. On the evening of February 21, the Ukrainian president had to flee to East Ukraine and then to Russia.

A sextile might not seem like enough to astrologically explain the ousting of a president. But it was the same aspect that Pluto had formed with Saturn at the time of his return to forward motion. The horoscope of a planet's departure from its most recent turning point should be considered a radical chart concerning all the celestial events that will occur until its station at the next turning point (or rather upon entering the zodiacal degree of its next station).

By the beginning of the week in the end of which President Yanoukovitch was ousted, Jupiter had arrived in the degree in which he would return to regular direction. So the refrain from signing the treaty with the European Union and the beleaguering of the government by protesters ensuing that refrain lasted until Jupiter was preparing to change direction again, while his previous change of direction right before the Ascendant of the Saturn-Neptune conjunction had suggested the refrain.

War Breaks Out

Jupiter's return to regular motion coincided well with Mars' change to retrogradation: Mars turned retrograde on March 1, 2014, and Jupiter returned to regular motion on March 6, 2014. The position of Pluto in the horoscopes of these changes of direction was in the same zodiacal degree where the Moon of the Saturn-Neptune conjunction is located, i.e. 13 Capricorn.

So the new government came to power by violence and force.

Kiev is part of western Ukraine, and in addition to its inhabitants, tens of thousands of western Ukrainians were blocking the central place, and their overwhelming number and increasing violence frightened the riot police and their commanders in the ministry of the interior until they suddenly withdrew. When President Yanoukovitch realized that his guards were gone and police were giving up their posts, he understood what this meant for his personal safety. He had to flee and to take refuge.

Mars is the planet of violence, physical threat, and fear. It was this that brought about a new government seeking to please foreign powers (except Russia, which in Ukraine is a power not as foreign as others) by doing what President Yanoukovitch had refrained from. Thus Jupiter's return to forward motion also meant that the influence of foreign powers resumed after a setback.

With Mars, powered by Pluto, war occurs. So it was in early March 2014, when in Russian-speaking eastern Ukraine, secession from the Ukrainian state and new Republics were proclaimed and civil war commenced.

The Crimea Peninsula

The position of Neptune in the horoscopes of Mars turning retrograde and Jupiter's return to forward motion in March 2014, is on the very close conjunction of Venus and the ascending lunar Node of the Saturn-Neptune conjunction in 4 Pisces. This horoscope computed for Kiev or any other post-Soviet capital city where the Ascendant may be found in Cancer, indicates that something *appending* (Node) to that post-Soviet state could be *gulped* down (Venus ruler of Taurus, sign of throat and gulping) in dramatic rapidity (close conjunction, sextile of Uranus). Venus ruling the cusp of the fourth house (Libra) involves the question of patriotism and to which family the territory belongs to. It's a conflict about family relationship—two strongly connective factors, Venus and the Ascending Node, compete in the same place (same zodiacal degree).

With regard to Russia (Neptune) and Ukraine (lunar Node, and the Moon, ruler of the Ascendant), the Node being in Pisces is part of the Neptunian sphere, and in Pisces this horoscope has an unquestionable significator for Russia as well: the Sun. The Node and what it means belongs to Russia by being in the same sign as the Sun, no less than it belongs to Ukraine by being the Node of the planet ruling the Ascendant. So we arrive at understanding that in this horoscope the ascending lunar Node symbolizes the Crimean peninsula belonging to Russia and Ukraine. The transit of Neptune to the radical lunar Node in Neptune's domicile, Pisces, symbolizes the (re-)unification (conjunction) of the peninsula with Russia.

When Neptune transited the lunar Node, the peninsula (sign belonging to the element water) was to be gulped down by the Neptunian force, big limitless Russia, which managed to perform this gulp smoothly with no physical hurt and with some deception, in a way only Neptune can.

Actually, there are two gulps, two parts of what the two countries consider to be part of their very own soil. For at the same time, Venus was also transited by Neptune. So we have to look at Taurus, where we find Mars and Jupiter. Both, in particular Mars, render the gulp concerning Venus rather violently or obstructed by violence. In this way Venus seems to represent those eastern, Russian-speaking parts of the Ukrainian Republic that resented that President Yanoukovitch, who is from the eastern area, was ousted and violence forced him to fear for his life and safety and to flee by refusing to acknowledge the new government because of its lack of legitimacy. This situation resulted in war, with European and American support for the people now in power at Kiev, and Russia's support for the secessionists. With Taurus and Pluto being involved, events evolve over a long time, even if initial actions were rapid (Uranus sextile Venus).

Russia's Current Mundane Radical Horoscope

Could it have been foreseen that the horoscope of the first conjunction of Saturn and Neptune in 1989 was and is important for Russia, even with no understanding that its function until then as center of communism, of the radical left in the world made it the natural main destination for this horoscope's suggestions?

If cast for Moscow, the Ascendant is in 0 Leo, and the Midheaven in 0 Aries.

A trial across the globe, casting this horoscopes for capitals of major powers, would have easily revealed that meanings of this horoscope were important for Russia's global position and rank as a superpower. All zero degrees of zodiacal signs mean public affairs (in the open air, on the road); however, this meaning is not, as Alfred Witte believed, reserved to zero degrees of cardinal signs. And Leo is the sign of competition for power, for royal brilliance. So 0 Leo is the superpowers' zodiacal degree: Great Britain when Great Britain ruled the biggest part of the globe; the United States and the USSR, when the power of each surpassed every other power; and of course Rome, when the Roman Empire was not matched by any other power or by just one competitor.

If 0 Leo is the position of a planet, node, or house cusp in a mundane horoscope, it indicates either that a superpower is involved in the course of events to happen under the rule of this horoscope. Or that a crisis is going to occur putting into question the options if not the status of a superpower. The latter is the case if the mundane horoscope is to become the mundane radical horoscope of that superpower. As the Saturn-Neptune conjunction of March 3, 1989, referred to the world center of the political left, which was Moscow, capital of the

Soviet Union, a superpower, the Ascendant in 0 Leo meant a serious crisis of that status. The Meridian in zero degrees meant that the crisis would heavily affect world politics and international relations and result in a new beginning (Aries), a reset for many countries.

Reason overcomes ideology, dire need of strict measures overcomes idealism, tough times for people guarded by the government, and the governmental system is renewed, according to the four planets in Capricorn.

Capricorn and Cancer are intercepted in the sixth and the twelfth houses, respectively. The absence of any house cusp in a sign means lack of control, independently acting people and people out of central control, and proclamations of independence as a state, regardless of consent or disagreement from the central government. Later on it poses the problem of maintaining control over the peoples and territories and states within the union whose radical horoscope it has become. We should note that the position within a house is similar to the specters of meanings attributed to Neptune and Pisces. Therefore, Neptune in his domicile promises a period of inner peace because of a lack of direct control. And it promises success in international affairs as a result of clandestine actions and silent, hidden support.

Cancer is intercepted in the twelfth house of the Moscow version of the March 3, 1989 horoscope, whereas Cancer is the sign of the Ascendant of the Kiev version. This could mean that Ukraine shed Russian control, especially a maritime part of it, the Crimean Peninsula. During Neptune's transit to the lunar Node, the lack of control could be exported to Ukraine.

As for other events in Russia's most recent history with no relationship to Ukraine, we see the radical function of this mundane horoscope for Russia confirmed by the Russian intervention in Syria. It began soon after Mars had transited 0 Virgo, i.e. the midpoint of the horizon (0 Leo and Aquarius)

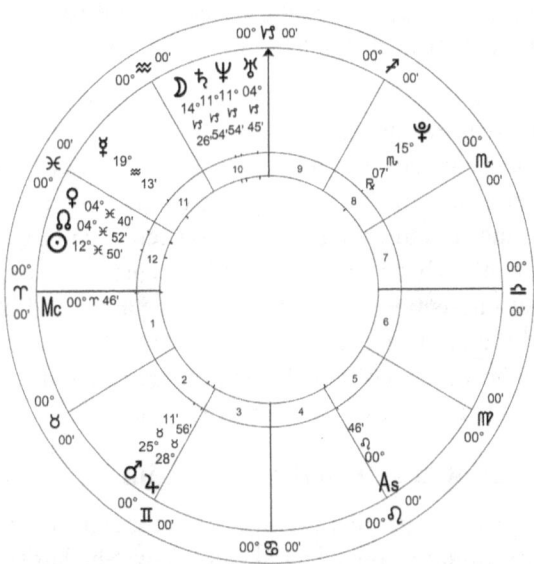

March 3, 1989. Topocentric 10:47:36 a.m. GMT, Kremlin, Moscow. First exact conjunction of Saturn and Neptune in 11 Capricorn 55.

and meridian (0 Aries and Libra), also aspecting both by semisextile and quincunx. Mars followed Jupiter, who had recently entered Virgo, and the hypothetical Transpluto, which meanwhile had arrived in 1 Virgo.

The first counterattack after Russia's intervention, the explosion of a Russian civil airplane in Egypt (again a peninsula, the Sinai) at the hands of an Islamic State agent, was executed while the lunar Nodes were in 0 Libra and Aries. A second counterattack, occurred when Turkey (a clandestine supporter of the Islamic State) downed a Russian bomber over Syria, claiming it had crossed Turkish territory and ignored a warning. The Sun had, in 0 Sagittarius, just formed a square to Mars' ingress position at the inception of the Russian intervention and a trine to the Ascendant and the Midheaven of the above horoscope. The obvious aim of this counterattack to block Russia's beginning military alliance with France against the Islamic State, a diplomatic success for Russia, indicates why a friendly aspect should be linked to a mournful event.

The major phases and turns of the Ukraine conflict can be understood from the horoscopes cast at the moment of exact aspects, changes of direction, and ingresses of the planets with reference to the Saturn-Neptune conjunction of March 3, 1989, as master radical chart, with no need to consider doubtful or doubtless birth and proclamation charts. This recount of how Pluto transiting the conjunction of Saturn and Neptune inspired the crisis and for the split of the Ukraine is an example of how the art of mundane astrology can perfectly work in the absence of known birth and of event times.

Hillary Clinton's Presidential Candidacy

Let me close with another example of a mundane forecast, that of Hillary Clinton's presidential candidacy. She has served as the first lady and as secretary of state, both positions ruled by Venus. So we look at the ingress of Venus into the sign it was in at the time she announced her candidacy.

In 2008, Venus was in Sagittarius, and in 2015, Venus was in Gemini. Both ingress horoscopes have in common the Moon void of course; her career was and is up to the people.

As for Hillary Clinton's presidential run, both Moons are void of course, so she ran in vain and is running in vain.

Horoscopes must be calculated for the topocentric positions of the planets, not merely geocentric ones. It is the topocentric position that we see in the sky, and this is therefore the position ancient astrologers worked with. The Moon's topocentric position may differ from the geocentric position by up to three degrees if close to the horizon, while the two positions are almost or exactly the same close to the meridian. There are cases where the Moon is void of course by her topocentric position but has already gone into a new sign by her geocentric position.

As for Mrs. Clinton's presidential run, the Moon in both Venus ingress horoscopes is void of course by topocentric position.

Topocentric planetary positions must not be confused with topocentric houses. Topocentric planetary positions are for a geographic position on the surface of earth (longitude, latitude), distinct from geocentric positions, which are in earth's center core.

Topocentric positions usually differ from geocentric ones, and they are different in different geographic positions. Consequently topocentric planetary events such as exact aspects and ingresses do not take place at exactly the same time at different geographic positions.

(In) Significant Aspects of the Reality and History of the Sidereal Zodiac

By Rui Miguel Fernandes

ABSTRACT: The usefulness of the sidereal zodiac versus the tropical one is not debated here. This article is a small and light mathematical study between the aspects to be considered to develop a possible sidereal model that might fit in a long time span in the past as in the future. Several astronomical data are presented in order to understand which major points are to be considered and an average model is presented. The historical background of the different computations, the anomalies, possible mistakes, and new, unanswered questions are presented in the article.

Introduction

It's almost impossible to establish the precise time when the so-called sidereal zodiac was defined in ancient history. We do know that the "wanderers," the sun, the moon, even the comets, were first referred to in their angular separation of a visible important star before any sidereal zero Aries point was defined. Here's an ancient example for the position of some usual celestial bodies by the Mesopotamians:

"19 from the Moon to the Pleiades; 17 from the Pleiades to Orion; 14 from Orion to Sirius..."

In fact, as it was very well stated, this does not define any kind of a zodiac as we know it.

The term sidereal comes from the Greek word "sidera," which means star. The secular discussion of the validity of these two systems in the astrology community seems endless. Some, like the Hindus, still use the ancient star-zodiac derived from the apparent fixed constellations, while the majority, mostly in the western world, joined the tropical-zodiac system anchored in the tropical 0 Aries point at the Vernal Equinox (spring). The difference is that in the tropical system, the Aries point seems to move backward toward the observer along the "fixed" stars pane and in the sun's path at a rate of about 50 arc seconds per year. This phenomenon has to do with the precession of the equinoxes caused by the tilt and rotation of the Earth's axis—precession is what the Indian astronomers call Akashchalana. So actually the tropical zodiac is directly connected with the tropical year, the seasons, etc.

The difference between the Vernal Equinox at a given epoch and the starting sidereal Aries point of any particular system of a sidereal zodiac it's called Ayanamsa by the Hindus (Sanskrit "ayanāmśa": ayana meaning "movement" and "amśa" meaning "component"; it's also called sometimes "ayanabhāga," from the sanskrit "bhāga," meaning "portion"). The most widely used planetary position in Vedic astrology (Jyotish) is not the one used by Western astrology. We have then two models of planetary position in use worldwide: The tropical model (Sanskrit: Sayana) used in Western astrology and the sidereal model (Sanskrit: Nirayana), used in Vedic astrology.

We don't know exactly which were the primary anchor stars

defining the origin of the first sidereal zodiac and it's very likely that this first definition gained various different interpretations and definitions among the several cultures that adopt it. We do suspect that it was substituted by the tropical zodiac by Hipparchus. Not only this bright mind had discovered the precession of the equinoxes, like, according to the "De re rustica IX, 14" of Columella (first century A.D.), he placed the Vernal point at 0 Aries—which is by definition the tropical zodiac. We may add to this Ptolemy's references that Hipparchus compared several times stars like Regulus and Spica referred to the tropical points—even if some authors choose to believe that the measurements cited by Ptolemy are conversions made by himself from the original polar coordinates to ecliptic ones. This is not very likely in my humble opinion.

In fact, if we think carefully and objectively about the subject, there's no accurate or correct Ayanamsa value defined so far since no ancient writings exist defining or mentioning its accurate position at a given time, not even a solid and unanimous reference about when the two zodiacs coincided. Despite this frustrating fact, we might count more than twenty different systems that attempt the computation of its value. Here are some examples of different calculations for October 27, 2006, according to the most popular systems (the reference year defines when the junction of the two types of zodiacs matched according to the stars references used):

Source	Ayanamsa	Reference Year
Fagan/Bradley	-24°50'10"	221 A.D.
Lahiri	-23°57'10"	285 A.D.
De Luce	-27°54'19"	1 B.C.
Raman	-22°30'24"	389 A.D.
Sassanian	-20°05'20"	564 A.D.
Ushashashi	-20°09'11"	559 A.D.
Hipparchos	-20°20'34"	545 A.D.
Djwhal Khool	-28°27'19"	41 B.C.

Yukteshwar	-22°34'28"	292 A.D.
JN Bhasin	-22°51'28"	364 A.D.
Babylonian, Huber	-24°43'43"	229 A.D.
Babylonian, Kugler 1	-25°55'43"	143 A.D.
Babylonian, Kugler 2	-24°31'43"	243 A.D.
Babylonian, Kugler 3	-23°40'43"	305 A.D.
Babylonian, Mercier	-24°37'03"	237 A.D.
Galactic Center	-26°56'55"	69 A.D.
Krishnamurti	-23°51'22"	292 A.D.
Aldebaran at 15 Taurus	-24°51'16"	220 A.D.
Chandra-Hiri8	-24°40'43"	233 A.D.
Tarun Chopra9	-11°53'43"	1153 A.D.
Dhira10	-23°09'48"	342 A.D.
Krushna11	-23°02'54"	350 A.D.
Wilhelm Ardra12	-23°30'16"	317 A.D.

Notice that the variations between the theories go from the -20°05'20" to -28°27'19" in the different systems, reaching a difference of more than eight degrees. As very well stated, and resumed, by Dieter Koch and Dr. Alois Treindl:

> "We have found that there are basically three definitions (for the Ayanamsa), not counting the manifold variations:
>
> "1. The Babylonian zodiac with Spica at 29 Virgo or Aldebaran at 15 Taurus: a) P. Huber, b) Fagan/Bradley, c) refined with Aldebaran at 15 Tau.
>
> "2. The Greek-Arabic-Hindu zodiac with the zero point between 10' and 20' east of zeta Piscium: a) Hipparchus, b) Ushâshashî, c) Sassanian.
>
> "3. The Greek-Hindu astrological zodiac with Spica at 0 Libra: a) Lahiri. The differences are:
>
> "between 1) and 3) is about 1 degree

"between 1) and 2) is about 5 degrees

between 2) and 3) is about 4 degrees

"It is obvious that all of them stem from the same origin, but it is difficult to say which one should be preferred for sidereal astrology.

"1) is historically the oldest one, but we are not sure about its precise astronomical definition. Aldebaran at 15 Taurus might be one.

"3) has the most striking reference point, the bright star Spica at 0 Libra. But this definition is so clear and simple that, had it really been intended by the inventors of the sidereal ecliptic, it would certainly not have been forgotten or given up by the Greek and Arabic tradition.

"2) is the only definition independent on a star—especially, if we take the Sassanian version. This is an advantage, because all stars have a proper motion and cannot really define a fixed coordinate system. Also, it is the only Ayanamsha for which there is historical evidence that it was observed and recalibrated at the time when it was 0.

"On the other hand, the point 10' east of zePsc has no astronomical significance at all, and the great difference between this zero point and the Babylonian one raises the question: Did Hipparchus' definition results from a misunderstanding of the Babylonian definition, or was it an attempt to improve the Babylonian zodiac?"

The official Ayanamsa approved by the Indian government, for instance, since 1956, is that of the Calcuttan astronomer and astrologer Nirmala Chandra Lahiri, member and secretary of the Calendar Reform Committee and compiler of India's official ephemerides, that review the establishment of the zero sidereal Aries point, and believed that the zero Ayanamsa year was at 285 A.D. This Ayanamsa was first proposed by the astronomy historian S. B. Dixit in 1896 in his work *History of Indian Astronomy* in accordance with the *Grahalaghava*, a work of the 16th century astronomer Ganesa Daivajna. This system assumes that the bright α star of the Virgo constellation, Spica (Chitra in Hindu), is always 180 degrees apart of the sidereal Aries point. Here's Spica's position in ecliptic longitude for 285 A.D.:

Date   Longitude   Latitude
01/02/285 AD, 00:00 TDB   179°59'59.9"   -1°56'15.63"
True obliquity of ecliptic: 23°39'24.79"

And in equatorial coordinates the junction happens 61 years later:

Date   Longitude   Latitude
27/12/346 AD, 00:00 TDB   11h59m59.99s   -2°07'10.12"
True obliquity of ecliptic: 23°39'11.82'

As we will see, this value disagrees completely with the Babylonian astronomical observations that place Spica always near the 29° inside Virgo, thus 179° from the start.

The "Main" Pproblem

The problem of defining a sidereal zodiac is not merely to establish a reference star associated with a fixed position inside its constellation, or even a set of them. This would be reasonable if the stars we're fixed in the sky like the ancient astronomers and astrologers believed. But mostly given to the sharp observation of Dr. Edmund Halley, we know that each star in the sky has its own movement, called the proper motion. Nothing is fixed in the Universe—at least that we are aware of. Stars have a "proper" movement in right ascension, declination, and radial velocity. We now have an extensive and reasonable accurate measurement of these quantities for milliards of stars.

Since Macrobius (about the 5th century A.D.), astronomers suspected this phenomenon. The first proof was provided in 1718 by Dr. Halley, who noticed that Sirius, Arcturus, and Aldebaran were over half a degree away from the positions charted by the ancient Greek astronomer Hipparchus roughly 1850 years earlier. There are no fixed stars for the observer—this is a proven fact. At most, there can be a few that might be so slow in their motion that we will take some time to detect its moving rate. In reality, all stars are in motion relative to each other and our galaxy, with typical velocities of a hundred fifty miles per second or so relative to the center of the galaxy, and a few tens of miles per second relative to each other.

Up until now, of all the catalogued stars, we have since the Barnard's Star with the fastest proper movement (of about 10.3 seconds of arc per year) to the average proper motion of the stars that can be seen with the naked eye, which is about 0.1" per year.

So when we reduce the position of a celestial body in our tropical system from a supposed single fixed anchor star to its original place, we're calculating the amount of precession and proper motion together. Not just the precession.

Ptolemy—and most likely all his ancestors—believed that, even if the sphere of stars was apparently moving along the ecliptic due to precession, the aspect ratios between them were fixed. As for its ecliptic declinations, these were considered constant, and thus the obliquity of the ecliptic as well. This is clearly stated in the *Almagest*. But this is not true facing our current astronomical knowledge. The axis Aldebaran-Antares, mentioned by many ancient astronomers, is not always around the exact 180° for instance. Neither are other established ratio relationships.

From a difference of about 25' in 13001 B.C., the Aldebaran-Antares axis starts to improve its fit to the 180°. It begins to be less than 10' apart around 5815 B.C., less than 5' from 3062

B.C., less than a minute between 482 B.C. and 1039 A.D. reaching the 180° opposition in 254 A.D., and then increasing up to 6' 25" around 9600 A.D. decreasing from there again down to 5' 52" in 13000 A.D.

Making the same comparison with Antares and Spica, which seem to have an harmonic angular separation of very near the 46 degrees, we begin with a variation of 7' 53" from the 46° in 13001 B.C., reaching the 6' at 589 B.C., the 5' at 1915 A.D., 4' at 3824 A.D., 3' in 5447 A.D., 2' in 6902 A.D., and 1' in 8250 A.D., and 46° in 9515 A.D. From this last point the angular separation starts again up to the 2'53" in 13000 A.D.

Looking just a little further (60001 B.C. to 57000 A.D.), the Aldebaran-Antares axis starts with a difference of 52' 37", reaching a new opposition (after 254 A.D.) around 25200 A.D, and a new maximum of 22' 53" in 57000 A.D. The Spica-Antares, on the other hand, starts with a 20'24" difference, and ends with 15' 35"—much better.

From here, studying some angular star separations along the path of the Sun, we find that Ptolemy most likely followed these apparent fixed historical values, considered as astronomical constants, along a careful millenary observation—as we'll see later.

A simple computation from the year 10000 B.C. to 1000 A.D. shows us how aspects evolve between the major stars and the apparent rate of its displacement in 11000 years to integer values or near the half degree. The criterion was to output only the shifts less than 30 arc minutes of a degree. Some examples are shown on the following pages.

Notice that the best models are curiously referred to Spica and to the relationship between Sheratan and Alcyone (the best in this time range) of 26°. The Aldebaran and Antares axis comes with a shift of about 18.5' (quite excellent indeed for a time span of 11000 years), but not as good as the previous combi-

Stars Pair	Angular Shift in 11000 years and Aspects (average and range)	Aspect near ½ or 1°
Sharatan - Alcyone	1.26' (26.01 [26.025 to 26.003])	26°
Zubeneshamali - Alcyone	1.5' (169.4 [169.412 to 169.387])	
Antares - Sharatan	1.98' (144.19 [144.207 to 144.173])	
Zubeneshamali - Sharatan	2.16' (164.58 [164.603 to 164.566])	164.5° (195.5°)
Spica - Antares	2.16' (45.89 [45.908 to 45.871])	46°
Alcyone - Praesepe	3.06' (67.18 [67.207 to 67.156])	
Antares - Alcyone	3.24' (170.2 [170.232 to 170.177])	
Zubeneshamali - Praesepe	3.36' (102.2 [102.236 to 102.179])	
Zubeneshamali - Antares	3.36' (20.4 [20.429 to 20.372])	
Spica - Sharatan	4.14' (169.91 [169.954 to 169.884])	170°
Sharatan - Praesepe	4.38' (93.19 [93.233 to 93.16])	
Spica - Zuben Elgenubi	5.1' (21.29 [21.337 to 21.251])	
Spica - Zubeneshamali	5.16' (25.48 [25.528 to 25.441])	25.5°
Spica - Alcyone	5.46' (143.9 [143.95 to 143.859])	144°
Antares - Praesepe	6.36' (122.61 [122.666 to 122.559])	
Aldebaran - Revati	6.54' (49.99 [50.046 to 49.937])	50°

Stars Pair	Angular Shift in 11000 years and Aspects (average and range)	Aspect near ½ or 1°
Zuben Elgenubi - Antares	7.32' (24.59 [24.657 to 24.534])	24.5°
Spica - Praesepe	8.58' (76.72 [76.794 to 76.651])	
Zuben Elgenubi - Sharatan	9.3' (168.78 [168.864 to 168.708])	
Zuben Elgenubi - Vindemiatrix	10.26' (35.03 [35.119 to 34.947])	
Zuben Elgenubi - Zubeneshamali	10.32' (4.19 [4.277 to 4.104])	
Zuben Elgenubi - Alcyone	10.62' (165.19 [165.287 to 165.11])	
Aldebaran - Praesepe	12.78' (57.53 [57.642 to 57.428])	
Zuben Elgenubi - Praesepe	13.74' (98.01 [98.131 to 97.902])	98°
Spica - Vindemiatrix	15.42' (13.73 [13.868 to 13.61])	
Aldebaran - Alcyone	15.9' (9.64 [9.779 to 9.513])	
Aldebaran - Zubeneshamali	16.2' (159.74 [159.878 to 159.608])	
Aldebaran - Sharatan	17.16' (35.66 [35.804 to 35.517])	
Antares - Vindemiatrix	17.64' (59.62 [59.776 to 59.482])	
Aldebaran - Antares	18.42' (179.84 [179.998 to 179.691])	180°
Regulus - Vindemiatrix	18.6' (39.92 [40.075 to 39.765])	
Praesepe - Revati	19.32' (107.52 [107.688 to 107.365])	107.5°

Sidereal Zodiac

Stars Pair	Angular Shift in 11000 years and Aspects (average and range)	Aspect near ½ or 1°
Sharatan - Vindemiatrix	19.62' (156.17 [156.343 to 156.015])	
Zubeneshamali - Vindemiatrix	20.64' (39.22 [39.396 to 39.052])	
Alcyone - Vindemiatrix	20.94' (130.16 [130.339 to 129.99])	
Aldebaran - Spica	21.36' (134.25 [134.436 to 134.079])	134°
Alcyone - Revati	22.44' (40.34 [40.532 to 40.157])	
Zubeneshamali - Revati	22.74' (150.26 [150.454 to 150.075])	
Sharatan - Revati	23.7' (14.33 [14.528 to 14.132])	
Praesepe - Vindemiatrix	24' (62.98 [63.183 to 62.782])	
Antares - Revati	25.74' (129.85 [130.074 to 129.645])	
Aldebaran - Zuben Elgenubi	26.52' (155.55 [155.773 to 155.331])	
Spica - Revati	27.9' (175.74 [175.982 to 175.516])	
Regulus - Zuben Elgenubi	28.92' (74.95 [75.195 to 74.713])	75°

nations. Aldebaran seems to be quite better with Revati (zeta Pisces) than Antares for that matter.

With the data gathered from this analysis, it seems safe to use Sheratan, Alcyone, Spica, Zuben Elgenubi, Zuben Eshamali, Antares, and only then Aldebaran and Revati, to make a comparison model of any kind with a possible fixed sidereal zodiac.

We'll use the reference values shown on the facing page for starters:

Extending a little further our results to the period between 60001 B.C. and 57000 A.D., we get the best fit results for an allowed shift inferior to one degree, as shown on the following page.

Spica and Antares maintain a good angle fit, as for Antares and Alcyone.

The annoying problem that arises from these calculations is that we must also account for all the other thousands of visible stars that don't have the same rate in proper motion and aren't moving in the same spatial direction. So any reduction will be false for all of them at the same time. Our reference star moved, for instance, an amount east, but our star reference B might have moved west. C moved southeast. So the degrees value of Star B won't be correct to the initial model. Neither will be C . . . and so on, multiplied by thousands of visible stars. Defining a sidereal system based in several established measurements thus becomes very difficult.

It's absolutely logical to presume that some kind of sidereal zodiac was first drawn by instituting a sort of rule, where a particular bright star was considered to be in a particular degree of its constellation—or a set of stars with several specific positions in the celestial sphere which formed "almost perfect" aspects between them. It's not likely that a mathematical point in space was the point of Aries. In this last case, there's only the remote possibility that a star unknown to us, extinguished a long time ago, was in the origin of the celestial wheel. Either way, the logic and the problem would be the same.

At this point arises an important remark we must also not forget: ancient celestial measurements were made regarding the equatorial plane at some times, but at other times regarding the ecliptic. And even other ones—as in the Hindu's Nakshatras system and in the Babylonian path of the Moon—stars were and still are referred to the plane defined by the path of our natural satellite, not the Sun—thus a small variation and oscillation of about five degrees below and above the ecliptic line, with the additional changing factor that comes from the shift of the ascending node of the moon along the ecliptic.

Ptolemy, for instance, gave a list of the position of the main stars relative to the path of the Sun. Hipparchus, on the other hand—and this is beginning to be most widely accepted—in polar coordinates. So when a star is referred as a reference point of x degrees in the zodiac, was it in one system or the other?

Nevertheless, let's emphasize for the sake of our arguments that relationships like the Aldebaran-Antares 180 degrees axis are only valid in the ecliptic system. Not in the equatorial frame. The same applies to other numerous angular separations.

If an ancient text speaks that Regulus, for instance, is at 125° and Aldebaran at 45°, they are talking in the Sun's path frame. We just only need to compare the equatorial coordinate's conversion values to easily realize that.

This was surely the first definition of the starting point. A simple rule or set of rules defined the medium zodiac across the centuries, across the millenniums, given the stars' positions and inner aspects that seemed stable and fixed.

The Vernal Equinox

> "Some place the tropics in the beginning, others about eight degrees, some about the twelfth, and others about the fifteenth." (Achilles Tatius, III century A.D., Isag. 23)

This first allusion of Tatius regarding the position of the Vernal Equinox in the sidereal zodiac really sums it up. Our astronomers and Western astrologers generally define the longitude of a celestial body as mainly referring to its tropical longitude from the Vernal Equinox of date (true or mean). We measure it in two kinds of coordinates: over the plane of the ecliptic, or in reference to the equator of Earth. Except for some specific astronomical calculations, a fixed point, or epoch, is used, such as the J1900, J1950, J2000, or B1850 epochs.

Our ancestors did exactly the opposite: given the fixed sky map, the spring equinox was placed within. So they speak that the Vernal Point is at 8 Aries, for example. From here we deduce that all the longitudes of the stars and celestial bodies are referred to the sidereal ground.

Following are some references of major authors that wrote about its position:

Censorinus (238 A.D.) tells us that "The Sun creates the winter solstice when passing through the 8th degree of Capricorn and in the 8th degree of Aries is in the vernal equiinox." (De Die Natali XXV.)

Columella (60 A.D.) writes: "Winter, which begins about viii kal. of January in the eighth degree of Capricorn....and I am not deceived by Hipparchus' argument which teaches that the solstices and equinoxes happen not in the eighth but in the first degrees of the signs. In this rustic science, I follow the Fastus of Eudoxus and Meton and the ancient astronomers, which fits the public festivals." (Columella IX 14, 12)

Manilius, the Roman poet-astrologer who flourished during

the reign of Augustus and Tiberius says, "So one degree in the tropical signs is to be marked out which moves the world and alters the seasons . . . some place this power in the 8 degrees, others prefer the 10 degrees and there has been a writer (probably Hipparchus) who has allotted to the first degree the alterations of the seasons." (Astronomicon Bk. III.)

Even the pseudo-Manetho, born according to the details of his own horoscope at 23h30, May 28, 80 A.D., and who dedicated his astrological poem, "Apotelesmatica" to his friend and countryman Claudius Ptolemy, whom he styles "King Ptolemy," shows, by the following statement, that he, too rejected the modern zodiac, invented by Hipparchus and which puts the Summer Solstice permanently in 0 Cancer: "The circle which turns the season of fiery summer is described in the sky by the all-seeing Sun in its course upon the 8th degree of Cancer." (Apotelematica II 72-87.)

According to Hipparchus, the Greek astronomer Eudoxus (4th century B.C.) defined the Vernal and Autumnal Equinoxes at 15 Aries and 15 Libra, respectively, and the Summer and Winter Solstices to be at 15 Cancer and 15 Capricorn, respectively. This ancient measure seems to be related to the Babylonian calendar according to some researchers: In the MUL.APIN solar calendar the equinoxes are placed on the fifteenth day of the months I and VII and the solstices on the fifteenth day of the months IV and X. This implies that the beginning of their calendar must have corresponded to the zero sidereal Aries. And since the sun moves around a degree each day, this places the Vernal Equinox at 15 Aries.

Meton and Euctemon (432 B.C.) speak of the midsummer sun located in Cancer. Euctemon places it explicitly at 8° in this constellation.

An interesting point to add is that the oldest zodiac systems don't start with the constellation of Aries. This only happened later. In the lunar mansions of the Hindus, named and numbered in the Atharveda, the starting point is Krittica (the third nakshatra associated with the star Alcyone of the Pleiades group) and not Ashwini (associated with Sheratan, and the Aries sign), which is placed last. Likewise, in the MUL.APIN tables, the constellations belonging to the path of the moon are counted from mul.mul, or the Pleiades, followed by mul. gu.an.na (the Bull of Anu), the Taurus constellation, finishing at last in mul.lu.hun.ga, Aries. Since the nakshatras are sidereal, the Atharveda is explicitly saying that the vernal point is at zero degrees Krittica, thus 25.71428 or 26.66667 sidereal degrees (with respect to the 28 or 27 lunar mansions used). Notice that the sidereal longitude of the vernal point is only around -17' to 40' the Alcyone-Sheratan aspect of 26°.

Let us be reminded at this stage that maybe one of the most important and exciting events in the history and development of the Greek astronomy happened when Callisthenes of Olynthus (c. 360-328 B.C.), nephew and pupil of Aristotle, sent to his uncle a large collection of Babylonian lunar and solar tablets from the time when Babylon had fallen to Alexander the Great's arms in 331 B.C. These included the ones of Naburiannu (Greek Naburianos) and Kidinnu (Greek Cidenas), two well respected Babylonian astronomers. More recently, copies of these tables were discovered by the German Jesuits J. Epping and F. X. Kugler, and by E. F. Weidner as well. A careful examination of their astronomical contents, namely by Paul Schnabel and John Knight Fotheringham, established that those of Naburianos were dated from circa 508 B.C., placing the Vernal Equinox always in 10 Aries (the so called System A), while those of Kidinnu were dated for about 373 B.C., placing it in 8 Aries (System B).

This raised some controversy among the Greek and Roman astronomers about the right place of the Vernal Equinox in its sidereal position, for their astronomical and astrological work purposes. Cidenas system B was, however, the most widely accepted and used according to the writings (we see it clearly in our descriptions above). Thus, the *Astronomicon* of the Roman Manillius and the *Apotolosmatica* of the pseudo-Manetho incorporate this Greek zodiac of eight degrees eastwards. Firmicus Maternus, Vettius Valens, and may other astrologers and astronomers joined this system, following it far "into the Middle Ages" according to Professor Otto Neugebauer.

Picking up our reference stars, like Spica for instance, we get its ecliptic longitude for the two epochs as follows:

Date: 01/01/508 BC
Longitude/RA: 169°02'31.6"/11h16m47.82s
Latitude/Declination: -1°53'35.81"/2°39'14.4"
True obliquity of ecliptic: 23°45'32.27"

Date: 01/01/373 BC
Longitude/RA: 170°54'43.96"/11h23m39.03s
Latitude/Declination: -1°54'01.4"/1°54'09.09"
True obliquity of ecliptic: 23°44'27.22"

If we add to the first computation 10 degrees, and eight degrees to the second, we get 179°02' and 178°54', that is, about 29 Virgo (+2'/-6') in ecliptic coordinates. In equatorial, we'll get 179°12' and 178°55' a bigger difference in the ecliptic, but less in the polar (+12'/-5').

In both cases Spica's position is nearer 179° than 180°.

The Main Stars Described in History

From the several astronomical ancient sources we have in our possession, we may reestablish some important star position measurements recorded by our ancestors, at least to the nearest degree of precision.

Aldebaran was recorded as being in the sidereal 15 Taurus on several writings as Antares, at Scorpio, being in the opposite side of the zodiac and thus at 15 Scorpio.

Cleomedes (mid-1st century BCE to 400 A.D.) clearly states (De motu I, 11, p. 106, 25 to 108, 5 Ziegler) that there exist two bright stars such that the rising of one coincides with the setting of the other: Aldebaran (α Tauri) and Antares (α Scorpii), both being located at the fifteenth degree of their respective sign (O. Neugebauer, HAMA ii, p. 960).

The Greek astrologer Hephaestion of Thebes (fourth century A.D.) also lists the longitude of Aldebaran as 15 Taurus (Cf. O. Neugebauer-H.P. van Hoesen, *Greek Horoscopes,* Philadelphia, 1959, p. 187).

The opposite positions of Aldebaran and Antares in 15 Taurus and 15 Scorpio, respectively, are also mentioned in a Greek treatise that goes under the name of the *Anonymous of the Year 379.* Though in this particular writing Aldebaran is not mentioned by name, it's clearly defined: "What happens if the bright star of Hyades which is in the circle of the zodiac at the 15th degree of Taurus, rises at the moment of delivery. *...+ In truth, only this star has a double force compared to other stars: in fact, when it rises, the shining star of Antares which is set in the diametrically opposed degree that is in the 15th degree of Scorpio sets; these stars are both in the circle of the zodiac." In this paragraph, the location of the Hyades is given between 11 and 15 Taurus (four-degree range). Aldebaran is not mentioned by name. Still, in *Almagest,* they go from 39° to 42°40' (3° 40' range), being called "the bright star of the Hyades, the reddish one on the southern eye," a clear reference to Aldebaran.

Anonymous 379, gives also some other referenced positions for several main stars:

Spica is referred as being at 29 Virgo. Pollux is placed at 29 Gemini. Arcturus at 29-30 Virgo.

From Peter Huber's analysis of the location of the first Aries point of the Babylonian zodiac, the longitudes of the first magnitude stars were carefully reconstructed. To the nearest degree, their positions in the Babylonian zodiac are assumed to be: Aldebaran (α Tauri) at 15 Taurus, Pollux (β Geminorum) at 29 Gemini, Regulus (α Leonis) at 5 Leo, Spica (α Virginis) at 29 Virgo, Antares (α Scorpii) at 15 Scorpio (R.A. Powell, *History of the Zodiac*, Cf. R.A. Powell, op. cit., apppendix 1).

Normal Star α Librae in terms of the system of zodiacal signs was mentioned as 20 Libra, i.e. the star α Librae is located at 20 degrees in the Babylonian (sidereal) sign of Libra. Similarly, the longitude of β Librae is 25 Libra or 25 degrees in the Babylonian (sidereal) sign of Libra (Cf. A. Sachs, *A Late Babylonian Star Catalogue, Journal of Cuneiform Studies 6* (1952), pp. 146-150, esp. p. 146).

From the famous *Almagest*, if we consider that the erroneous or unclear transformation of the stellar coordinates affected all the major stars but at least some kind of uniformity was achieved, we then have the initial miscalculated positions for some major stars at the time of Ptolemy (c. 138 A.D.):

Sharatan: 7°40'
Alcyone: 33°40'
Aldebaran: 42°40'
Pollux: 86°40'
Regulus: 122°30'
Spica: 176°40'
Arcturus (α Boote): 177°00'
α Librae (Zuben Elgenubi): 198°00'
β Librae (Zuben Eschamali): 202°10'
Antares: 222°40'

From Hipparchus' observations described by Ptolemy, Spica is referenced as being six degrees westwards from the Autumnal Equinox. This happened in ecliptic coordinates in 17/2/150 B.C. 17h TDB, and in equatorial at 18/1/129 B.C. 2h TDB (the presumably time of Hipparchus life time by most authors). If we were to admit that Ptolemy's epoch is around 138 A.D., this would have happened 265 years earlier, at 128

B.C. (so nearer of 129).

Here we might try to establish the correct epoch for Hipparchus observations from the polar declinations of the original text: Ptolemy clearly says that Hipparchus found that Aldebaran (the bright star of the Hyades) was at his time at $9+1/2+1/4°$ north of the equator—$9.75°$ north. This value is consistent with the observational value of Aldebaran calculated nowadays for 129 B.C.: $9.7054°$ (2.6' difference). The value of 150 B.C. gives a value of $9°36'58.1"$ ($9.616138°$ - 8' of difference) much more far from the value of Hipparchus. The Ptolemy value of 11 degrees is close to the value in 138 A.D. of $10°48'41.86"$ (11.3' of difference).

The *Almagest* also speaks of Regulus being at $29+1/2+1/3°$ eastward from the summer tropic point (thus $119.8333°$ - $119°$ 50') 265 years before, again at Hipparchus time. If we add the $2+2/3°$ mentioned by Ptolemy, we reach $122.5°$, the value of the *Almagest*.

The problem is that if Ptolemy made the reduction from the polar coordinates directly given by Hipparchus, his results would not be in ecliptic coordinates, but equatorial instead.

Notice that for Spica the calculations were straightforward: he summed $2°+2/3°$ (the calculated rate for 265 years) to the $180-6=174°$ of Hipparchus observation, thus giving the result of $176°+2/3°$ ($176°$ 40'). This would correspond to the right ascension of Spica not its ecliptic longitude. Unless he had converted between coordinates first, the results would be wrong—as for all the other ones that followed the "fixed" angular separations.

In fact we have for Spica:

Date: 01/01/138 AD, 00:00 TDB
Longitude (longitude and difference: $177°57'27.28"$
    ($177.9575777°$ - $1.9°$)
Latitude: $-1°55'44.1"$

Date: 01/01/138 AD, 00:00 TDB
RA (RA in degrees and difference): 11h49m25.24s
  (177.355166° - 41')
Declination: -0°56'48.32"

It's clear that an erroneous reduction was made from the polar coordinates.

But let's examine further the positions given by Ptolemy for the stars list above.

Notice that Antares is exactly 180° from Aldebaran as mentioned by the Greek astronomers and accordingly to our median calculations. Spica is placed 134° from it, which places it at 179° (29 Virgo) in the sidereal zodiac which considers Aldebaran being at 15 Taurus in the middle of the constellation. Spica is 46° from Antares and 25.5° from Zuben Eschamali.

Sharatan, however, comes 169° before Spica. Not 170° apart like our calculations show (it's a matter of computing their positions for around 138 A.D.).

Why this displacement of minus one degree away from Spica? Why is Alcyone (correctly 26° apart Sharatan) 143° apart (instead of 144°), also diminished by 1°? Their angular separation toward Zuben Eschamali is also reduced by one degree. Roughly, Sharatan would have to be also about 35°40' from Aldebaran, but instead is placed exactly at 35°. Why?

Sheratan: A Mystery to be Solved?

This anomaly in the *Almagest* may come from confusion generated from the systems employed by the Greeks, previously mentioned, where Sheratan could have been placed at 10 Aries sidereal and Spica at 180° at 448 B.C.

We know that probably Sheratan, meaning "the two signs," was named when it was aligned with the Vernal Equinox, separating two distinct signs (Aries from Pisces), like many other stars were before (and after). Still, I found it very peculiar that a star has this specific name, and not a general or common one. Why the "two signs"? Sheratan doesn't fit in a sidereal zodiac model as its starting point; its angular separation from the Pleiades, from Aldebaran, Antares, Spica or its place in the Ashwini nakshatra is too long.

But what about the hypothesis that this particular star was also named this way because it marked a specific astronomical rate between the tropical and sidereal zodiacs?

As we have seen, the medium distance between Spica and Sheratan is 170°. This is not a magical number. It's just a significant astronomical observational quantity. Thus is a simple arithmetic operation to realize that if the Virgin's main bright star was considered to be at 0 Libra in some epoch, Sheratan would be placed at 10 Aries, or 10 Ashwini in the Hindu system. Sheratan was at 0 Aries tropical in ecliptic longitude around 21/10/448 B.C. (and in equatorial coordinates at 22/10/178 B.C.). The Greek system A of Naburianos, as we'll see later, states a difference of precisely 10 degrees between the two zodiacs roughly 60 years earlier. Can this just be a coincidence? If in fact Spica was considered at 180° by the Hindus, Sheratan would mark the tropical Aries point at 10 degrees sidereal.

Also, 448 B.C. might be the most commonly accepted date for the establishment of the sidereal zodiac. "Within two centuries after King Ashurbanipal collected the Enuma Elish, Enuma Anu Enlil, Mul.Apin, and other cuneiform texts into his great library, the Babylonian priest-astronomers had made a further refinement of their picture of the *Paths of the Gods*. In two cuneiform texts dating from 475 B.C. and excavated from Babylon, the zodiacal constellations are divided into 12 30-degree signs. This is the original or sidereal zodiac (sidereal means "pertaining to the stars"). The sidereal zodiac places the star Aldebaran ("Bull's eye") at the center (15°) of the constellation of Taurus, and places the star Antares ("Scorpion's heart") at the heart of the constellation of Scorpio (15°)." (*Astrological Revolution: Unveiling the Science of the Stars as a Science of Reincarnation and Karma*, Powell, Robert, Dann, Kevin, 2010).

As we'll see later, in the 27 nakshatras system, most widely used, Sheratan must be at least at

10.666° sidereal in order to Antares fit the sidereal zodiac in the beginning of the right nakshatra. It's just a difference of 40' from our 10° aspect.

In the 28 mansion style, it can't be more than 10°, in order for Spica be at 180°—in the junction of Chitra and Svati.

If we reduce the given Sheratan, Spica and Aldebaran positions by Ptolemy to Hipparchus time (whether we use the dates 150 B.C. or 129 B.C.), then they would be, respectively, at 5°, 174°, and 40° tropical. Assuming that the red star of Taurus was indeed referred as being in the middle of the Bull constellation (45° sidereal), the 0° sidereal point would be at 355° tropical (25 Pisces), thus placing Sheratan again in sidereal 10 Aries—even if the corrected value would place it at 9° since its longitude is of about 4° (4.0995° to 4.39°, 6' to 23' of difference). Spica would be at 179° (29 Virgo).

If, on the other hand, we considered at this time Spica at 0 Libra, the true tropical longitude of Sheratan on these epochs, very near the four degrees tropical, would again become 10 degrees sidereal.

Did Ptolemy makde a simple mathematical mistake of one degree in the aspects regarding Sheratan and Alcyone (even if their angular separation of 26° was accurate), and even for Mesarthim, or was he trying to maintain an ancient correlation, namely the 10° of Naburianos which could be in use at Hipparchus time?

One more possible conclusion is that apparently Ptolemy might have reduced one or just a few anchor stars to his epoch at the rate of 2+2/3° per 265 years (like he demonstrated with Spica), and applied the supposed fixed angular separations (which our computations showed) erroneously assuming—as he states—they were fixed for all eternity.

These events and assumptions might be in the origin of the current difficulties of understanding the star positions listed in the *Almagest*, especially the ones in the zodiacal belt.

Fitting the Stars in the Hindu System

The study of the angular separations (from -7000 to 1500), searching for the most fixed integer aspects leads us to these results:

Best shifts:

Stars Pair	*Shift and Best Aspect*
Aldebaran - Antares	0.204 (179.89)—near 180°
Regulus - Zuben Elgenubi	0 .373 (75.03)—near 75°
Spica – Zuben Elgenubi	0.085 (21.3)—about 21.3°
Spica – Zuben Eshamali	0 .05 (25.5)—near 25° ½
Spica - Antares	0.036 (45.89)—near 46°
Spica - Sharatan	0.065 (169.9)—near 170°
Spica - Alcyone	0.078 (143.89)—near 144°
Zuben Elgenubi - Sharatan	0 .138 (168.81)—near 169°
Sharatan - Alcyone	0 .013 (26.01)—near 26°

Applying these shifts to the nakshatras, we find that in the 28 old system mentioned in the Atharveda, Sheratan must lie between 2.572° to 10° maximum.

Here's the sequence:

Sheratan, 2.572, 2.572 [0 to 12.8571428571429]

Alcyone, 28.572, 2.857 [25.7142857142857 to 38.5714285714286]

Aldebaran, 38.572, 0 [38.5714285714286 to 51.4285714285714]

Regulus, 118.872, 3.157 [115.714285714286 to
128.571428571429]
Spica, 172.572, 5.429 [167.142857142857 to 180]
Zuben Elgenubi, 193.872, 1.014 [192.857142857143 to
205.714285714286]
Zuben Eschamali, 198.072, 5.214 [192.857142857143 to
205.714285714286]
Antares, 218.572, 0 [218.571428571429 to
231.428571428571]

to

Sheratan, 10, 10 [0 to 12.8571428571429]
Alcyone, 36, 10.285 [25.7142857142857 to
38.5714285714286]
Aldebaran, 46, 7.428 [38.5714285714286 to
51.4285714285714]
Regulus, 126.3, 10.585 [115.714285714286 to
128.571428571429]
Spica, 180, 12.857 [167.142857142857 to 180]
Zuben Elgenubi, 201.3, 8.442 [192.857142857143 to
205.714285714286]
Zuben Eschamali, 205.5, 12.642 [192.857142857143 to
205.714285714286]
Antares, 226, 7.428 [218.571428571429 to
231.428571428571]

In the 27 system, Sheratan must lie in 10.667° to 13.333°:

Sheratan, 10.667, 10.667 [0 to 13.3333333333333]
Alcyone, 36.667, 10 [26.6666666666667 to 40]
Aldebaran, 46.667, 6.667 [40 to 53.3333333333333]
Regulus, 126.967, 6.967 [120 to 133.333333333333]
Spica, 180.667, 7.333 [173.333333333333 to

186.666666666667]
Zuben Elgenubi, 201.967, 1.967 [200 to 213.333333333333]
Zuben Eschamali, 206.167, 6.167 [200 to
213.333333333333]
Antares, 226.667, 0 [226.666666666667 to 240]
to

Sheratan, 13.333, 13.333 [0 to 13.3333333333333]
Alcyone, 39.333, 12.666 [26.6666666666667 to 40]
Aldebaran, 49.333, 9.332 [40 to 53.3333333333333]
Regulus, 129.633, 9.633 [120 to 133.333333333333]
Spica, 183.333, 9.999 [173.333333333333 to
186.666666666667]
Zuben Elgenubi, 204.633, 4.633 [200 to 213.333333333333]
Zuben Eschamali, 208.833, 8.832 [200 to
213.333333333333]
Antares, 229.333, 2.666 [226.666666666667 to 240]

Notice first of all that in the 27 system Spica can't be at 180° in the sidereal zodiac (even if it's often putted in the middle of the Chitra nakshatra). Why? If we give it that value, Antares will have a longitude of 226—less than the 226.666° of its nakshatra. In this system, Spica must be positioned between 180°40' and 183°20'.

However, in the old 28 system, Spica might be fitted at 180° if we consider it at the limit of Chitra—beginning of Svati.

If we are to take Aldebaran with a sidereal longitude of 45°, and relate this value with the Hindu's nakshatras, we're placing it at exactly 5° in Rohini in the 27 mansions system or at 6.428° in the 28 system, right in the middle of Rohini.

Even if Spica is referred in almost all the Mesopotamians writings as being in the twenty-ninth degree of Virgo, it is placed, however, at the twenty-eighth in the Babylonian table

BM 46083, published by Abraham Sachs in *A Late Babylonian Star Catalog*, JCS, VI (1952), 146-150. α and β Librae are placed at 20 and 25 Libra, respectively, as we've seen before. β Virgo at 151°, ν Virgo at 166° and θ Leo at 140° (also consistent with Anonymous 379).

We think that the only explanation here is that the coordinates of Spica were given in right ascension—not ecliptic ones. If we consider Spica at 178° RA, with an average declination of -2.1°, we get the ecliptic coordinates of 179° 00' 02" and -2° 43' 20".

Spica was—and is—largely studied by the Hindus, namely in astrology. In the Suraya Siddhanta treatise, Spica (Chitra) is placed in the middle of Nakshatra Chitra. This would place it at exactly 0 Libra: $13*360/27+360/54 = 180°$, if we would to consider 27 nakshatras. We have already seen that this is not possible.

But if Aldebaran is apparently the fifteenth degree of Taurus, the reference sidereal point would be shifted by the excess of 45°54' (ecliptic longitude of Aldebaran at 285 A.D.) minus 45, about 54'. So the suppose location of 0 Libra would be 180° 54' from the Aries tropical point. The difference of 54'—almost a degree—places Spica at 29 Virgo.

Coincidently, Varāhamihira, the author of Pañcasiddhāntikā (or Pancha-Siddhantika, "[Treatise] on the Five *Astronomical+ Canons"), refers Chitra in a polar longitude of 180° 50' in Chitra nakshatra, at 7°30' ($13*360/27+7+30/60 = 180.833333333333°$, the 180°50', very near ours 180° 54') with a latitude of 2°43' South—going against other opinions like the 183° of Brāhmasphumasiddhānta, the 184° 20' of Sisyadhivrddhida, and the modern Surya Siddhanta 180°.

Let's remember that the nakshatras are sidereal, not tropical. In the case of Varāhamihira, the calculations are clear: Spica was at 180°, in right ascension, in 27/12/346 A.D. 0h

TDB, with a declination of -2.119480431132810°. If we translate this coordinates to ecliptic ones, we get 180°51'02.34", and a declination of -1° 56' 28.88". Using an average obliquity of 23.2° we get 180° 50' 07". Thus the latitude of Spica is being referred in equatorial coordinates (more than 2° South), and the longitude in ecliptic ones. Even so, the declination given is almost 38' larger than the real one. And he lived according to the records in about 505-587 A.D. (159 years later).

Conclusion

It's not really a big mathematical problem to try to define a theoretical geometric sidereal zodiac. There's no plausible possibility, given the available data (and probably is useless I'm afraid) to define a precise system with an accuracy of tenths of arc seconds of precision. The data is really insufficient, rounded, and the differences will be always of some arc minutes or even degrees.

As we travel in time, stars will always move regarding a fixed point east or west (or any other possible 3D direction), and the constellations shapes will change. If we take one star as reference we won't be solving the problem, because the change rate of that star is not the same as another one. As I've said, the reader must multiply this problem by thousands of stars. Being the starting sidereal point whether a star or a mathematical point, the problem will always remain the same. . . . So we actually have three choices if we wish to work in an approximate sidereal model:

The hardest way: stop doing the math, dump the computers, rise your eyes up and start looking at the skies instead of a piece of paper filled with creepy algorithms or a PC screen with a fine and confortable software that makes all the computations for you. Return to past, and the ancient ways. Redefine the zodiac each day. Study it. Evolve with it.

The simple but eventually misleading way: choose a star as an anchor reference, and disregard the accuracy of all the others when reducing their position (as in the Lahiri Ayanamsa).

The easy and safe way: create an average mathematical model. Establish an adaptable and malleable sidereal mathematical model generating an ideal geometric point—a fictional point that coincided once with a particular set of aproximative positions of the stars but that is calculated over time with the average of their original and current coordinate's differences. Use the best fitted values computed in this article if you wish. The Aldebaran and Antares opposition axis is a good start; Spica and Antares angular difference of almost a semi square (46°) also.

There's no way around these methods for the time being.

I think that the idea of a consistent sidereal model is achieved with this third choice, at least over a long period of time. And it's in fact almost independent of establishing a starting epoch.

But it will eventually fail due to deviations. It may take milliards of years for this to happen. Still the primary logic will be respected.

Our reference point—initial sidereal point—will be placed in the average of the tropical longitude of the most important stars we choose, each one of them reduced by its supposed original and documented longitude in the zodiac.

So we can make a model, for instance, where the start of the sidereal point is given by adding the tropical longitudes of Aldebaran and Antares minus the sum of their supposed zodiacal longitudes, 45° and 225° respectively, and dividing the result by 2.

We might increase the accuracy of our model, if we add Spica tropical longitude decreased by 179°, for instance, to the previous ones (each diminished by their and divide the whole result by 3. And so on.

The only important remark to make is that if one wishes to use the Hindu model, it's necessary to add a degree to the result S (variable defined below) thus increasing the subtraction by one. This has to do with the Spica different values of 180° or 179° that we've seen in the article as a result of the Vedic and Western systems.

If there was a truly fixed star, without any kind of proper motion, this calculation would be worthless. But since there's none—everything in the cosmos moves—it's the best choice we have. This model adapts itself through time.

It's much simpler to choose the slowest star in the sky as reference, and deal with the error, particularly when we're faced with a small apparent reality: there's none to choose.

Here are some computational models examples where the considered stars are Aldebaran, Antares, Spica, Regulus, Pollux, α and β Librae.):

System Aldebaran + Antares (Babylonian): Ayanamsa in 2000 A.D.: -24°46.3'; S: Value to subtract to the average of the stars true longitudes: 270/2

System Aldebaran + Antares + Spica (Babylonian): Ayanamsa in 2000 A.D.: -24°47.6'; S: Value to subtract to the average of the stars true longitudes: 449/3

System All stars (Babylonian): Ayanamsa in 2000 A.D.: 24°41.7'; S: Value to subtract to the average of the stars true longitudes: 1068/7

System All-stars, with the Ptolemaic corrections: Ayanamsa in 2000 A.D.: -24°44.5'; S: Value to subtract to the average of the stars true longitudes: 1067° 40'/7

Average of the models: Ayanamsa in 2000 A.D.: 24°45'

A simple and rough comparison with other systems gives the following differences:

Fagan-Bradley: Ayanamsa: -24.7365°; difference from Ptolemy system (example): 0.31'

Krishnamurti: Ayanamsa: -23.7620°; difference from Ptolemy system (example): 58' (1.2' if we add 1° to S)

Lahiri: Ayanamsa: -23.8531°; difference from Ptolemy system (example): 53' (6.6' if we add 1° to S)

The results will be more accurate as we input more stable values and dismiss the discrepant ones (like Regulus or Pollux).

The calculation was made by adding in the different systems the following stars tropical values, divided by 2,3 or 7 (according to the system) and subtracting the respective S value (S being the supposed original longitudes of the considered stars). In the Ptolemy system, n is equal to 7 (stars).

Babylonian records:
Aldebaran at 45°
Antares at 225°
Spica at 179°
Regulus at 125°
Pollux at 89°
α Librae at 200°
β Librae at 205°
Sum = 1068, n = 7, S = 152° 34'

Ptolemy records (each value was increased by 2° 20' to obtain the 45 degrees for Aldebaran; the aspect ratios are kept the same this way):
Aldebaran at 45°
Antares at 225°
Spica at 179°
Regulus at 124° 50'
Pollux at 89°

α Librae at 200° 20'
β Librae at 204° 30'
Sum = 1067° 40', n = 7, S=152° 31.4'

Finally, analyzing the different systems towards the position of Aldebaran (as an example), we can see that some of the systems that achieve a best fit change with time:

Year	System
-8000 to -3000	Babylonian Aldebaran-Antares
-3000 to 600	Corrected Ptolemy
600 to 5850	Babylonian Aldebaran-Antares-Spica
5850 to 8000	Babylonian Aldebaran-Antares

About the Authors

José Luis Belmonte

A telecommunications engineer, publisher, writer, international lecturer and author of four books, José Luis Belmonte's interest in astrology began more than thirty years ago. He studied at Kepler College, where he earned a master's degree in astrology. Currently he conducts astrological research on the history of astrology, paganism, gnosticism, mythology, symbolism, archetypes, and Jungian psychology. Apart from being a guest on radio and TV shows, he conducted a weekly radio show on astrology in Miami from 2013 until early 2014. He currently lives in Barcelona, Spain, with his wife and daughter and works as an astrologer, writing papers and lecturing on astrology, and teaching astrology at Marilo Casals school of astrology.

Ronnie Gale Dreyer

Ronnie Gale Dreyer is an internationally known astrological consultant, lecturer, and teacher specializing in both Western and Indian (Vedic) astrology, based in New York City. She is co-author and author of numerous books, including *Healing Signs: The Astrological Guide to Wholeness and Well-Being*, *Vedic Astrology: A Guide to the Fundamentals of Jyotish*, *Your Sun and Moon Guide to Love and Life*, *Venus: The Evolution of the Goddess and Her Planet*, and *Indian Astrology*. She has served as editor or contributor to numerous anthologies, and has written articles for *The Mountain Astrologer*, *American Astrology*, *Horoscope Guide*, NCGR *memberletter*, *Geocosmic Journal*, and the *Astrological Association of Great Britain Journal*.

Ronnie lectures extensively for astrology groups, conducts ongoing courses and workshops, and is also a faculty member of ACVA (American College of Vedic Astrology) and an instructor for ACVA Online College.

Ronnie is a former presiding officer of AFAN, and is currently editor of NCGR's *memberletter* and a boar member of ACT (Astrological Conference on Techniques). She holds a bachelor of arts in English/theater arts from the University of New Mexico, and a master of arts in south Asian languages and cultures from Columbia University, where she studied Sanskrit and Hindi.

Rui Miguel Fernandes

Rui Miguel Fernandes is a self-taught student and researcher who has explored several distinct areas of study. From astronomy and math to the mystic, mythological, religious, archeological and spiritual, he has always tried to achieve an equilibrium point of understanding and balance between the two areas in order to form a whole. The accumulated knowledge was used in a professional Web site of astronomy and celestial mechanics research program, and in a journal dedicated to all the subjects of interest mentioned that at first sight would seem to conflict. He is dedicated to scientific and occult studies, with the simple and plain philosophy that "there's no religion superior to the truth."

Miguel attended the University of Sciences of Porto (FCUP—Faculdade de Ciências do Porto) in Portugal, earning the equivalent of a bachelor's degree in physics/applied mathematics, variant astronomy.

Peter Gadek

Peter Gadek has a master's degree in mechanical engineering and more than 30 years experience in the design, development, and analysis of heavy equipment. He emigrated from Poland to the United States in 1989, as a political refugee, and later became a U.S. citizen.

Peter's interest in astrology dates to 2002, when he received his first astrological consultation. By 2005, he was studying on his own, and in 2010, studied with Christine Arens and Joe Polise, and joined the Friends of Astrology, for which he serves as a board member, and the NCGR (Northern Illinois chapter). In the fall of 2010, he began a formal program of study with Kepler College and obtained certificates in the fundamentals of astrology, astrological chart calculation, moving the chart in time, and counseling and relationships. He expects to earn a Kepler Diploma in 2016. Peter has also presented three lectures on harmonic astrology in practical applications.

His hobbies include history, music (classical and jazz), natural healing (working with prana), and meditation—but his passion is astrology.

Julie Grant

Julie Grant has an extensive background in finance and business, having worked as an administrative leader at large educational institutions for more than 25 years. She has a bachelor's degree in business, and master's degrees in finance and conscious evolution. She also holds a diploma from the Academy of AstroPsychology, where she developed an Excel program that precisely calculates the developmental age and date for each planetary location in the birth chart in accord with Glenn Perry's Developmental Age Method. She is currently enrolled at Pacifica Graduate Institute in a Ph.D. program in depth psychology, Jungian, and archetypal studies. Julie also does astrological consultations.

Glenn Perry

Glenn Perry, Ph.D. is a professional astrologer and licensed psychotherapist in East Hampton, Connecticut. He received his doctorate in psychology from Saybrook Institute in San Francisco. In addition to private practice, Dr. Perry is founder of the Academy of AstroPsychology, an online school that offers courses and training in psychological astrology. He has written eight books, including *An Introduction to AstroPsychology*, and lectures internationally on the application of astrology to the fields of counseling and psychotherapy. Glenn is a board member and qualitative research advisor for ISAR. Contact: www.aaperry.com

Lutz Rathke

Lutz Rathke is a German astrologer who studied composition of classical music, Semitic languages, and physics before deciding to become a professional astrologer and researcher. After studying medieval astrological works in Latin, Greek, Arabic, and Persian, he was an astrological counselor in Munich in the 1980s, and published a magazine for research in astrology until the early 1990s.

He is a member of Kosmobiologische Akademia KAA (founded by Reinhold Ebertin) and speaks on advanced astrological and sometimes on other scientific subjects.

From age 36, he was able to entirely focus on research and has developed his own system, concentrating on interpretation in clear, verifiable or falsifiable, and precise words, including the vocabulary of modern life. He twice lived in the United States and has been living in France for more than 20 years.

Using his approach, mundane astrology can be based on mundane horsocopes only, and charts of personalities and proclamations are interesting but not necessary to predict the fate of countries, regions (such as the post-Ottoman regions including Syria and Iraq), wars and campaigns, governments, political factions and parties, and other events in the course of history. He has found radical mundane horoscopes for powers like ISIL, Hesbollah or al-Qaeda, Islam, Christianity, the Roman Empire and many European nations and states to be valid. His method is effective even with historical data of little precision. The astrogeography of German astrologer Hans

Jürgen Andersen is one of the principle means he uses to determine localities where events will or will not occur.

Bruce Scofield

Bruce Scofield began a lifelong study of astrology in 1967, and since the mid 1970s has been an astrological consultant specializing in psychological analysis, relationships, and electional astrology. He has authored seven books and hundreds of articles on astrology and has served on the education committee of NCGR since 1979, as both member and director, presently serving as president of PAA. He has Level IV certification from NCGR-PAA, professional certification from AFA, holds an M.A. in history and a Ph.D. in geoscience, and has taught science at the University of Massachusetts and currently teaches courses for Kepler College. His website www.onereed.com contains information on Mesoamerican astrology and other topics.

Alex Trenoweth

Alex Trenoweth earned a master's degree in cultural astronomy and astrology at Bath Spa University, and has gained recognition as an outstanding teacher for her tireless and innovative education of adolescents. Her unique expertise in both astrology and teaching, coupled with ground-breaking research, led her to her write *Growing Pains*, a book aimed at helping parents and teachers support and guide young people into maturity. Alex's articles have appeared in astrological magazines across the globe and in addition to her many writing accomplishments, she was voted Best International Astrologer, 2015 by the Krishnamuti Institute of Astrology in India for the energetic presentation of her original and thought-provoking investigation into astrology and education. Alex continues to lecture on a variety of astrological topics at various conferences around the world and enjoys meeting other astrologers from different cultures.

www.ingramcontent.com/pod-product-compliance
Lightning Source LLC
Chambersburg PA
CBHW021342230426
43666CB00006B/381